PAUL WALLACE

Tanked

Why the British Economy is Failing and How to Fix it

The
Bridge
Street
Press

To Shirley, Imogen, Joseph, Bridget and Sylvia

THE BRIDGE STREET PRESS

First published in Great Britain in 2024 by The Bridge Street Press

1 3 5 7 9 10 8 6 4 2

A CIP catalogue record for this book
is available from the British Library.

ISBN 978-0-349-13635-6

Typeset in Garamond by M Rules Ltd

Printed and bound in Great Britain by
Clays Ltd, Elcograf S.p.A

Papers used by The Bridge Street Press are from well-managed forests
and other responsible sources.

MIX
Paper | Supporting
responsible forestry
FSC
www.fsc.org   FSC® C104740

The Bridge Street Press
An imprint of
Little, Brown Book Group
Carmelite House
50 Victoria Embankment
London EC4Y 0DZ

An Hachette UK Company
www.hachette.co.uk

www.littlebrown.co.uk

Contents

Introduction

Forty-nine days of madness

For over four decades there was no question about when Britain's post-war economic fortunes reached their nadir. It was September 1976, when Jim Callaghan's Labour government had to ask the International Monetary Fund (IMF) for a record loan to prevent the pound and the economy from collapsing. But during her forty-nine-day premiership in the autumn of 2022, Liz Truss managed to outplumb that low.

Unlike Chancellor of the Exchequer Denis Healey, who didn't make it to the IMF conference in Manila in 1976, memorably having to turn back from Heathrow, Truss's chancellor Kwasi Kwarteng did attend the IMF gathering in 2022 held in Washington DC. But he was recalled early to be sacked by Truss. He had been chancellor for little more than a month, making his stint at the Treasury the second shortest in modern times. Casting him aside so brutally did not save the prime minister: soon after appointing Jeremy Hunt in his place she was forced to resign, making her premiership the shortest on record.

For both Callaghan and Truss, the financial markets had passed a vote of no confidence in a government living beyond its means. When Truss became prime minister in early September, she adopted the Facebook motto, 'Move fast and break things'.

Following plans she had worked out in advance, she and her chancellor did indeed move fast. And the 'mini-budget' delivered by Kwarteng on 23 September 2022, less than three weeks after Truss had become prime minister, certainly broke things.

Britain's trip to fiscal la-la land

What went wrong?

First and foremost, Kwarteng cut a whole range of taxes – including bringing the top rate of income tax down from 45 to 40 per cent – without corresponding spending cuts to balance the books. He reversed an additional National Insurance levy that had only just been introduced, and cancelled a big impending increase in the main corporation tax rate. Altogether, the lost revenue amounted to £45 billion a year, making it the biggest package of tax cuts (as a share of gross domestic product [GDP]) of any budget in half a century.[1]

Second, this maxi- rather than mini-budget dodged scrutiny by the independent Office for Budget Responsibility (OBR). That followed a pre-emptive strike against the top civil servant in the Treasury. On his first day in his job, Kwarteng, with the backing of Truss, sacked Tom Scholar, the respected permanent secretary of the Treasury whose experience would have come in handy in the crisis that erupted.[2] In Truss's brave new economic world, institutions such as the OBR and an independent civil service no longer seemed to count.

The radical budgetary measures were supposed to jolt a sluggish economy back to life and put it on a trajectory of stronger growth. That, at least, was the case Truss and Kwarteng made. But it had the exact opposite effect. The financial markets went into turmoil as they witnessed a government seemingly transported to economic la-la land, where massive unfunded tax cuts would miraculously pay for themselves through higher revenue from a bigger economy.

Just as in 1976, a sinking pound indicated a loss of faith in the British government. The day after Kwarteng had unwisely told the BBC's Laura Kuenssberg on her Sunday news show that there was 'more to come', sterling fell to its lowest-ever value against the dollar, trading at $1.035 in Asian markets.[3] But it was the gilt market, in which dealers buy and sell government bonds, that really sounded the alarm.

The effect of Kwarteng's unfunded tax cuts would be to increase already high public borrowing, meaning that the Treasury would have to issue even more debt. Investors took fright and started to sell gilts, driving down their prices. Since yields (the returns to bond investors) are inversely related to prices their yields were driven up.

Long-term bond yields are usually slow to move because so much of their value lies far in the future. They are also loosely connected to short-term borrowing costs set by the Bank of England. Yet in a matter of days the thirty-year gilt yield vaulted from around 3.5 per cent to over 5 per cent, the highest level in two decades.[4] That jump was all the more astonishing because the Bank of England's base interest rate was still only 2.25 per cent.

All pain, no gain

This was where the mini-budget got close and personal for two sets of people. Disquietingly, pensioners learned that their final salary company pension funds were in trouble: they were having to make payments on over-clever schemes supposed to protect pensions, forcing them to dump gilts at a loss to release the money. The second was homeowners with fixed-rate mortgages, typically for either two or five years. Since those rates were priced off the shorter-term gilt market, they rose sharply for anyone re-mortgaging. For those with existing loans not immediately affected, pain loomed menacingly ahead since the loans had been taken out when interest rates were unusually low. It would be all the more punishing because mortgages were now so large, reflecting inflated house prices driven ever higher by cheap borrowing costs.

But almost all the population stood to suffer. Inflation was already surging and the last thing the economy needed – contra Truss and Kwarteng – was an injection of more demand. British households were facing a desperate cost-of-living squeeze as energy bills threatened to become unaffordable after an extraordinary increase in European gas prices. Truss had pledged a two-year guarantee to hold down household energy prices. But this involved yet more borrowing. And if the British state remained under siege in the markets, would it even be capable of honouring its promises?

We will never know what the full disastrous impact of the mini-budget might have been because the proposals were dropped like hot bricks – starting with the provocative cut in the top rate of income tax. The only measure of note that went ahead was the abolition of the extra National Insurance levy; and that was partially offset by dropping a previously announced plan to cut the basic rate of income tax from 20 per cent to 19 per cent. The costly energy price guarantee offered by Truss and Kwarteng was restricted to cover just the winter to come rather than two years.[5]

Once Truss was herself replaced by Rishi Sunak in October 2022, both the new prime minister and his chancellor Jeremy Hunt went out of their way to represent themselves as trustworthy custodians of the public finances. When Hunt issued his autumn statement in mid-November, the jilted OBR was fully back in the fold. It painted a bleak picture of the nation's finances.

Even with the fiscal adults back in charge there was reason to rue the costs of Truss and Kwarteng's fit of delinquency. The concerns of pensioners proved to be short-lived, not least since the Bank of England intervened to cool things in the gilt market. But even though long-term interest rates came down, the impact on mortgages endured. At the height of the panic, lenders had withdrawn swathes of new mortgage products. When they returned to the market, loans had become more expensive, providing banks with a bigger safety margin protecting against future volatility.[6]

All in all, it had been a close-run thing. For a time during the premiership of Truss, Britain had lost all fiscal credibility. The new partnership of Sunak and Hunt made a big difference. The jump in long-term interest rates now resembled a spike. By the end of the year, the 'moron premium' – a term coined during the autumn madness to describe the additional yield that international investors were demanding for British gilts – had largely disappeared.

Unlike in 1976, Britain had avoided having to go cap in hand to the IMF and then having to impose the harsh economic and fiscal conditions attached to such loans. But maybe that was what was needed? In June 2023, Adam Posen, an American economist and a former member of the Bank of England's Monetary Policy Committee that sets interest rates, suggested it was 'time for the UK to think like an emerging market' – quite a comedown for arguably the first developed economy. Specifically, those in charge 'should now act as though they are under a self-imposed IMF stabilisation programme'.[7]

A tale of two turnarounds

The wheel had turned full circle since 1976. Yet for a good stretch of the period after that first crisis, the British economy had confounded the pessimists. In particular, the fifteen years following the recession of the early 1990s were an exceptionally good period with sustained growth and low inflation, delivering in turn steadily rising living standards.

But any self-congratulation – and there was plenty of it about in the mid-2000s – was premature. Following the financial crisis that came close to toppling Britain's banking system in the autumn of 2008, there was no more summertime when the living was easy. Rather, the fifteen fat years were followed by fifteen lean years of stubbornly low growth. Those past fifteen years – and how to break the negative spiral that has become the new norm – are the subject of this book.

One consolation during the 2010s was that inflation generally remained low. But that unnatural calm was abruptly shattered after the pandemic when consumer prices took off. Inflation reached 11.1 per cent in late 2022, the highest for forty years; but for the government cap on home energy prices, inflation would have reached a peak of 13.6 per cent in early 2023.[8]

The leap in inflation tore a hole in family finances. Living standards, measured by real household disposable income per person, declined in 2022–23 by the most in any financial year in records stretching back almost seven decades.[9] The Trussell Trust reported that it distributed almost three million emergency food parcels across the UK between April 2022 and March 2023, over half as many again as the 1.9 million in 2019–20. The number of people using one of its food banks for the first time was 760,000.[10]

Other depressing figures suggested that gains in health had also slowed. In the 1990s and 2000s, there were steady and appreciable gains in life expectancy at birth. That reflected lifestyle changes such as falling smoking rates as well as medical advances. But even before the pandemic, demographers and actuaries were taken by surprise as improvement petered out during the 2010s.[11]

Too much wishful thinking, too little resilience

One explanation for this dire record (favoured by Conservative ministers) was that Britain had been battered by a succession of extreme international shocks. These had started (under Labour) with the financial crisis of 2007-09, the worst since the early 1930s. Then there was the outbreak of Covid in 2020, another once-in-a-century event. The shortages and bottlenecks resulting from lockdown triggered the rise in inflation, which was then turbocharged by an unprecedented rise in European gas prices associated with Russia's invasion of Ukraine in February 2022, and the clampdown on Russian gas exports that followed.

However, Britain's record in coping with these international shocks was poor. Financial services had long made up an unusually large proportion of national output and became even more prominent in the run-up to the banking crisis. That meant the economy was especially hard hit following the 2008 crash. Much the same could be said of the pandemic's impact. At best, Britain's overall performance judged by excess mortality was middling. But during the first wave in the spring of 2020, England's was the worst among European countries.[12] Yet it had had advance warning from Italy where the new disease had struck earlier.

The collateral damage to the NHS was also worse than in other European health services. Figures from the Organisation for Economic Co-operation and Development (OECD) showed that 'elective' (planned) operations in 2020 slumped far more in Britain than in the rest of Europe. On average, among twenty-three EU countries, hip replacements dropped by 14 per cent in 2020 compared with the number in 2019, whereas they fell by 46 per cent in the UK; for knee replacements, the respective declines were 24 and 68 per cent. Among all the countries compared, the falls for such treatments were biggest in the UK.[13]

Put to the test, the NHS had clearly done a lot worse than other health systems in looking after patients who were not ill with Covid. That contributed to the extraordinary jump in the hospital waiting list, which rose in England from an already high 4.6 million before the pandemic to well over seven million in 2023.

Even though a lot more money was belatedly going into the NHS it was still underperforming.

The upsurge in inflation following the pandemic was also particularly severe in Britain. Not only was the peak in 2022 of 11.1 per cent higher than the eurozone's 10.6 per cent and America's 9.1 per cent, inflation stayed higher for longer, only coming down to single figures in April 2023, months after the eurozone.

A common factor in all these crises was a lack of resilience born of complacency. Ahead of the financial crisis, too little attention was paid to the risks of hosting an outsize international banking centre in the City. The pandemic exposed a woeful state of public health preparation. The inflation shock was especially acute in Britain because it was the fourth most dependent economy on gas in Europe. Yet scarcely any provision was made to store reserves: just a few days' capacity compared with over a hundred in the Netherlands.[14]

The habit of wishful thinking that lay behind this lack of resilience was also apparent in Brexit. The casual way in which then prime minister David Cameron promised a vote on Britain's most crucial economic relationship was matched by the careless way in which the referendum itself was conducted. The vote and the chaotic paralysis that followed it revealed deep structural weaknesses in the British state itself.

Charting a way back

This book will explore how and why the British economic success story of the early millennium turned sour while the public finances deteriorated at a frightening pace. It will answer crucial questions. Is the City too big for its boots? Does Britain make enough things? Could more immigration be the answer? How damaging has Brexit been and was there ever an economic case for it? Is there a better way of funding the NHS? What are Britain's economic strengths and how can they be built upon? As important, how can longstanding weaknesses such as poor vocational skills throughout the country and lagging regions in central and northern England be put right?

In the pages that follow I analyse what went wrong – and what we need to do to recover our former status as an economic powerhouse. I end with a ten-point plan that our political leaders – whatever their party affiliation – could start putting into action right away.

Britain turned itself around after 1976 and it can turn itself around again. But what that will require is a coherent set of reforms and a rethink of the way that the country is governed. Above all, it will require a consistency of purpose that has been conspicuous by its absence in the last fifteen years.

Chapter 1

From hero to zero: a brief (recent) history of the British economy

When Tony Blair won his landslide victory in 1997 to the thumping soundtrack of 'Things Can Only Get Better', it turned out that he was right – at least in one respect. During his decade as prime minister the economy continued on the upward trajectory that had started after the recession of the early 1990s. New Labour presided over a new economy.

GDP rose consistently and strongly. Inflation, the bane of post-war governments, lost its sting. Unemployment was low. The City was a world financial centre vying only with New York. Living standards in Britain, which had fallen well behind those in other big European nations in the post-war period, caught up with Germany's and surpassed those in France and Italy.

The boom meant extra revenues poured into the Exchequer which Labour spent on public services. The sovereign remedy of cash worked in the NHS: waiting times fell and treatments rose. Other public services such as schools also got a lot more money. All this was possible without busting the national finances. In fact, in the mid-2000s public debt was at a very reasonable 35 per cent of GDP.

The good times came to a juddering halt during the financial crisis of 2008. That triggered a severe recession. Worse, when the economy recovered, it shifted down a gear to much slower growth. Then came the Brexit vote in 2016, which sapped business investment owing to prolonged uncertainty over the UK's status. Boris Johnson's hard trade deal with the EU at the end of 2020 inflicted more damage.

By the early 2020s Britain had tumbled down the prosperity league table: living standards were now markedly lower than in Germany. Prolonged austerity had taken its toll on the public services with the NHS, in particular, stuck in a year-round winter crisis. The public finances were also strained, with debt hovering close to an unwelcome 100 per cent of GDP, the highest in six decades.

Why did things go so right for so long? And why since 2008 have they gone so stubbornly wrong?

The exceptional decade-and-a-half

The British economic success story for most of the 1990s and 2000s broke the post-war template of relative economic decline. By historic standards, growth in the 1950s and 1960s was more than respectable. But there was no *Wirtschaftswunder* or *les trente glorieuses*, when the German and French economies respectively boomed as never before. British attempts to emulate their success generated a stop-go cycle. Fiscal easing through measures such as cutting taxes and monetary loosening through lowering interest rates ('go'), opened a hole in the balance of payments and put the pound under pressure in the foreign exchange markets; that prompted a 'stop' as the brakes were put on.

Already by 1960, West Germany had caught up with the UK in terms of prosperity, an astonishing achievement for an economy that lay in ruins after the war.[1] Over the next two decades, Britain lagged behind. In 1979, GDP per person was 16 per cent lower than in West Germany, 13 per cent less than in France and had even fallen below Italy's.[2] Britain was the sick man of Europe, suffering not just from weak growth but rampant inflation: a toxic combination known as stagflation.

The economy was also wracked by three wrenching recessions, in the mid-1970s, the early 1980s and the early 1990s. The worst was the middle one when, from peak to trough, output fell by over 5 per cent.[3] Unemployment rose to a post-war high of above three million. Over 10 per cent of the workforce were jobless for much of the 1980s.[4]

But following the third recession in the early 1990s, the economy jumped out of that dismal groove. For almost sixteen years until the start of 2008, GDP grew steadily without a single dip. Labour chancellor Gordon Brown boasted that this was Britain's longest uninterrupted boom in three centuries.[5] The claim required some historical arm-wrestling with the stats, given that quarterly GDP figures began only in the mid-1950s. Still, his point was well made.

While growth was high and stable, inflation was low and stable. In the summer of 1975 inflation had reached an eye-watering 27 per cent (a rate at which the real value of your savings would halve in just *three years*) but that now appeared a distant aberration. For most of the 1980s inflation was in single digits. After briefly returning above 10 per cent during 1990, it started a long retreat, so much so that people started to worry about it being too low.[6]

Unemployment touched 3 million again following the recession of the early 1990s. But the recovery brought it down to 1.4 million in 2004. Meanwhile, pay rose on average by more than 4 per cent a year between 2001 and 2008. Given low inflation, that translated into real earnings rising by close to 2.5 per cent a year.[7]

Britain appeared to have reached the sunlit uplands of sustainable growth. There were two crucial elements in this success:
workers were producing more through continuing increases in
productivity; and labour resources rose, whether measured in
higher employment or more hours worked.

American economist and Nobel laureate Robert Solow famously
quipped in 1987: 'You can see the computer age everywhere but in
the productivity statistics.' This was a time when American productivity was increasing much more slowly than in the post-war era
until 1973. But in the late 1990s, IT advances did show up in the
figures: productivity growth surged.[8] Britain stepped up its investment in IT in the late 1990s and early 2000s. Unlike in America
this did not push up labour productivity growth noticeably – it
remained on average at around 2 per cent a year. But that steady
increase in output per worker was still better than in continental
Europe where the pace slowed to around 1 per cent in France and
Germany.[9]

Combined with higher employment and longer working hours,
Britain was able to catch up in terms of living standards with
Germany and to overtake France by the middle of the 2000s.

Victory has many fathers

The received narrative about the new economy was that it reflected
a new economic policy model. After the long post-war struggle to
revive Britain's flagging economic fortunes, the government had
apparently stumbled on a winning formula. Instead of the state
trying to engineer growth, it would be left to private enterprise.
Government would step aside and confine its role to refereeing
markets. Its main job was to ensure that inflation was kept low
and the public finances in good order.

Naturally, both main parties sought to take credit for the new approach. The Conservatives pointed to the reforming zeal of Margaret Thatcher who curbed the trade unions and imposed market discipline. Thatcher abandoned an industrial strategy, dismissing it as a doomed attempt to 'pick winners', and privatised large chunks of the public sector including telecoms, energy and water. New Labour paid tribute to Thatcher by essentially accepting her economic settlement. In opposition, Blair abolished the party's historic commitment to nationalisation embodied by clause four of its constitution. Unlike previous Labour administrations, his government would not try to steer the economy through old-school growth plans or industrial policy.

A crucial part of the new economic model was a revolution in how inflation was controlled. Both main parties had a hand in this. The Conservatives had initially sought price stability by trying to put a lid on the amount of money in the economy, on the grounds that inflation was 'always and everywhere a monetary phenomenon' as Milton Friedman, the high priest of monetarism, once declared. After that turned out to be unworkable – the money supply was a fickle friend – they tried to restrain inflation by tying sterling to the German mark through membership of the European Exchange Rate Mechanism (ERM). That ended in the ignominy of 16 September 1992 – Black Wednesday – when the pound was forced out of the ERM. Only then did the Treasury finally adopt an approach that worked. Britain became an early pioneer of inflation targeting – setting an explicit goal for inflation and thus creating a discipline for the government to achieve that, as well as an expectation among the public that price rises would be kept under control.

Labour built on that innovation by freeing the Bank of England to set interest rates and giving it the job of meeting the Treasury's inflation target. Brown's surprise move in his first week as chancellor bolstered the government's credibility on low inflation. In the following decade, the fastest that consumer prices (which in 2003

replaced the older retail prices measure for the inflation target)
rose was 3.1 per cent in March 2007. A sharp increase in global
oil prices drove inflation up to 5.2 per cent in September 2008;
but it then swiftly fell back since the economy was, by then, in a
severe recession.[10]

Brown introduced two fiscal rules to allay market fears that he
would play fast and loose with the public finances: public debt
should not exceed 40 per cent of GDP; and the Treasury would
borrow only to invest, the so-called 'golden rule'. During the
decade that Brown was chancellor, the government met the first
target and just about managed the second, though this required
some jiggery-pokery with the fine print. (To save the blushes of
the chancellor, in 2005 the Treasury fudged the golden rule by
re-dating the 'economic cycle' over which it was supposed to be
met.)[11]

Brown also sought to make the economy flourish through a
range of supply-side reforms (affecting production as opposed to
demand). These included a big regulatory shake-up to heighten
competition with the aim of spurring productivity improvements.[12]
The chancellor commissioned studies on increasing house building
and improving skills. But too often these worthy initiatives ran
into the sands.

Instead, the central domestic mission of New Labour turned out
to be spending tax revenues generated by a strong economy. Blair
sought public sector reform, especially in the NHS; but the public
services got better mainly because of more generous funding. This
made possible, for example, the recruitment of more doctors and
teachers. The need to improve the public services was undeniably
urgent. Although mostly counted as current expenditure, education and health spending is also an investment in the human
capital and health of the nation. But there was an unanswered
question about New Labour's approach: what would happen if
the money ran out?

The three tailwinds

In practice, the new economic model was less decisive in changing Britain's fortunes than its architects claimed. Three underlying forces were helping to drive the economy.

The first was demographics. Although there was an immediate post-war spike in births in the late 1940s, the main baby boom was in the second half of the 1950s and the 1960s. The birth rate peaked in England and Wales in 1964.[13] As that generation matured, it boosted the labour supply both in numbers and in quality, since it had benefited from better state education. The timing of the baby boomers' entry into the workforce was unfortunate, however, since it coincided with the weak labour market of the early to mid-1980s. Indeed, high youth unemployment was an unhappy feature of that decade – baby boomers didn't have it all their own way, as is now so widely claimed.

But during the 1990s and 2000s the economy benefited from a bulge in the number of people in their most productive years (roughly twenty-five to fifty-five).[14] This is when earnings typically rise reflecting greater individual productivity in the workplace.[15] That home-grown effect was reinforced by a surge in migration, especially from Europe following the accession to the EU of eight east and central European countries in May 2004. The new migrants were young and keen to work.

The second force was globalisation. A world where markets and trade were opening up also played to British strengths. English was the *lingua franca* of commerce, and Britain was unusually well connected globally owing to its former far-flung empire. The City had always been outward-looking and could cash in on the boom in international finance as new supply chains snaked round the world.

Globalisation became especially intense in the two decades

following the fall of the Berlin Wall in 1989 and the collapse of the Soviet bloc. That released reserves of cheap labour among the former members of the Warsaw Pact. More important still was the increasing integration into the global economy of China and its huge low-wage workforce, a development accelerated further by its accession to the World Trade Organisation (WTO) in 2001. By one reckoning, the global labour force doubled in the 1990s.[16]

Britain benefited from globalisation mainly through lower import prices. By the early 2000s, this downward pressure meant that the Bank of England was grappling with inflation being too *low* rather than too high. In an early warning that the inflation targeting regime might be flawed, the Bank was forced to bring down interest rates in the second half of 2003 to 3.5 per cent, the lowest rate for almost half a century. This, in turn, generated a boom in house prices that was good for older homeowners but less so for first-time buyers.

The third tailwind was the delayed benefit of joining the European club in 1973. British industry was exposed to more intense competition and compelled to get its act together. At first, this was a rude awakening as underperforming companies came under pressure. But those that survived were more productive and had the opportunity to sell goods throughout the European community.

The fillip to the economy was increased by the drive to create a genuine European single market from the mid-1980s to the early 1990s by removing regulatory barriers to trade. This contributed to the rush of companies setting up operations in Britain both to seize the new opportunities and to avoid being locked out of 'fortress Europe' if the single market was protected by higher barriers, a fear that turned out to be misplaced.

There have been several attempts to work out how much the British economy benefited from joining the European club. Shortly before the June 2016 referendum, economic historian Nicholas

Crafts of Warwick University, an authority on Britain's growth record, reviewed these studies. He judged that membership had over time lifted GDP by around 10 per cent (compared with staying outside the bloc). That was a handsome return in greater prosperity on the 'membership fee' of being in the EU – the net contributions to the budget plus the cost of European regulations that were badly designed, which he put at about 1.5 per cent of GDP.[17]

The good times masked underlying flaws

The standard explanation of Britain's economic relapse in the 2010s is that everything changed with the financial crisis, the worst since the early 1930s. When banks start collapsing there can be massive economic harm, not just through triggering severe recessions but also by curbing recovery as businesses and households become much more cautious. Given that, it was unsurprising that a crisis of the magnitude of the one in 2008, affecting not just Britain but the rest of Europe and America, took its toll. In particular, there was a notable deceleration in productivity growth across Europe and America. But that slowdown was especially marked in Britain because the banking crisis had been so severe thanks to the City's intimate involvement in dodgy financial engineering.

Productivity – output per worker – fell by almost 1 per cent in 2008 and 3 per cent in 2009. This in large measure reflected the sharp economic downturn induced by the financial crisis. But it was what happened next that caught economists by surprise. After recovering by just over 2 per cent in 2010, productivity made only stuttering progress in the rest of the decade. The main engine of GDP growth was idling.

In fact, the gloss was already peeling off the British economy before the crisis. In October 2003, Bank of England Governor Mervyn King dubbed the previous ten years the 'nice' – non-inflationary consistently expansionary – decade (he was a central banker). Speaking in Leicester, King said that the economy had experienced ten years of 'unparalleled stability of both growth and inflation'. But his observation came with a warning: 'Will the next ten years be as nice?' he asked. 'That is unlikely.'[18]

With hindsight, King looks prescient (though he was wrong-footed by the financial crisis). By the middle of the decade the gilded years were losing their lustre. For one thing, Britain still hadn't fully caught up in the productivity race with comparable big economies. For another, there were familiar imbalances. The nation's current account ran persistent deficits in the 2000s. That was all the more worrying since business investment was surprisingly weak in the first half of the decade given the buoyancy of the economy. Growth was, instead, driven by consumers together with politicians directing more resources into public spending. The consumer boom was in turn underpinned by a strong housing market. Most important, the underlying performance of the economy was less impressive than it appeared to be. In the mid-2000s the City was on steroids. The financial sector as a whole grew by almost 10 per cent a year between 2003 and 2007, far outstripping annual GDP growth of around 2.5 per cent.[19] This was unsustainable.

Even though the economy was flattering to deceive before the crisis, few people predicted just how badly the British economy would do in the 2010s. Growth slowed from above the historical average to well below it. In 2002, the Treasury had pushed up its estimate of trend growth from 2.5 per cent a year to 2.75 per cent, an estimate it renewed in late 2006.[20] This appeared reasonable given how well the economy was doing. But between 2007 and 2022 growth was little more than 1 per cent a year (see box).

Given the slowdown in productivity improvements, overall GDP growth performance was better than might have been expected. This was because employment increased strongly in the

2010s. One reason for this was the sharp rise in the state pension age for women, from sixty at the start of the decade – an age set during the Second World War – to sixty-six by 2020. Men's retirement age of sixty-five, originally set in 1925, rose to sixty-six in the same year. Another was that more people came to work in Britain, especially from the EU.

The growth slowdown in numbers

Britain's poor economic performance in the past fifteen years is usually described in terms of GDP, or national output. Going back half a century to 1973, when the first oil crisis ushered in a new period of lower growth, there have been three distinct phases. From 1973 to 1992, Britain's GDP grew by 1.8 per cent a year. Between 1992 and 2007, growth accelerated to an annual rate of 2.9 per cent. But in the following fifteen years until 2022, GDP grew by only 1.1 per cent a year.

Businesses look at GDP to gauge demand for their products. Markets obsess over it as a guide to economic performance. But as an indicator of prosperity, it is *GDP per person* that matters. What this showed was annual growth of 1.7 per cent between 1973 and 1992; 2.5 per cent between 1992 and 2007; and 0.4 per cent between 2007 and 2022. Especially in the past fifteen years, a rising population has been dragging down growth in GDP per person.

The main yardstick of long-term economic performance is labour productivity – how much is produced per worker. As the economist Paul Krugman once observed: 'Productivity isn't everything, but in the long run it is almost everything. A country's ability to improve its standard of living over time depends almost entirely on its ability to raise its output per worker.'

So what do the British productivity numbers show us? Between 1973 and 1992, output per worker grew by 1.7 per cent a year. In the fifteen years to 2007 that picked up to almost 2 per cent before collapsing to an annual rate of 0.4 per cent in the fifteen years to 2022. Excluding the short-term impact of the financial crisis, between 2010 and 2022 it still grew by a measly 0.6 per cent a year. Another way of measuring labour productivity – output per hour worked – tells a similar story.

The British economy was not alone: the same trends can be found in other G7 members. Where Britain stood out was in the extent of the slowdown. By the early 2020s, our living standards were considerably lower than in Germany and roughly similar to France's.[21]

Tailwinds into headwinds

More people were being employed but the figures showed a sharp deceleration in the growth of output per worker. Why? Trying to solve what became known as the 'productivity puzzle' became a popular pastime for economists.

After much wracking of brains, a solution began to emerge. The City's travails played a big part – just as its excesses had exaggerated growth ahead of the banking crisis. Perhaps surprisingly, another underperforming sector was information technology and communications. Altogether, there was a widening gap between firms at the forefront of productivity and those trailing behind. As Andy

Haldane, the Bank of England's chief economist, said in 2018: 'Companies previously gliding in the slipstream are now floundering in the wake of frontier firms.'[22] Best practice and innovation were no longer diffusing so readily into the mainstream.

The tailwinds that had supported growth in the golden period before 2008 were also turning into headwinds. Demographics were becoming less favourable. From 2010, the second wave of baby boomers started to turn fifty-five, an age when individual labour quality can start to deteriorate. An IMF study in 2016 highlighted the potential drag on productivity growth from such 'workforce ageing', in particular the rising proportion of fifty-five- to sixty-four-year-olds among Europeans.[23] Ahead lay the 2020s when they would retire in large numbers – an eminently predictable fact that nonetheless appeared to come as a shock to politicians.

The second tailwind had been globalisation. But the opening up of the global economy lost momentum in the early 2010s. Instead of racing ahead of GDP growth as in the previous two decades, world trade only just kept pace. Globalisation turned into 'slowbalisation'.[24]

Under Donald Trump, things deteriorated further as America embarked on a self-defeating trade war with China that led to tit-for-tat trade tariffs. Behind the scenes, the US government sought to weaken the WTO by sabotaging its role as an adjudicator in trade disputes. Anyone hoping that Trump's successor Joe Biden would turn the clock back was swiftly disabused. Under his presidency, relations between America and China got even worse. Meanwhile, the misleadingly named Inflation Reduction Act introduced lavish protectionist subsidies for green energy. In another sign of Trump–Biden continuity, the new president made little attempt to revitalise the WTO. As the *FT*'s Gideon Rachman argued in August 2023, Bidenomics built upon Trumponomics. [25]

In addition to the White House, multinationals were having

second thoughts about globalisation. After the disruptions of the pandemic, supply chains that prioritised cost savings no longer seemed such a brilliant idea. Security of supply also mattered. Resilience became the new watchword, pushed hard by management consultancy McKinsey and the World Economic Forum at its annual summit held at Davos in the Swiss Alps. Offshoring anywhere that was cheapest was out; 'friendshoring' with added security was in.

Then there was Brexit. Foreign exchange markets have been called a continuing referendum on economies. Their verdict on the Leave triumph in 2016 was damning. When the markets closed in London on the day of the vote, the pound was worth $1.48 and €1.30. When the result was announced the next day, it dropped by 8 per cent against the dollar and 6 per cent against the euro. The decline against the dollar was the biggest 24-hour fall since the pound started to float against other currencies in the middle of 1972.

That fall in the pound's value pushed up import prices over the next two years. This directly affected living standards. One estimate from economists is that by June 2018 consumer prices were 2.9 per cent higher than they would otherwise have been, imposing an enduring cost of £870 a year on the average household.[26] Another malign effect was that firms cancelled or postponed plans to boost capital spending. After collapsing during the recession in 2008 and 2009, business investment made a vigorous recovery, rising sharply in the first half of the 2010s. But following the vote it stalled for the rest of the decade as the country became politically paralysed.[27]

Brexit finally took effect at the start of 2021 when Britain began to trade with the EU under the agreement negotiated by Boris Johnson. Brexit was a 'unique' example of deglobalisation, Mark Carney argued in an IMF lecture delivered in September 2017.[28] Although the Bank of England governor said its effects could be anticipated, he could scarcely have imagined that the trade deal struck on Christmas Eve 2020 between Britain and the EU would be quite so damaging.

Churn, baby, churn

The upsurge in inflation following the pandemic and the Russian invasion of Ukraine in February 2022 was a global phenomenon. However, Britain stood out for both its severity and persistence: in the year to June 2023, inflation was still almost 8 per cent compared with the euro area's 5.5 per cent and America's 3 per cent. It didn't help that the Bank of England was far too slow to anticipate and respond to the threat of inflation following the pandemic. Admittedly, it wasn't alone among central banks in getting its forecasts wrong. But its failure undermined a crucial plank in the new economic policy model. The fiscal plank had also rotted, with soaring interest payments on public debt.

Britain, it appeared, had come back full circle to the stagflation disaster of the 1970s. Although inflation fell back sharply in the second half of 2023, ending the year at 4 per cent, that was still double the inflation target. Meanwhile, the economy slipped into recession in the second half of the year, according to initial estimates from the Office for National Statistics (ONS) in early 2024.[29] The economy had flatlined over 2023 as a whole, growing by just 0.1 per cent compared with 2022, which in turn meant a sizeable fall of 0.7 per cent in GDP per head.

By the early 2020s, it was clear that Britain's economic policy model was well past its sell-by date. Shrinking the state and rejecting its role in orchestrating growth might have made sense when the government had tried to do too much in the post-war era up to the 1970s. Persisting with the free market approach was also understandable while the economy was on a roll from the early

1990s to the financial crisis of 2008. However, the economy's stuttering performance since that shock testified to the fact that the model of 'private good, public bad' no longer worked. The privatisation programme had initially yielded benefits as inefficiencies in previously state-run industries were eliminated and private ownership permitted higher investment than the Treasury had been willing to allow. But these were one-off gains.

The fundamental flaw of the model was that there was too little investment in either the good or the bad times. The state itself was far too stingy, a false saving since infrastructure investments underpin growth. For all its flaws, Britain's old statist model had at least built lots of affordable homes, criss-crossed the country with motorways and educated baby boomers to basic standards of literacy and numeracy as high as the generation that followed them – unlike almost every other advanced economy where younger adults were well ahead.[30] But businesses, too, were guilty of short-termism.

Neither the state nor the private sector had worked out a coherent strategy for equipping people with the skills needed in a modern economy. As much as anything, it was the uncertainty created by incessant policy churn that was now dragging the economy down. Britain's shiny new economic model had turned out to be no better than the one it had replaced. If Britain was to pull itself out of the mess there would have to be a comprehensive rethink of what the government should do – as opposed to what it shouldn't do.

Chapter 2

Brexit blues: how to devalue a country

A year before the fateful Brexit vote of 23 June 2016, the world's attention was focused on the looming danger of Grexit. The risk of Greece leaving the euro mounted when the radical left Greek government held a snap referendum on the bail out it was being offered – and the public emphatically rejected it. In the event, though, Greece stepped back from the brink whereas Britain stepped over it.

A crucial reason was that they were very different cliff-edges. Grexit was a sudden death prospect: a restored drachma would have immediately collapsed against the single currency, making it impossible to honour euro-denominated Greek debts and causing GDP to plunge by over 10 per cent. By contrast, Brexit was a slow-motion event because Britain was leaving the EU rather than the more tightly woven monetary union. Indeed, it took until the very end of 2020 for Britain to actually leave the customs union and single market. Even then the process was incomplete: at the start of 2024, the government had still not imposed full border controls on imports from the EU.[1]

The bitterly protracted nature of Brexit made it hard to assess the eventual economic impact. Would it be as damaging as the Remainers had suggested? Or could it yield the benefits that the Leave camp highlighted? Even if there was some economic harm would that be outweighed by the political gains of restoring full national sovereignty?

In the first few months after the vote, each side pointed to evidence backing its case. On the one hand, the foreign exchange markets delivered an instant thumbs-down. On the other, the wider economy avoided the punishment beating that George Osborne had predicted. As part of what Brexiters called 'Project Fear', the chancellor published a Treasury analysis a month before the vote warning that the economy would be tipped into recession if Leave won.[2] As Remain nerves jangled still further with the vote only a week away, Osborne claimed there would also have to be an emergency austerity budget – with taxes going up by £15 billion and spending cut by the same amount.[3]

Neither dire prediction materialised. The economy did not come close to recession, not least since the Bank of England rode to the rescue in August with a package of measures including a cut in interest rates and a new scheme to support bank lending. There was no emergency budget. When delivering the usual Autumn Statement in late November, the new chancellor Philip Hammond set looser fiscal targets rather than tightening budgetary policy.

But what mattered was the longer-term impact of leaving the EU. Who came out best in this contest between claims and counter claims? Have any of the supposed benefits of Brexit materialised?

The economic case for Leave

Although the economic establishment – from the Treasury to the OECD – strongly backed Remain, the Leave campaign did have some formidable proponents. These included former chancellor

Nigel Lawson, a towering figure in the Thatcher government of the 1980s, and David Owen, a former foreign secretary and one of the founder members of the pro-European Social Democratic Party, which broke with Labour in 1981. Another person to reckon with was Rishi Sunak, a fledgling MP who disappointed David Cameron by backing Brexit. On becoming chancellor in February 2020, Sunak showed his respect for Lawson (who died in 2023) by hanging a picture of him above his desk.[4]

The economic case for Brexit made by Lawson focused on three potential benefits.[5] First, Britain would untether itself from Europe's dysfunctional monetary union. Second, as the world economy was tilting eastwards, trade deals could be struck with fast-growing countries in Asia and elsewhere. Third, freed of interference from Brussels, Britain would be able to rewrite onerous regulations supposedly hindering economic performance. We could become a bigger version of a light-touch Singapore (though in fact Singapore is a lot more statist than its free-market fans like to admit).

In the run-up to the vote, Brexiters made much of the eurozone's woes. The panic about a potential Grexit in 2015 followed half a decade in which Europe's monetary union had stumbled from one crisis to another. Starting with Greece in spring 2010 and soon followed by Ireland, several countries in the currency union were unable to cope with soaring borrowing costs inflicted by investors and traders reckoning that they could no longer cope with the rigours of membership. In all, five required humiliating bailouts from sounder European economies and the IMF. In return, they had to swallow unpalatable economic and fiscal medicine. The travails of the eurozone undoubtedly contributed to the UK's sluggish recovery in the early 2010s. But was this reason enough to leave the EU? In or out of Europe, Britain would still be influenced by its biggest trading partner.

A more credible fear was that Britain might get financially

dragged into the euro's travails. Yet this concern was greatly exaggerated. For one thing, the IMF committed to over a quarter of the first Greek rescue package. The remainder came from the other euro countries, above all Germany. Britain's sole exposure to the other bailouts was indirect, through an EU fund backed by the European budget and thus all the member states, including those outside the euro area. But this fund, which would raise money by borrowing from the financial markets, could mobilise only up to €60 billion – little more than half the €110 billion pledged to Greece in its first bailout. Separately, the Treasury contributed later that year to Ireland's rescue, but only because it was in Britain's direct interests to do so.

Crucially, the opt-out from joining the single currency, which John Major secured at the European Council meeting in Maastricht in 1991, remained intact. Moreover, neither Denmark nor Sweden had adopted the euro. Several of the twelve countries joining the EU in the 2000s also retained their currencies. The original decision to stay outside the monetary union was by no means cost-free. Inevitably, Britain lost influence compared with the countries that had pressed ahead with the euro when it was launched in 1999. But there was no reason to forfeit the benefits of EU membership altogether for fear of some dystopian future in which the inner ring of the union held the UK to ransom. That was like razing your house to stop it being burned down. Even if a blaze started, Britain could fight it better from within.

As it happened, the Greek confrontation of 2015 proved to be the final flare-up of the euro crisis. Even during its worst years, the monetary union had continued to expand its reach, with the three Baltic states joining. In 2023, Croatia became the twentieth member, less than ten years after it had joined the EU.

More important still, the eurozone economy rallied, putting behind it the trauma of the early 2010s. Despite having to impose yet more austerity, Greece was on the path to recovery. Brexiters had been too hasty in writing off the currency union, mainly because they underestimated the depth of the political commitment to it – above all Germany's.

You can't buck economic gravity

The second Brexit benefit was supposed to be more trade with fast-growing emerging economies. The objective was a sensible one: the EU had been sluggish in pursuing new trade deals. However, there was nothing to prevent Britain pushing for faster progress.

A crucial advantage of securing a trade agreement as an EU member was that the bloc had a market five times as big (without Britain) as the British economy. For example, the EU's deal with South Korea, which came into force in 2011, included a concession that helped Britain's legal firms, which the east Asian economy was prepared to make because it was keen to get better access to Europe's huge car market.[6]

This awkward truth about relative negotiating power became embarrassingly clear after Britain formally left the EU at the end of January 2020 (while temporarily staying in the single market and customs union for the rest of the year) and started negotiating its own trade deals. Trade minister Liz Truss, more intent on buffing her image as a prospective prime minister than on the nitty-gritty of trade negotiation, bragged about how many deals she had secured as she dashed around the world. But the vast majority of the seventy or so 'new' trade agreements that were signed were rollovers from the ones Britain had in the EU.[7]

The first new deal – of sorts – was with Japan, which came into force at the start of 2021. However, this was essentially the same as the one inherited from the EU apart from a new section about digital trade.[8] By contrast, the agreement signed with Australia in December that year started with a blank slate, presenting an opportunity for British negotiators to show their mettle. But Johnson's political need to show Brexit was working by securing a quick deal weakened an already weak hand. The negotiation resembled a lacklustre England cricket team being thrashed by the Aussies. They must have been pinching themselves when they won eventual full access to Britain's food market – a concession that prompted howls of anguish from British farmers.[9] George Eustice, a devout Brexiter and environment secretary under Johnson, subsequently condemned the agreement, saying the UK 'gave away far too much for far too little in return'.[10] Britain also appeared to come out the worse when striking its next new deal with New Zealand in February 2022.

Leaving the EU in the hope of better deals was, in effect, to defy the laws of economic gravity. Just as the force of gravity is stronger when two objects are closer together, the same is true of trade. The pull of neighbouring Europe's big single market would always outweigh that of a distant and smaller economy. Brexiters seemed blind to the fact that around half of Britain's trade was with the EU.

The new trade deals would yield economic gains so scanty they barely registered. The government's own impact assessment calculated that the Australian deal would raise GDP in the long term (2035) by £2.3 billion – a meagre increase of 0.08 per cent.[11] This barely counted as small change in the national accounts.

The finding chimed with official estimates leaked in early 2018 when prime minister Theresa May was working out in earnest what she wanted Brexit to mean.[12] These showed that the biggest prize of all, a deal with the United States, would produce a long-term gain of merely 0.2 per cent of GDP, a negligible amount compared with the loss arising from Brexit. A host of other deals in the Asia-Pacific region and the Gulf states would bring a gain of between 0.1 and 0.4 per cent.

Indeed, as with so much to do with Brexit, there was something very old-fogeyish about its advocates' view of trade. Johnson claimed on Christmas Eve 2020 that his deal would 'allow UK goods and components to be sold without tariffs and without quotas in the EU market'. Technically, that was an oversimplification because bilateral trade would be subject to 'rules of origin' which, if broken, could mean tariffs – for example, on car exports if the proportion of the value created in Britain (which could include EU parts) was too low.[13]

But more important, Johnson's focus on tariffs (taxes on imports) and quotas was outdated. Following successive global trade rounds, industrial tariffs were generally no longer high. But just as a receding tide exposes hidden rocks, this highlighted the importance of 'non-tariff' barriers such as product standards. The aim of the many bilateral trade deals negotiated since the last big global agreement concluded in Morocco in 1994 was to lower such barriers as well as to liberalise markets in services (on which tariffs are not charged) and to allow more mutual investment.

In July 2023 the government added to its modest tally of three new trade deals (the ones with Japan, Australia and New Zealand) one that sounded more impressive. It agreed to join the Comprehensive and Progressive Agreement for Trans-Pacific Partnership (CPTPP), a free-trade area between eleven countries. However, Britain already had bilateral deals with nine of them. The government's own estimate for the long-term boost to the economy – £2 billion – was as modest as the one for the Australian deal.[14]

On becoming president in January 2021, Joe Biden swiftly made it clear that he didn't want a trade deal with Britain. Maybe that was a mercy in disguise. The notoriously hard-boiled American trade negotiators would have run rings round a government trying to show the point of Brexit. In any case, an updated estimate in 2020 suggested a deal with the US would yield a long-term boost of between only 0.07 and 0.16 per cent of GDP, depending on how ambitious it was.[15]

Meanwhile, the EU was itself negotiating new trade deals. Agreements with Japan and Singapore came into force in 2019. A deal with New Zealand was signed in 2023 while one with Chile was updated that year.[16] Jolted by Britain's departure, the EU had stepped up a gear.

Ruletaker, not rulemaker

What of the third supposed advantage of Brexit: the ability to make rules that fitted Britain's needs rather than those of the EU?

In another brutal reality lesson, British firms told ministers they did not want bespoke product procedures even for their home market: that would simply impose a further regulatory burden. Given the size of the European market, UK businesses would, in any case, have to comply with EU rules, so separate British ones would overcomplicate matters. After determined lobbying by business groups, the government shelved indefinitely plans to replace the EU's product safety mark (CE for Conformité Européenne) with a UK mark (UKCA for UK Conformity Assessed) for most goods sold in the British market.[17]

This inglorious retreat revealed something long appreciated by British business, if not Westminster politicians: the EU was a regulatory superpower. Simply by virtue of the size of the single market, rules set in Brussels held sway beyond European borders. Ministers liked to boast that Britain was a country that could punch above its weight. If ever that phrase had any substance Brexit voided it, as John Major pointed out in 2020.[18] But beyond question the EU was capable of punching above its weight through its regulatory clout.

Inside the EU, Britain could exert real influence over common rules: for example, before the banking crisis it was the main author of financial regulations. Outside the EU, it started to alter the financial rulebook but that was only because banks could no longer provide services to European countries out of London. Furthermore, there had always been scope to vary financial rules between member states: for example, in Britain, ringfencing of big banks' domestic retail activities was introduced after the 2008 crisis but not in the rest of the EU.

The issue of Britain's regulatory future came to a head when Jacob Rees-Mogg, in his brief stint as business minister under Truss, introduced a bill to scrap 2,400 pieces of legislation inherited from the EU by the end of 2023 after which they would automatically expire through a 'sunset clause' unless specifically preserved.[19] That number increased to around four thousand as more were discovered: Brexit was a learning process.[20] This scorched-earth strategy brought consternation among lawyers and despair among environmental groups and businesses. Under pressure from a host of organisations, the 'bonfire of the rules' was in effect extinguished under Sunak in May 2023 when the government got rid of the sunset clause and slashed the number of scrapped laws to six hundred or so, many already largely defunct.[21]

Whatever happened to Singapore-on-Thames?

Among the rules that Britain retained were those governing the labour market which had long riled Brexiters. A *bête noire* for even the milder species of eurosceptic was the working time directive that imposed a weekly limit of forty-eight hours on average (though individuals could opt out). But there were plenty of other regulations stemming from Europe, especially after Tony Blair agreed soon after taking office in 1997 to adopt the Social Chapter, which for example enhanced the rights of part-time workers.

The suspicion in Brussels was that Boris Johnson's Britain would rip up its labour standards and become a bargain basement

competitor – a lightly regulated, low-tax 'Singapore-on-Thames'
on Europe's shores. Even though Johnson was aiming for no more
than a bog-standard trade deal covering goods, Europe demanded
that Britain play by the same rules on environmental and labour
standards.

But there was no compelling reason for Britain to dismantle its
labour market rules. The OECD found that in the early 2010s they
were among the least stringent among comparable economies.[22]
Other member states such as Germany – the largest economy in
the bloc ahead of the UK and France – had amongst the most
exacting rules. Precisely because British regulations were already
comparatively light, the OECD said ahead of the referendum that
gains from further liberalisation would be 'limited'.[23] The moral
was that membership of the European club did not in practice
prevent Britain from going its own way on labour standards.

Could Brexit Britain follow Singapore's example and turn itself
into a low-tax competitor with the EU? At first, that seemed to be
the logic when Philip Hammond stuck with Osborne's strategy
of bringing down the main corporation tax rate, which duly fell
from 20 to 19 per cent in 2017. When he left office together with
May two years later, a further reduction, to 17 per cent, was due
in April 2020.

But again Britain didn't need to leave the EU to tailor its own
tax regime. As a member, it had to follow the main rules about
VAT – a minimum standard rate of 15 per cent and a reduced
rate no lower than 5 per cent.[24] There were also minimum rates
for excise duties, such as those levied on alcohol. These aside, the
Treasury essentially had a free hand to set whatever taxes it chose
and to levy whatever rates it wanted. Moreover, like any other state,
Britain could veto a European tax proposal.

In the event, Brexit brought a change of mind on corporation
tax. The planned cut to 17 per cent in April 2020 was ditched
while Sajid Javid was briefly chancellor. Then, in a screeching

U-turn in the spring of 2021, Rishi Sunak raised the tax rate from 19 to 25 per cent, due to take effect in 2023. (This was the rise cancelled by Kwarteng and reinstated three weeks later in the autumn chaos of 2022.)

The corporate tax *volte face* showed how far removed the bogey-man of Singapore-on-Thames was from reality. Just as the British government's fear of being sucked into supporting the euro was unwarranted, so was the EU's of a deregulated, low-tax Britain. The key point to bear in mind was the conflicted politics of Brexiters: those who backed leaving the EU had very different priorities from those leading the cause. The referendum featured a revolt by people who felt economically marginalised and wanted *more* rather than less help from the state. That inevitably meant higher taxes – on someone else, they hoped – a vision of Britain far removed from the laissez-faire fantasies of the Brexiters.

The paradox of Brexit: it made Britain more European

The economic discontent that fuelled the Leave campaign reflected the poor overall performance of the economy in the preceding eight years. First there was the wrenching recession in 2008-09, the deepest decline in GDP in post-war history. (The pandemic-induced economic collapse eclipsed that record in 2020.) The subsequent recovery was disappointing, mainly because of the sustained setbacks to productivity growth. For decades people had become used to their living standards rising year on year.[25] That expectation had been dashed.

There was also a distinct regional dimension. Anand Menon of King's College London, who heads the UK in a Changing Europe think tank, recalled addressing a pre-referendum debate in Newcastle. When he spoke about the risk to GDP if Leave won, a woman in the audience cried out: 'That's your bloody GDP. Not ours.'[26] The heckler had a point. Even in the good times, growth had been lopsided with London pulling ahead of the rest of the country. That continued in the bad times – to no one's advantage since the capital paid for its economic prowess through congestion and higher house prices.

The post-referendum governments of May and Johnson differed in their approach to regional balancing. Under May, an ambitious industrial strategy was supposed to improve local and regional outcomes. Under Johnson, that strategy was ditched but he and his lieutenant Dominic Cummings were gung-ho about using the public purse to champion British technology companies.[27] Indeed, a bid to have a free hand over state aid in the trade deal being negotiated with Brussels was a prime reason why at one stage in 2020, Johnson threatened to break international law by breaching provisions about Northern Ireland in the exit treaty with the EU. The crude tactic brought obloquy from all quarters and was dropped later that year.[28]

Both prime ministers were committing a cardinal heresy for those who still revered Thatcher's liberalising legacy. They were also bringing Britain more into line with Europe, where countries such as France and Germany had long spent much more on state aid. Post-Brexit Britain was becoming *more* rather than less European in its economic approach.

Another galling similarity was growth. Before Brexit, Britain outperformed the eurozone economy. That was no longer the case. On figures published in early 2024, GDP in the UK was 1 per cent higher in the final quarter of 2023 than four years earlier in late 2019, just before the pandemic. That was worse than the euro area's 3 per cent.[29]

That growing resemblance was evident most of all in taxes. In the early 2020s, headlines screamed that taxation as a share of GDP was on course to reach its highest since the late 1940s. Less commented upon was the fact that Britain was drawing closer to

European countries that had long raised more in tax. In 2015, taxation in the Netherlands was 37 per cent of GDP compared with Britain's 31.9. In 2022, the Dutch tax take was 38 per cent compared with 35.3 in Britain – the gap had narrowed to less than three points. Similarly, compared with the average of the fourteen other EU states before enlargement in 2004, a gap of seven percentage points in 2015 shrank to four points in 2022.[30]

This was the paradox of Brexit. A belief in British exceptionalism fuelled the vote to leave the EU. But the effect of the vote was for Britain to become less exceptional.

'Fuck business'

According to Jean Monnet, a founding father of the EU, Britain's failure to shape the European club's ground rules when it was formed in the 1950s was the 'price of victory' in the Second World War. What would the final price of Leave's victory be? Even by the early 2020s that remained unclear – though clearly the price tag was high. The difficulty in putting a precise number on the cost of Brexit reflected the delay in reaching a deal. It also reflected the fact that the adverse consequences of Brexit would take effect gradually.

Although the Treasury's analysis a month before the referendum turned out to be quite wrong, its previous report on the longer-term impact of Brexit remained highly relevant. Published in April 2016, this explained how any departure would reinstate barriers to doing business with the EU. The result would be lower trade and a drag on growth over the next fifteen years compared with Britain staying in the EU.[31]

Some forms of departure were worse than others. The Treasury analysis helpfully set out the alternative relationships that might replace Britain's membership of the customs union (eliminating tariffs on trade within the EU while setting common ones on all other countries) and the single market (the mutual acceptance of regulatory standards and tests among EU states).

At best, Britain might remain in the single market (but not the customs union) on terms similar to Norway, which followed the rules set in Brussels without having a meaningful say on them. At worst, it would leave without a deal, trading with the bloc on the bare minimum WTO terms. Johnson misleadingly tried to sugar the bitter pill by calling the WTO terms an 'Australia-style' deal since Australia had no free trade agreement with the EU. In between these two poles, Britain could strive for an arrangement similar to Switzerland (better) or Canada (worse).

The story of the negotiations that finally got under way in mid-2017 and ended at the end of 2020 can be summed up by these options. Neither May nor Johnson contemplated 'Norway' since this would leave Britain as a ruletaker. After initially trying for a more ambitious version of a Canada-style deal (dubbed Canada-plus-plus-plus by David Davis, the first Brexit secretary), May plumped for 'Switzerland', whereby Britain would in effect stay in the single market for goods. May's inability to win enough parliamentary votes for her plan doomed her premiership. Johnson discarded that approach for a barebones 'Canada' deal (Canada-minus was the verdict of Citigroup economists when the agreement was unveiled), while claiming during the negotiation that Britain could 'prosper mightily' under an 'Australia-style' arrangement.[32] That was a bluff because obviously Britain traded far more intensely with the EU than distant Australia did.

In 2016, the Treasury projected that the long-term cost of a Canada-style agreement would be 6.2 per cent of GDP, not far off the worst-case scenario of leaving without a deal which would inflict a 7.5 per cent hit – in both instances compared with staying in the EU. These estimates might have erred on the gloomy side, but they were in the right ballpark. As the eventual deal took shape in

2020, the Office for Budget Responsibility projected a substantial loss of 4 per cent.[33] The OBR estimated that about a third of that loss had already occurred through the effective stalling in business investment since the referendum. The reason for that reluctance to invest was clear: uncertainty. Long after the vote, the question remained over what exactly Brexit would mean in practice. Even in the closing months of 2020, no deal appeared to be as likely as the trade agreement eventually concluded.

The disadvantages of the new trading arrangement immediately became apparent after it came into force at the start of 2021. While Britain was a member of the EU, firms did not have to worry about showing they complied with rules such as safety when they traded with other EU countries. Outside, it was a different matter. Smaller businesses were worst affected since the cost of complying with the new regime was high compared with the value of their trading activity (see box). Many simply abandoned exporting to the EU. A study of the first year (2021) of the new trade deal published by the LSE's Centre for Economic Performance spoke of 'the destruction of low-value trade relationships'.[34] Bigger firms could cope better although the increased costs made doing business with Europe less profitable.

Losing the will to trade

When the new agreement between Britain and the EU came into force at the start of 2021, it showed that the devil was in the detail. Yes, goods could, by and large, still be traded free of tariffs. But businesses still had to fill in customs declarations that even the government accepted were 'complicated'. Firms had to comply with 'rules of origin' by demonstrating that their products had sufficient local content (this varied but was roughly half their value) to prevent Britain becoming a staging post for foreign suppliers seeking to avoid EU tariffs. They also had to show that their products were safe. Rules were especially tight for plant and animal products.

A Cabinet Office guide to the new system ran to over 250 pages. This new heap of hassle weighed heavily on smaller firms. A survey in July 2022 by the British Chambers of Commerce painted a dispiriting picture. Over half (56 per cent) of small and medium-sized firms trading goods with the EU said they faced difficulties arising from the trade deal. A small manufacturer in Dorset complained that 'the bureaucracy makes it no longer worthwhile' to export to the bloc. If anything, the impact got worse in the following year. A medium-sized manufacturing firm in the West Midlands lamented: 'Our experience has been that EU companies view the UK in a different way and are more reluctant to buy from us. We used to exhibit in Europe but now have stopped as European companies are very reluctant to start any form of dialogue with UK companies if there are European alternatives.'

In early 2024, Patrick Minford, one of the few economists to back Leave, claimed in a letter to the *Financial Times* that significant negative Brexit effects 'are simply not to be found in statistical time-series modelling of the UK data on trade and other macro variables'. One of the newspaper's readers retorted: 'All I know is that since Brexit came into effect, Bettys of Harrogate has been unable any longer to send me (here in Belgium) its excellent Christmas cakes.'[35]

Even so, the overall impact of the Brexit deal was difficult to determine. Trade patterns were hugely distorted by Covid. Official statisticians changed the methods for recording trade, which made it harder to interpret the data. However, the OBR noted in the spring of 2022 that Britain had 'missed out' on much of the recovery in world trade following the pandemic. The evidence, it suggested, was consistent with Brexit eventually depressing 'trade intensity' (the ratio of trade to GDP) by around 15 per cent (compared with where it would have been if Britain had remained in the EU). That would in turn lower GDP by 4 per cent (again compared with not leaving the EU). Updating the analysis in March 2024, the OBR concluded: 'Overall, our assumptions about the impact of Brexit appear to be broadly on track.'[36]

One welcome surprise was that exports of services, though neglected in Johnson's trade deal, were doing well. Still, Britain's overall trading performance trailed that of the other G7 economies compared with the pre-pandemic year of 2019, making the economy less open. And since trade openness is linked to productivity that would depress GDP.

There were wider damaging consequences. For a generation there was a cross-party consensus on the need for government to work with business. Before the 1997 election, Labour courted the City, through its famous 'prawn cocktail offensive'. Since the 2008 crisis, relations with financiers had soured. But it was only after Brexit that business as a whole fell out of favour since, apart from a few high-profile bosses, it mostly backed Remain. Notoriously Johnson even spelled out what at least some Brexiters felt when he declared 'fuck business'.[37]

Nostalgia dressed up in rhetoric

Whatever the economics of Brexit there was a political case for leaving the EU. Even if 'take back control' was pitched to exploit anti-immigration sentiment, there was a grain of truth in the slogan. By leaving the EU, Britain would once again be able, for example, to represent itself at the WTO in Geneva rather than being represented by the EU (even though along with the other European states it had always had its own seat there).[38]

Setting aside the awkward fact that Britain had actually ceded sovereignty during the negotiations by agreeing to a border in the Irish Sea, the flaws in the political liberation argument were two-fold.[39] First, after two devastating world wars, Europe had decided to pull together and pursue a common destiny. Like it or hate it, the EU wasn't going to go away. Since a constant thread in British history was to avoid the threat posed by a continental hegemony, it made strategic sense to be within rather than outside the EU.

Second, there was a wilful conflation of formal sovereignty with actual power. This was a distinction that featured prominently in the first in–out referendum in 1975, when Margaret Thatcher, then a pro-European, warned that leaving the club would diminish Britain's control over its future. That was a lesson hard learned by the government after snubbing the European project in the 1950s. It was one that had to be painfully relearned following the Brexit vote as British influence waned both within and outside Europe.

In the wake of the referendum, first May and then Johnson held out the vision of 'Global Britain', returning to its roots as a buccaneering country trading around the world. In a speech at Greenwich in February 2020, Johnson spoke of Britain 're-emerging after decades of hibernation as a campaigner for global free trade'.[40] But this was nostalgia dressed up in rhetoric. The time had long passed since Britain could assume such a role.

Insubstantial trade deals following Brexit proved how illusory this prospect was. Come what may, the EU would remain Britain's main trading partner – and now on much worse terms than before. All along, the only agreement that really mattered was the one Britain already had as a member of the most integrated multi-state market in the world.

One consolation was that a democratic vote had been respected. But the seemingly endless disputes that had ensued after the referendum left a country so bruised that it no longer wanted to revisit the question. Politicians simply avoided talking about the subject. Yet there was plenty to talk about. Altogether, the economic costs of Brexit were immense. Take one easy measure of a country's standing: its currency. In the seven years following the vote sterling never regained its pre-referendum levels against the dollar and the euro. Brexit had devalued Britain.

Chapter 3

Debt Wish

In July 2023, nine months after the disaster movie starring Truss and Kwarteng was pulled, the Office for Budget Responsibility still had plenty to fret about. Even with sanity apparently restored in the shape of Rishi Sunak as prime minister and Jeremy Hunt as chancellor, the fiscal watchdog that Truss and Kwarteng had sought to bypass issued grave warnings in its annual 'Fiscal Risks and Sustainability' report. Its chair Richard Hughes said: 'The 2020s are turning out to be a very risky era for the public finances.'[1]

The report was a litany of woes, but most worrying was the state of the government's coffers. Public debt had risen to its highest in six decades. Even though taxes were at a seventy-year high, the government would be hard pressed to meet its modest new objective of getting debt to start falling within five years. At the same time, public services were under immense strain, requiring still more spending. Looking further ahead, the OBR was even gloomier. It published the fiscal equivalent of a long-range Met Office weather forecast predicting what debt would look like in fifty years if nothing changed. That projection showed a gathering storm, with debt spiralling out of control to 310 per cent of GDP and conceivably closer to 400 per cent by the mid-2070s. But though the 310 per cent figure duly made the headlines, it was a pretty meaningless stat: no government could allow debt to balloon that high. What the journalists missed was the OBR's story of what had already happened: the extraordinary increase in public indebtedness.

Britain was no stranger to debt burdens reaching 100 per cent or more of GDP, but these were necessary conditions of fighting existential wars. Shortly after the Napoleonic Wars, debt reached 194 per cent; in 1946, it reached an all-time peak of 259 per cent. Such high indebtedness was then worked down during the long periods of peace as the economy expanded. By the start of the new millennium, debt was less than 30 per cent of GDP, close to its lowest in living memory. But between 2000 and 2023 it rose by some 70 percentage points. 'Such a large increase in debt over such a short period is unprecedented in peacetime,' the OBR pointed out.

How on earth had things come to such a pass? The two once-in-a-century global shocks – the financial crisis of 2008 and Covid pandemic in 2020 – played a big part. But there were also deeper, structural reasons why things had gone wrong.

In the decades after the humiliation of the 1976 IMF loan, Britain clawed back its reputation for sound fiscal management. Under the Conservatives in the 1980s and 1990s, tough measures were adopted to keep borrowing down. When New Labour took over in 1997, Gordon Brown set two apparently tough fiscal goals, for both debt (the cumulative amount owed) and the deficit (how much is borrowed each year) and vowed to meet them. But as successive chancellors of both parties brandished their budget day red box full of yet-to-be-revealed goodies, their biggest secret was a shared failure to prepare for the future. There was too much wishful thinking – including resorting to fiscal conjuring tricks – and too little grappling with hard choices. Not least the timebomb of an ageing population in the 2020s and 2030s, the impact of which on the public finances could be as bad as a war.[2]

Why public debt matters

At the start of 2023, the BBC published a review of its economic coverage by economist Andrew Dilnot and journalist Michael Blastland. Among other things, it found fault with the way that some BBC reporters assumed that debt was 'simply bad, full stop'. However, they also insisted: 'this does not mean we advocate going the other way and saying debt doesn't matter, or that a government has carte blanche'.[3]

The authors were right to caution against simplistic storytelling. It's hard not to gasp when you're told that public debt has reached £2.5 trillion (enumerating it in full, £2,500,000,000,000), as it did in early 2023.[4] But what matters is how big debt is in relation to the value of national output or GDP. Since these were roughly the same, the debt-to-GDP ratio was close to 100 per cent. In other words: we owed as much as we earned. It was, in fact, worse than it appears because debt had *already* reached £2.5 trillion almost two years earlier in April 2021 according to a different measure. Definitions matter (see box).

How much does the government owe?

The headline measure for public debt is net rather than gross. (It also leaves out the liabilities of banks that came under public control during the financial crisis.) What this means is that liquid (and therefore easy to turn into cash) financial assets that the government holds – including, for example, foreign exchange reserves and local authority deposits with banks – are subtracted from gross debt. Since the autumn of 2021, the Treasury has been targeting a version of this measure that excludes the Bank of England's contribution to net debt on the grounds that it is a better guide to the underlying picture.[5]

This focus on net debt doesn't make much difference because in Britain, liquid financial assets are relatively small (as these things go), typically amounting to around 10 per cent of GDP. Still, it does modestly flatter the picture compared with gross debt, the measure that reached £2.5 trillion in April 2021, and the one generally used in international comparisons. In other countries, notably Japan, it makes a big difference. Japan's gross debt was almost 250 per cent of GDP in 2022; its net debt was a lot less, though still high at about 135 per cent.[6]

Debt is valued in cash terms. This means that the measure of GDP used in debt-to-GDP ratios is not the one that features in most of the coverage of what's happening to the economy. When a reporter tells us that GDP has risen or fallen in the most recent month or quarter, they mean in real terms, stripping out the effect of inflation. By contrast, the debt ratio is based on nominal GDP – the cash value of the economy – which rises through both real growth and inflation.

For example, after the Second World War (and despite Britain's engagement in the Korean War of the early 1950s), the debt ratio fell sharply, from above 250 per cent in 1946 to around 100 per cent at the start of the 1960s. This wasn't because the actual debt itself fell over that period (it rose). Rather the magic was a mix of both real growth and inflation increasing nominal GDP, the denominator.[7]

However we define debt, it's important to bear in mind the other side of the national balance sheet. That can be grasped through looking at 'net worth', a broad measure of government assets minus liabilities. If Britain had over the decades built new infrastructure to match the scale of its debt then the ratio to GDP would have been healthier, because that would have promoted higher growth. But the reverse was true.

The British state had not only piled on debt but also under-invested across the board. Figures for public sector net worth showed it moving into negative territory in the 2010s, with overall indebtedness increasingly exceeding the total value of the public realm, counting physical assets such as highways and hospitals as well as the full range of financial assets held by the state. International comparisons published by the OBR in late 2021 showed Britain in an unfavourable light: among twenty-four advanced economies it had the most negative net worth as a share of GDP.[8]

But why does debt matter in any case? Primarily, it matters because it provides a resource for spending. Rather than paying their way through the amount of taxation that can be levied each year, governments can borrow extra from the markets. In effect, they can spread the costs with future taxpayers – which is especially helpful during emergencies. When Covid struck, the Treasury was able to support a stricken economy through massive borrowing, which reached a colossal £315 billion in 2020–21, a peacetime high of 15 per cent of GDP. This easily exceeded the previous record, in 2009–10, when the deficit amounted to 10 per cent of GDP. In 2019–20, before the pandemic affected the public finances, borrowing had been just £61 billion, less than 3 per cent of GDP.

So we shouldn't make the mistake of thinking that debt is automatically a bad thing. Historically speaking, Britain's growing power in the eighteenth century was made possible through the superior borrowing capacity of the British state. Indeed, the Bank of England was founded in 1694 to help finance wars in Europe.

Accounts of conflicts such as the Seven Years' War (1756–63) when Britain prevailed over France focus on military exploits like the victory of James Wolfe on the Plains of Abraham outside Québec City in 1759. But those efforts were bankrolled by borrowing, which accounted for 37 per cent of British military spending in the war, according to economic historian Charles Kindleberger. [9]

We must also remember, though, that piling up more debt isn't consequence free. Generally, lenders are more than ready to finance governments because of their power to tax. That's why countries can usually borrow at cheaper rates than companies. Typically, they do so by issuing a range of bonds with maturities (the time until the original sum of money borrowed is repaid) running from one to thirty or even fifty or so years in Britain where these are called gilts because the paper certificates used to be gilt-edged.[10]

As public debt mounts, however, lenders become wary. There is a long history of states defaulting on their debt. Notoriously, Philip II, who ruled Spain in the second half of the sixteenth century (ironically nicknamed Philip the Prudent) defaulted no fewer than four times. Lenders kept on lending since they paid more attention to the treasure arriving from the Spanish empire in Latin America than to his terrible track record. In more recent times, serial offender Argentina has defaulted three times since 2001 (and nine times in its history). Greece's default in 2012 was the biggest on record. What's more, governments can renege on their debt without formally defaulting by letting inflation rip, which devalues the worth of the bonds they have issued.

The precise level at which public debt becomes a concern is hotly disputed. Under the Maastricht fiscal rules underpinning Europe's monetary union, 60 per cent of GDP was set as an upper limit – but the rationale for that figure was contested at the time by leading economists such as Willem Buiter.[11] Even before the financial crisis, eurozone countries honoured that supposed limit more in the breach than the observance. On the other hand, the very fact that five member states (first Greece, then Ireland, followed by Portugal, Spain and Cyprus) subsequently had to be bailed out between 2010 and 2013 suggested that concern about debt was warranted, even if it wasn't the only reason why they got into trouble.

Does the experience of households provide clues about what is sustainable debt? Though beloved by some politicians the maxing-out-the-national-credit-card analogy is fundamentally misleading. Although mortgage loans as a share of income can be considerably higher than 100 per cent, regulators do worry about very high loan-to-income ratios.[12] In any case, mortgage loans are secured on properties: borrowers have to stump up deposits and eventually repay the full amount. By contrast, states can always rely on an income thanks to their power to levy taxes and never really have to repay loans since they simply refinance maturing debt. Dilnot and Blastland, in their BBC report, rightly cautioned that 'household analogies are dangerous territory'.

During the 2010s public debt gradually lost its sting and those still bothered about it were dismissed as worrywarts. As interest rates fell lower and lower, finance ministries found that rising debt could be accompanied by lower servicing charges. This emboldened the Treasury to raise investment. In March 2020, Rishi Sunak's first budget set out an ambitious plan to increase capital spending calling it 'the biggest programme of public investment ever'. For those who had become blasé about debt, the precipitate rise in interest payments between 2021 and 2023 was a rude awakening. Suddenly, it became clear again why governments have always had to care about how much they owe. In 2022–23 the Treasury paid £112 billion in interest, double the £57 billion in the preceding financial year. That outlay was more than the entire education budget for the whole of the UK, which came to £106 billion in 2022–23.[13]

Chronicle of a debt foretold

Debt contains its own story, both past and future. It is the cumu-
lation of past borrowing and the decisions and untoward events
that have contributed to that outcome. But that is possible only
because the debt will be honoured by future taxpayers, including
generations as yet unborn. For example, in 2015 the government
redeemed all the outstanding undated (i.e., with no obligation to
repay at a specified maturity) gilts, at a cost of £2.6 billion. Most of
the debt had been incurred during the First World War, but some
could be traced back as long ago as the early eighteenth century.
This was essentially a PR exercise by George Osborne, who wanted
to present himself as a chancellor getting on top of debt old and
new. However, it showed vividly how far back the story of debt
might begin.[14]

Looking to the future, a fiscal crisis of some kind in the 2020s
was far from unexpected, owing to the predictable nature of population ageing. This would be the decade when the second big wave
of the baby boomers, born between 1955 and 1972, would start
retiring en masse. That increased the burden on younger taxpayers
who would now have to fund their state pensions and healthcare.
What was not inevitable was the public finances already being so
weighed down by indebtedness by the early 2020s. The starting
point should have been low rather than high debt. Why didn't we
see what was coming?

Most of the debt increase since the start of the century was the
result of two extraordinary shocks: the financial crisis and the
pandemic. In the financial year of 2007–08, public debt stood at
36 per cent of GDP, not that much higher than the 28 per cent at
the start of the decade. Two years later, it had nearly doubled to 65
per cent – excluding the liabilities of the banks that the Treasury
had had to rescue. Despite the austerity inflicted by Osborne while

he was chancellor between 2010 and 2016, debt had risen by the end of the decade to 85 per cent. In 2020–21, the year when the pandemic struck the public finances, it jumped to 96 per cent. Just three years accounted for forty of the almost seventy percentage points increase in debt to GDP over two decades.

But not everything could be blamed on these two (mostly) unpredictable misfortunes. These had, after all, affected all major advanced economies. Since the start of the century, Britain saw the second largest increase in (gross) debt among the G7 countries, exceeded only by Japan.[15] This was mainly because the financial crisis had been especially harmful to Britain's public finances. However, it also reflected the failure to shore up the coffers in the non-crisis years.

The poor state of Britain's public finances bore witness to lost opportunities and wishful thinking. In September 2022, Labour set out a proposal for Britain to have a 'national wealth fund' investing £8 billion of public money in green projects working in partnership with business. It stuck with this plan when abandoning the wider commitment to invest £28 billion a year in green projects in early 2024 (blaming the U-turn naturally on Sunak and Hunt 'promising to "max out" the country's credit card').[16]

Another advocate of a sovereign wealth fund was financier Nicholas Lyons, who said in late 2022 that he would use his one-year term as lord mayor of the City of London to campaign for one raising as much as £100 billion, split between private sources such as pension funds and the government.[17] Although Lyons's job was honorific (his ancient office stretches back more than eight centuries), his role included acting as an 'ambassador' for financial and professional services and he had to be taken seriously.

But both ideas were several decades too late. The time to have introduced a sovereign wealth fund was forty years earlier when the North Sea oil and gas fields briefly turned Britain into a petro-state. By the early 1980s, a gusher of petroleum taxes and royalties was flowing into the Exchequer.[18] The short-term fix was to use this bonanza to flatter the public finances. The better choice from a longer-term perspective would have been to put aside the windfall in a fund.

Sovereign wealth funds serve several purposes. First, they stabilise the public finances from the boom-and-bust vagaries of the oil price. Second, they can be used to invest in domestic infrastructure as well as in overseas assets to diversify their holdings. Third, they prepare for the predictable expense of an ageing society, providing a resource that can be drawn down when that cost materialises. Finally, they recognise that revenues from oil and gas fields will eventually dry up. Most importantly, such a fund shields the public finances from the political temptation to lower taxes or to increase spending. (Strictly speaking the money could also be used to pay down debt but this rarely happens.) By contrast, a fund builds up net worth. It can be raided – but at a political cost.

Norway, the other beneficiary from the underwater wealth of the North Sea, legislated in 1990 to set up exactly just such a fund. Thirty years later, the Norwegian fund, which invested only in overseas assets, was a powerful investment force with assets worth $1.6 trillion at the end of 2023 – equivalent to around $280,000 per person and 300 per cent of GDP.[19] Admittedly, Norway had a far smaller population and economy. But it had looked ahead and taken action to prepare for the predictable fiscal pressures of an ageing population.

The Norwegian fund stood as a rebuke to the course that Britain had pursued two years earlier. In 1988, Nigel Lawson announced sweeping tax cuts, including lowering the top rate of income tax from 60 to 40 per cent. His controversial budget contributed to an overheating economy, which allowed inflation to take off again. The British government had chosen to prioritise short-term budgetary giveaways over long-term economic development and fiscal stability. In 2018, Michael Heseltine, who had been a minister in

Thatcher's cabinet, deplored the way the 'incredible windfall of North Sea oil' had been squandered.[20]

A decade or so later, North Sea oil reserves had been considerably depleted, but there was another chance to set up a fund. Britain's public finances, now under Labour management, swung into surplus for two financial years between April 1999 and March 2001 – a rare event. Although revenues from the North Sea were now much lower they were bolstered by higher oil prices, which jumped threefold between the start of 1999 and the autumn of 2000 and went on to surge to an all-time peak of $147.50 per barrel in July 2008.

Once again, the opportunity wasn't seized. Gordon Brown liked to depict himself as the 'prudent' chancellor and he was – initially. In Labour's first two years in office, the public finances remained under tight control. But he then set in motion a ten-year boom in spending: while it helped to repair our decrepit public services, it failed to recognise that the good times would eventually end. (His mantra? No more boom and bust.) Debt remained within the limit of 40 per cent of GDP Brown had set as a fiscal rule. But given the unusual buoyancy of the economy debt should have been falling rather than rising. This was the period when the baby boomers were in the most productive years of their lives. Furthermore, the borrowing figures were flattered by outsized revenues from taxes on property and financial services, which were bound to be flaky.

Clever accounting

Rather than genuinely preparing for the future, chancellors from both the main parties took refuge in accounting conjuring tricks that disguised harsh budgetary realities. Such 'fiscal illusions' – a term introduced by the IMF in 2012 to highlight a practice by no means confined to Britain – became prominent, leaving an expensive legacy that would make the crisis of the 2020s worse.[21]

A case in point was the Private Finance Initiative. Originating in 1992 when Norman Lamont was chancellor, the PFI got private consortia to finance public works. Early examples included transport projects such as the M6 toll road, where the contractor would be repaid through tolls. But the PFI was also used to refurbish and then maintain buildings, such as the Treasury's itself, the cost of which would be settled through payments typically made for twenty-five to thirty years (in the Treasury's case thirty-five). Under Labour, the PFI was greatly expanded, covering, in particular, the renovation of hospitals and schools. The Treasury consistently argued at the time that getting private firms to finance these public projects made sense because they would be more efficient both in constructing and maintaining the buildings. By using the PFI, the government would avoid cost overruns and the inclusion of maintenance would incentivise private contractors to minimise lifetime costs.

This rationale was phoney because the government could always borrow more cheaply than the private sector, given the state's power to tax and its greater capacity to shoulder risk. Claims about overall savings turned out to be as tendentious as they appeared to many critics at the time. The long-term contracts tied the hands of the public providers such as hospitals and schools. For example, Liverpool City Council was paying around £4 million a year for a school that was no longer being used, pointed out the National Audit Office (NAO) in January 2018.[22]

The real appeal to both Conservative and Labour chancellors was that the Treasury didn't have to finance the investment immediately, keeping down the high-profile borrowing and debt figures.[23] That would help Brown, for example, meet his much-trumpeted fiscal goal about debt not exceeding 40 per cent of GDP. But this was targetry turned sophistry. It would have been better to have set a higher debt target that could encompass the cost of up-front public investment, financed at lower cost than the private sector.

When the PFI was finally abandoned by Philip Hammond in October 2018, the chancellor said there was 'compelling evidence' that the scheme neither delivered value for the taxpayer nor genu-inely transferred risk to the private sector.[24] Its legacy was the continuing payments on the seven hundred or so projects it had already financed. These were running at £10 billion a year and would amount to £199 billion from 2017-18 to the late 2040s, according to the NAO. Such bills added to borrowing and debt that would have to be settled by future taxpayers.

Another example of fiscal illusionism was student loans. When these were used to cover the university tuition fees introduced by Tony Blair's government, there was a case of sorts for them. They offered a means to expand higher education by tapping a new source of finance: students' future earnings. New Labour was keen to emphasise the fairness argument. Why should young people leaving school to work right away contribute through the taxes they paid to the cost of university courses from which stu-dents could expect higher wages? Why should a trainee bus driver subsidise an arts student?

But after tuition fees tripled under the coalition government, to £9,000 a year (strictly a maximum but it became the norm) from 2012–13, another consideration became paramount. The student loans were financed by the Treasury borrowing from the markets. That added to the official figures for debt but, crucially and counter-intuitively, not to the headline budget deficit.[25] The cash borrowed to finance student loans could be excluded from the deficit because it was swapped into another asset, the student loans themselves, making it a purely financial transaction. Helpful accounting, indeed.

However, that accounting made sense only if the loans were

repaid in full. But repayments were based on how much students subsequently earned, from 2012, over thirty years, turning them in effect into a graduate tax. In practice, though, many graduates would not repay in full. Yet that shortfall would be recognised in the deficit figures only in the distant future when any arrears on the loans were written off. Belatedly, a new more accurate accounting approach was introduced in 2019 that acknowledged the reality of student finance. The reform added £12.4 billion – 0.6 per cent of GDP – to the deficit for 2018–19.[26]

It wasn't just the credibility of the government's own figures that was harmed by this exercise in fiscal illusionism. The very fact that so many students were expected not to pay off their loans suggested that too many people were attending university with little prospect for financial gains. Whatever the wider benefits of higher education (which are considerable), it was not boosting their earning power sufficiently; some might have done better going down the vocational route through a good apprenticeship.

Meanwhile, universities also found themselves in a financial trap as it proved politically impossible to raise tuition fees beyond a small increase to £9,250 in 2017–18. That meant the value of the fees was eroded in real terms, at first gradually and then dramatically after the leap in inflation in the early 2020s. Serendipity funding had ended up sapping the finances of Britain's universities, widely regarded as one of the economy's strong cards.

The austerity illusion

The biggest exercise in fiscal illusionism was the persistence with austerity policies by George Osborne between 2010 and 2016 and then, to a lesser extent, under Philip Hammond until 2018 – long after they had ceased to make sense. Some fiscal retrenchment was essential following the financial crisis because the economy would

be smaller than previously expected. Labour chancellor Alistair
Darling had already set out a plan to bring the public finances
under control. Osborne's contribution was to intensify the squeeze
mainly through deeper and faster spending cuts.

At first, the austerity programme was bearable. The years of
Labour largesse had left some fat in the system. There was scope
to improve productivity by operating with fewer staff. Following
a period of generous wage settlements, pay restraint in the public
sector was tolerable for a while. The mistake was to persevere
with austerity for so long. Reductions in spending started to cut
into muscle, leading to a deterioration in the quality of public
services.

Both Osborne and Hammond persisted with policies that made
sense only on fiscal spreadsheets, rather than in the real world. The
Treasury was executing yet another bust in its own boom-and-bust
world, where clampdowns are held in place for too long, paving
the way for an eventual breakout to higher spending. That had
happened in the 1990s and was happening again in the 2010s. In
the middle of 2018, prime minister Theresa May announced a big
five-year increase in NHS spending, to start the following year. It
was the end of austerity, but the damage had been done.

A risky gamble on low inflation

The doubling in debt interest in the financial year of 2022–23 was
extraordinary not just from a historical but also an international
perspective. According to credit-rating agency Fitch, the ratio of
debt interest to revenues in Britain was second highest among
twenty or so advanced economies in Europe and North America
in 2022, and the highest in 2023.[27] This was remarkable for two
reasons. First, debt was still a lot lower than in some countries – in
Italy it was 140 per cent of GDP. Second, a longstanding strength

of our public finances has been the extended maturity – the time until repayment – of its debt. The longer the maturity of debt, the more the public finances should be insulated from rising interest rates. That's because every year a lower proportion of debt needs to be refinanced at the higher rates.

At the end of 2021, the average maturity of British debt, ranging from short-term bills repayable within a few months to longer-term bonds coming due over fifty or so years, was fifteen years. This was much longer than among other G7 economies where average maturity lay between six and eight years.[28] This, in turn, reflected the prominence of private pensions provided by companies in Britain whose schemes needed to hold long-term safe assets such as gilts to match their pension obligations.

Why, then, was the rise in debt interest so much worse than in other comparable countries? The main reason was another unusual feature of Britain's debt: the high proportion of gilts that were issued offering protection against inflation. Such bonds were called 'index-linked' because they were tied to a price index, meaning that when the index rose because of inflation, so, too, did the principal (the amount initially borrowed by the government) and the interest payments. By contrast, both the principal and interest on conventional gilts stayed the same when prices rose. Index-linked debt made up 25 per cent of the outstanding value of gilts in Britain, twice as high as the 12 per cent share in Italy, the second-biggest issuer in the G7.

Britain was the first big advanced economy to issue such bonds, in March 1981. Nigel Lawson, then a Treasury minister but not yet chancellor, was a prime mover. The rationale was to convey to the markets that the government was serious about keeping a grip on inflation, which the Thatcher government had been battling since taking office in 1979. Gordon Richardson, the Bank of England governor, strongly opposed the idea, regarding it as 'redolent of a banana republic', according to Lawson in his memoirs.[29] However, the issuance of index-linkers soon became common across advanced economies.

Once the Bank was made independent and asked to set interest rates to keep inflation low in 1997, index-linkers were no longer needed to buttress the government's anti-inflationary credibility. But they continued to be issued. There was a ready market for them in the form of pension funds wanting to secure protection against inflation. And as inflation repeatedly came in lower than expected, they proved a good bargain for the Treasury.

While debt itself was relatively low, the Exchequer wasn't that vulnerable to a substantial chunk of gilts being index-linked. But that changed after the leap in debt resulting from the financial crisis. In July 2017 the OBR highlighted the risk to the public finances through higher debt interest if inflation was higher than expected.[30] Although the Treasury's Debt Management Office acknowledged that danger, the share of index-linkers remained high. This left the public finances exposed when the low inflation era ended with a bang. Index-linking meant that the principal as well as the interest on the bonds were regularly uprated. Suddenly, a quarter of Britain's debt became subject to punishingly high rates of interest.

Making matters worse, the price index used to uprate the bonds was the old Retail Prices Index (RPI), which had been largely superseded by the more recent Consumer Prices Index (CPI). This mattered because since the early 2010s it had become clear that RPI exaggerated inflation owing to methodological flaws in the calculations used to compile it. Mindful of the contractual difficulties of changing the price index, the government had put off such a reform until 2030. The delay was expensive. In 2022 the RPI recorded inflation of 11.6 per cent whereas CPI recorded 9.1 per cent.

Another vulnerability was that quantitative easing had, in effect, drastically shortened the maturity of the debt stock, making the public finances much more exposed to rising interest rates. When the Bank of England conducted QE, starting in March 2009, it bought gilts by creating money in the form of central bank reserves held by banks. What this meant was that the bonds it had purchased – an astonishing £875 billion by December 2021, worth about two-fifths of all gilts – were now being financed at a daily rate paid to the banks.[31] As long as interest rates remained low this was profitable for the Bank, which received the interest payments due on the bonds; and it didn't take the Treasury too long to snaffle those profits, which reduced debt interest and thus borrowing.[32] Yet, even more than with the North Sea oil revenues, the case for setting aside the original gains from QE was strong because they were a windfall that would in all likelihood have to be repaid. That was because the government, which had indemnified the Bank against any losses, was now vulnerable to the rise in interest rates needed to curb inflation.

Altogether, the Treasury had received £124 billion in cash profits, but since October 2022 it was having to transfer money back to cover losses, amounting to £49 billion by January 2024. Further shortfalls lay ahead as the QE programme was wound down – losses that were likely to exceed the original gains by a wide margin.[33]

In a fiscal fix

The budgetary impasse in which the Treasury found itself in the wake of the pandemic and energy-price shock was profound. Even though Hunt announced tax cuts focused on lowering the main rate of employee National Insurance contributions (NICs) in both November 2023 and March 2024, the overall increase in tax revenues as a share of the economy was still on track to be the biggest in any parliament of the past seventy-five years, according to the

Institute for Fiscal Studies (IFS).[34] Even so, the Treasury could manage to hit its latest (and hardly stretching) fiscal target – for 'underlying' debt (the measure excluding the Bank of England as a share of GDP) to be falling within five years – only by setting unrealistically tight overall day-to-day spending plans and planning real-terms cuts in investment. All this when more rather than less needed to be spent, especially on infrastructure and public services already emaciated by a decade-long squeeze on budgets.

In the past, inflation had been the chancellor's friend, raising taxation automatically as earnings rose and the cash value of purchases increased. This 'fiscal drag' was reinforced by the Treasury's extended freeze of the income tax allowance and higher-rate threshold since April 2022, boosting revenues that enabled Hunt to hand some back to working taxpayers. But now inflation was double-edged, owing to the cost of servicing index-linked bonds. Meanwhile, higher wages and procurement costs also raised the expense of public services. In any case, no one wanted to repeat the post-war experience of persistent high inflation.

The Treasury's room for manoeuvre was constrained by the changing ownership of its debt. In the past it had been held predominantly by domestic institutions such as British insurance companies. In that sense, Britain simply owed money to itself – one reason why many economists urged not getting too worked up about the 'national debt'. But especially in the past two decades that reassuring story was rewritten. At the start of 2004, 13 per cent of British public debt was in the hands of foreign private owners (excluding central banks). By 2022 that had doubled to 25 per cent, the second highest after France in the G7.[35]

British insurers and pension funds buy government bonds to be sure they can honour promises to pensioners and other long-term savers, which will be paid in pounds. That generally makes their holdings more stable than foreign investors who lack this need to match assets and liabilities in sterling. Although the behaviour of

British pension funds in the autumn of 2022 was anything but stable owing to complex hedging strategies they had adopted, that was an exception to the rule. One reason why Japan had long been able to live with very high public debt was that the great majority was held by domestic creditors; in 2022 less than 10 per cent was in private foreign hands.

Among other things, the build-up of foreign holdings of debt reflected the persistent current account deficit on the balance of payments, meaning that Britain wasn't paying its way and required inflows of funds from overseas creditors and investors to close the gap. In June 2017, Mark Carney, governor of the Bank of England, warned that Britain had come to rely upon 'the kindness of strangers' at a time when risks to trade and investment were on the rise.[36]

Tarnished fiscal credentials were not conducive to such kindness. Britain no longer belonged to the elite group of countries with a 'triple-A' (AAA) credit rating. In the autumn of 2023 two of the three big rating agencies, Fitch and Moody's, gave the UK the fourth highest grade (AA-) while the other, Standard & Poor's, gave it the third highest (AA). The only comfort was that both Moody's and S&P had removed the 'negative outlook' – warning that a further downgrade could be on the way – they had adopted a year earlier as Truss and Kwarteng trashed Britain's budgetary reputation.[37]

Fiscal targets had been set and abandoned with increasing frequency by successive governments. The one constant was that once it became clear they could no longer be met, chancellors would then adopt another set of objectives that appeared more achievable – until they weren't. The widespread use since 2010 of rolling targets set three or five years ahead meant that in practice the date for meeting them never arrived.[38] This brought a progressive loss of credibility.

The underlying reason for the budgetary impasse and the

erosion of Britain's standing in managing the public finances was lower growth. Brexit certainly hadn't helped. The main culprit, though, was the step change down in growth following the financial crisis. This was the fundamental reason why Osborne's austerity programme ran into the sand. In another sustainability report published in 2020, the OBR highlighted just how dramatic the recession and subsequent sluggish recovery had been. In early 2013, the economy was 14 per cent smaller than the Treasury in 2008 had forecast it would be by then.[39]

If anything, the prospects for the 2020s were even worse since the Exchequer would no longer benefit from low interest rates. Even though debt interest was forecast by the OBR in March 2024 to fall from the highs of 4.4 per cent of GDP in 2022–23 and 3.8 the following year, it was expected to be between 3 and 3.5 per cent through to the late 2020s – well above the level in the 2000s and 2010s when it averaged 2 per cent.[40] Britain now faced deteriorating 'debt dynamics' as the relationship between interest rates and growth that is a crucial determinant of how debt as a share of GDP changes worsened.[41]

Could tax reform brighten the picture by improving growth prospects? Truss and Kwarteng had already shown that unfunded tax cuts were self-defeating. Financial markets didn't buy into the notion that such reductions would miraculously pay for themselves by spurring growth. But there was no shortage of ideas for simplifying Britain's complex tax system and getting it working better for the economy without losing revenues. The snag was that tax reform typically produces losers as well as winners, making it harder when tight budgets mean there is little scope for giveaways to sugar the pill.

The inconvenient truth is that, if anything, taxes need to rise still further. One apparent way of achieving this – without inflicting general pain – would be through a wealth tax levied on how much people own less what they owe. But working that out is tricky; for example, how do you value future pension rights? International experience suggested this would not raise all that much money. And in any case, the trend across the OECD club of mainly rich economies had been away from levying such taxes, falling from twelve countries in 1990 to just three (Norway, Spain and Switzerland) in 2022.[42] To rake in substantial extra amounts, the Treasury would have to turn to the three big taxes – income tax, National Insurance contributions and VAT – that together raise three-fifths of overall revenues.[43] That made Hunt's cuts in NICs paid by employees and the self-employed all the more questionable, let alone his 'long-term ambition' to eliminate them altogether (though that would still leave intact the larger portion of NICs paid by employers – and passed on to workers in lower wages).[44]

Britain has long tried to provide European-style public services financed by American-style taxes. But the failure to prepare for population ageing, the rise in debt, and the unpromising outlook for growth and interest rates made that no longer feasible. Even though taxes had already risen so much, higher taxation affecting the bulk of taxpayers was the only realistic way to escape the fiscal fix.

Chapter 4

The City: blessing or curse?

During the 1990s and most of the 2000s, the City of London was on a roll. You could trace its expansion as an international financial centre by looking at the capital's changing skyline: in the old square mile, weirdly designed new towers like the Gherkin, replacing the old Baltic Exchange in 2004, stood cheek by jowl with medieval churches and livery company halls. Crowded trading floors with high-tech screens and dealers shouting into phones became a beehive for smart, ambitious young people keen to become very rich, very quickly. From the City of bowler hats and gentlemen's agreements emerged something new: a glossy global hub.

All that changed when the financial crisis broke in the summer of 2007. Soon the City was viewed with hostility rather than fascination. The skyscrapers that had once stood for economic regeneration now symbolised the out-of-control greed that had fuelled a banking collapse and a nationwide downturn. The lesson was clear: finance left to its own devices could bust an economy. The UK was plunged into its worst recession since the war. Rescuing banking behemoths such as the Royal Bank of Scotland (RBS) – which, on the eve of the crisis had a balance sheet as big as the entire UK economy – put immense strain on the public finances.

A prolonged sobering-up period lay ahead in which the financial sector, rather than turbocharging growth, would act as a drag on the economy. Inevitably there was also a political backlash. The 2016 vote to leave the EU, fuelled by the left-behinds' resentment of well-heeled metropolitan bankers, put London's role as a global financial centre further at risk.

Given that the City has been a mixed blessing for Britain, would it be so bad if the industry was humbled for good? What would we actually lose? Tempting as it might be to do away with it, though, there are good reasons to be cautious. Britain can still capitalise on its underlying strengths in international finance – provided that tougher rules and oversight are upheld. In addition, there is a powerful case for the financial sector to do more to support the rest of the economy, promoting start-ups and middle-sized businesses and providing long-term finance for infrastructure investment. While it may prove impossible to tame the tiger, it should be possible to ride it.

An unlikely success story

The rebirth of the City of London as a global hub after the Second World War was, in many ways, unexpected. International financial centres tend to be based in the country whose currency is pre-eminent, which is why the City was so dominant in the late nineteenth and early twentieth century when the gold standard was in effect a sterling standard run by the Bank of England. On that basis, once the dollar reigned supreme New York should have prevailed. Instead, London grabbed the prize. Already in the 1960s and 1970s it was hosting more and more foreign banks keen to participate in 'eurodollar' markets, where lending was done in dollars held outside the US. These banks were taking advantage of Britain's relatively relaxed regulatory approach, which contrasted with tougher US rules.

Although London had become the world centre for foreign

banks – by the 1970s there were more American banks in the City than in New York – it started to fall behind in the new growth sector of the cross-border issuing and trading of equities (company shares). That changed with Margaret Thatcher's deregulatory 'Big Bang' in October 1986, which tore apart the way the London stock exchange used to work. Previously, it was a cosy carve-up between 'jobbers', dealers who made their living by selling shares at a higher price than they had paid when buying them (a margin called the jobber's 'turn'), and brokers who brought orders to buy or sell on behalf of clients and were paid by fixed commissions. But now a wave of mergers ensued and a new era of investment banking, combining broking and dealing together with helping companies to raise money, had begun.

A novel threat to the City's sway as a global financial centre loomed in the 1990s following the decision at the Maastricht summit in 1991 to create a single currency by the end of the decade. European resolve became clear when the new currency was named the euro at the Madrid summit in December 1995. Fears mounted that Frankfurt, where the European Central Bank would be located, could challenge London's financial hegemony. But despite the UK's reluctance to adopt the euro as its own currency, the City became the offshore centre of the euro markets, just as it had done with the dollar. Furthermore, the new currency gave a shot in the arm to eurozone lenders such as Deutsche Bank which sought to build global rather than national businesses – all of which benefited London as a finance hub.

How did the City reinvent itself so profitably? Helpfully, it was underpinned by sturdy foundations. London is in a favourable time zone, able to pass on trading positions to New York in the afternoon and to pick them up from Asian and Australian markets in the morning – one reason why early starts became standard for City workers. Britain's imperial past bequeathed connections through corresponding banks around the world as well as overseas branches of UK banks. And English was the language of global finance.

Financiers need lawyers to nail down their deals and there was no shortage of them clustered in and around the City. Crucially, international financial contracts are typically written under English law and when disputes arise they are subject to courts in London. When the eurozone countries had to set up an emergency rescue fund in the spring of 2010, they did so through a special purpose vehicle established under English law. London was also an international media hub – markets move depending on the news. But most important of all was a large workforce with the wide array of skills needed to assemble financial deals and trade in markets. City firms could draw on workers not just living in London but also within commuting distance of the capital as well as anyone from the EU. Some had long-established professional skills, such as the actuarial qualifications needed by pension funds and insurance companies. But increasingly banks and hedge funds recruited 'rocket scientists', such as physicists, to apply their expertise to financial products.

Success built success. The Victorian economist Alfred Marshall noted the tendency of firms to congregate in industrial districts because of something 'in the air', both sharing the 'mysteries of the trade' and spreading innovation: 'If one man starts a new idea, it is taken up by others and combined with suggestions of their own; and thus becomes the source of further good ideas.'[1] A century later, in 1990, Michael Porter of Harvard Business School highlighted the importance of local clusters in driving national economic performance in his influential doorstopper, *The Competitive Advantage of Nations*.

Whether through accident or design, Britain appeared to have created a financial cluster in London that was driving the national economy. The bustling City and its outposts in Canary Wharf and Mayfair had wider spin-offs as other business, services such as management consultancy and accounting, set up shop close to the big financial firms. Its success was a gift to the Treasury, which could pluck the golden goose on its doorstep. What could possibly go wrong?

Clusterf*ck

Even before the financial crisis, a number of downsides had become evident. For one thing, the astonishing salaries and bonuses you could earn in finance made it an obvious destination, especially for those with science and maths degrees. One estimate in 2006 was that 4,200 City workers would pocket million-pound bonuses for that year.[2] Such largesse spilled over into the upper end of the London property market as well as speeding its way to top-of-the-range car showrooms.

The City's gain was a loss for other parts of the economy, including public services. No school could compete with a bank when trying to hire physics or maths graduates. 'Such a high proportion of our talented young people naturally think of the City as the first place to work in,' the Bank of England governor Mervyn King told the Commons Treasury select committee in April 2008. 'It should not be. It should be one of the places, but not the only one.'[3]

The big bucks to be made in the City also contributed to widening inequality. Company executives looked at the earnings of investment bankers and wanted some of that. An upward spiral got under way that fuelled resentment all the way through society.

The coarsening culture of the new City had wider drawbacks. The intense focus on deals and trading sent a get-rich-quick message, even though enduring economic advances come about through sustained hard work and long-term investments. The no-holds-barred approach of the 'big swinging dicks' gambling with the bank's money sent a similarly undesirable message about risk-taking. When bets turned sour, someone else was landed with the bill. When that 'someone else' turned out to be the taxpayer, the biggest downside of all was exposed.

The banks which had allowed this frenzy of deal-making had put aside far too little capital to absorb potential losses. In October 2008 the Treasury had to rescue two of Britain's biggest banks, RBS – at the time the world's largest by size of balance sheet, following its ill-timed takeover of ABN Amro, a big Dutch bank, a year earlier (subsequently described by the bank's new chairman as 'the wrong price, the wrong way to pay, at the wrong time and the wrong deal') – and Lloyds, which ministers had encouraged to make a mercy merger with shaky HBOS less than a month earlier, acquiring big losses in the process.[4] Looking back a decade later at RBS's number one position in 2008, Howard Davies, the chair of the nationalised bank, said: 'In retrospect we can see that was precisely the worst moment to be top of the league,' adding ruefully, 'we are now at number twenty-nine.'[5]

Ahead of the crisis, there had been talk about banks being too big to fail (meaning that when push came to shove they would get bailed out by the government). But in 2008, the worry was that the banks were too big to rescue. The bailouts pushed public debt up from around £700 billion in August to £2 trillion in October, a jump of getting on for 100 per cent of GDP.[6] This didn't show up in the headline figures because they were presented excluding the banking liabilities; and those figures, in any case, weren't presented formally until January 2011. Whether it showed up in the stats or not, though, the strain on the public finances was immense. In the event, actual losses for taxpayers were relatively modest. An estimate in 2018, ten years later, put the net cost of the bailouts at just £23 billion.[7] The real cost of the banking crisis emerged through its effects on the economy, inflicting a savage recession from early 2008 until mid-2009 followed by a sluggish recovery. That, in turn, weakened the public finances.

Of course, excessive risk-taking and insufficient capital were hardly confined to the UK: the crisis was global. The acute phase was triggered by the collapse of the American investment bank Lehman Brothers in September 2008: one of the defining images of the crisis was shellshocked Lehman staff clutching cardboard boxes as they left their swanky City office for the last time. There were also casualties among European banks that had been eager participants in the boom, including supposedly cautious state-owned regional banks (*Landesbanken*) in Germany that had to be rescued. One of Switzerland's top two banks, UBS, ran into trouble and required emergency help. (Ironically, a decade and a half later, in 2023, UBS had to take over its rival Credit Suisse, which had got into a self-inflicted mess.) But the City's special role as an international hub made it – and therefore the British economy overall – especially vulnerable.

Financial meltdowns cause enduring harm in two ways. First, buoyant borrowing overstretches both households and companies, which then have to work down excessive debt. Second, banks have to mend their own balance sheets, putting a dampener on further lending for viable companies and important projects. The scale of the 2008 crisis was such that both effects were especially pronounced. It soon became clear that some of the financial sector's growth before the crisis had been meretricious. Banks had been busy doing 'financial engineering' through ingenious techniques such as the securitisation of loans, parcelling them up by risk category and then selling them in the markets. These were supposed to take risk off their balance sheets; but in practice there was a 'return to sender' when things went wrong, meaning that the banks had to bail out the 'conduits' through which this activity had been funnelled.

As the crisis was reaching its peak in the autumn of 2008, Adair Turner became chair of the Financial Services Authority (FSA), which had been responsible for regulation since the late 1990s. A year later he condemned the pre-crisis City in a scathing interview in *Prospect*, describing some of its activities as 'socially useless'. The financial sector had become 'swollen' as a result of 'oversimplistic financial deregulation'.[8]

Everywhere the response was a regulatory clampdown. Banks now had to set aside much more capital to provide buffers in the case of losses. They also had to hold more liquidity, to avoid the predicament that Northern Rock had experienced in September 2007, when customers queued to take out their money, the first serious bank run in Britain since the collapse of Overend Gurney in 1866. Instead of there being just one regulator in the shape of the FSA, there would now be two. Supervision of banks would return to the Bank of England, which would also be responsible for insurers, through its Prudential Regulation Authority (PRA). A new Financial Conduct Authority (FCA) would do the less glamorous work of ensuring better behaviour and monitoring of smaller financial outfits.

This drastic overhaul was arguably unnecessary and certainly caused duplication and confusion. It owed much to politics. George Osborne wanted to pin the crisis on the FSA, which Gordon Brown had created as part of his 1997 reform, when the Bank of England was handed the keys of monetary policy but lost banking supervision. But this was to scapegoat the FSA for a light-touch approach that had long been a City tradition – and which had been smiled on by ministers. Inevitably, the new FCA was regarded as the also-ran regulator and came to suffer from low morale and high staff turnover.[9]

Brexit and the City

The City that emerged from the crisis was a somewhat humbler place: regulators, not bankers, were now in charge. This was vividly demonstrated when Mervyn King insisted on a change of leadership at one of Britain's top banks in the summer of 2012. Bob Diamond was forced out of his job as chief executive at Barclays because he represented the kind of risk-taking investment banking that King – soon to wear his new regulatory hat (the Bank resumed bank supervision in April 2013) – wanted to discourage at a big British bank.[10]

The regulators had been empowered by a change in their remit. Under legislation passed in 2000, the FSA had to 'have regard' when rulemaking for 'the international character of financial services and markets and the desirability of maintaining the competitive position of the United Kingdom'. That stipulation, which had opened the door for the banks to lobby for laxer rules, was dropped for the two new regulators.

In general, Britain's tough new approach was similar to that adopted by other countries. The new banking rules on capital and liquidity followed international standards hammered out at Basel in 2010 and were implemented as common regulations in the EU. It seemed that the City could still prosper in this new era. Instead of offering a light-touch environment, it could make the most of the safety now being provided by financial firms operating out of London.

The real threat to the City came from the political realm. Ahead of the crisis, the general rise in living standards had made more tolerable the high earnings of bankers. But post-crash, real wages sagged, leading to sharp disgruntlement at the relatively big money still to be made by working in the City – despite a cap on bonuses to only (only!) double your basic salary. That sour mood found its outlet in the Brexit vote of 2016.

The outcome of the referendum was unambiguously bad for the City. European negotiators took a hard line on access to the single market for London-based financial firms. In October 2006, David Walker, a senior City figure who had played a key role behind the scenes at the Bank of England preparing for the Big Bang twenty years earlier, told *The Economist*: 'London is more than a network: it's become a knot and it's very difficult to disentangle a knot.'[11] But if anything was likely to undo the knot it was Brexit.

In a June 2018 speech, Mark Carney, who had taken over at the Bank of England five years earlier, spelled out the full dimensions of the City's global role. It accounted for 40 per cent of foreign exchange volumes and trades in over-the-counter interest-rate derivatives. More international banking activity was booked in London than anywhere else. The City was Europe's investment banker, with UK-based banks underwriting half the debt and equity issued by EU companies. Britain hosted the world's second largest asset-management industry and fourth largest insurance industry.[12] Carney, both central banker and financial regulator, was bullish: 'the UK's financial system remains both a national asset and a global public good'. He pointed out that two-thirds of financial sector jobs were based outside London. Financial services ran a healthy trade surplus and contributed a tenth of government revenues. His 'public good' aspect alluded to the new regime of stricter standards and supervision for the City that brought wider benefits to international users of its services.

Carney was speaking at a time when it was possible to envisage a constructive exit deal with the EU that would preserve the City's access to the single market. Prime minister Theresa May was preparing a close future economic relationship with the bloc. Carney certainly sounded hopeful: the Bank believed 'an ambitious future financial services relationship, founded on commitments to achieving equivalent outcomes and supervisory cooperation, remains both feasible and in the interests of the UK, Europe and the world'. But Carney's hopes were crushed when May's overtures to the EU were spurned that autumn at the Salzburg summit and her strategy undermined at home by Brexit diehards in the Tory Party. The relationship that Carney had optimistically considered 'feasible' turned out to be impossible when May's successor Boris

Johnson negotiated a trade deal with the EU in the closing days
of 2020 that secured nothing meaningful for financial services.

Where did all this leave the City?

Already, financial firms had announced plans to move £1.3
trillion of assets out of London owing to Brexit. A further adverse
effect emerged at the start of 2021. Gallingly, Amsterdam overtook London in January to become Europe's biggest share-trading
centre as business in euro-denominated shares moved to the Dutch
city. Although London briefly regained its top place in the summer
it fell back again by the year's end.[13]

But some of the worst outcomes were dodged. For the time
being, London retained its role as a centre for trading in and set-
tling derivatives used by European banks. These were primarily
interest rate 'swaps' in which banks sought to manage the risk of
interest rates moving up or down. The ECB had long been uneasy
about this big chunk of sensitive financial activity going on outside the eurozone. But moving the clearing operation away from
London turned out to be impractical and the trading continued
for the time being.

Most important, the exodus of staff out of London was considerably smaller than had once been feared. Figures doing the rounds
in 2016 estimated that between 70,000 and 100,000 jobs could
be at risk.[14] But in the event, only 7,000 job relocations had been
announced by early 2022, according to consultancy EY's 'financial
services Brexit tracker', which was based on public statements by
around 220 of the biggest financial firms.[15]

Moreover, it seemed unlikely that any one European capital
could supplant London's unique constellation of activities. If
Amsterdam had won favour for equity trading, Dublin led for
asset management. Meanwhile, Paris and Frankfurt vied for
banking. Luxembourg was another popular choice for relocations,
according to EY. But if anything, New York was the real winner.
In September 2022 and March 2023, according to Z/Yen's Global

Financial Centres index, the City lagged behind Wall Street whereas before Brexit it had been head-to-head for the top spot.[16]

Even if the short-term impact was more bearable than expected, there were fears that the City would experience a slow puncture. London's grip on the derivatives markets remained vulnerable given the European desire to shift the euro-denominated business, even though the deadline for doing this had been extended to mid-2025. Rivalry between Paris and Frankfurt prevented a big grab in early 2024, but this was a precarious position for London to find itself in.[17]

Brexit also meant that the City was missing out on a promising new opportunity. European states had recognised that their financial systems were too reliant on banks, whose weaknesses had contributed to the euro crisis in the early 2010s. That prompted a move to forge a 'capital markets union' within the EU, which would provide alternatives to traditional loans made by local banks. The aim was to make it easier for firms to tap finance from outside their countries by issuing tradable bonds and equities and providing new and safer ways to securitise loans. The EU also wanted to beef up its venture-capital industry, which was far smaller than America's. The capital markets project played to British strengths in market-based finance. Moreover, Britain was well placed to shape this, thanks to the appointment in 2014 of Jonathan Hill, a Tory peer who knew his way round the City, as the European commissioner in charge of financial services. But in the aftermath of the Brexit vote, Hill resigned. There was no point in Britain leading an effort in which it would no longer be able to participate. And without Britain the whole project lost momentum.

Lessons unlearned

Once it became clear that the EU would not offer Brexit Britain special treatment for financial services, there was a case for reviewing domestic regulation. The legacy of over four decades of membership was a set of cumbersome rules that had been written for the bloc as a whole. Even though the UK had generally taken the lead in these matters, it made sense to think again about whether some of these could be tailored to better fit the City's unique status without compromising on essential safeguards.

Since the government liked to make much of the independence of the City's two regulators, the FCA and the Bank of England, this was a task that could simply have been handed to them. Instead the Treasury, by then led by Rishi Sunak, whose own background was in investment banking and hedge funds, decided to take the lead. One controversial proposal was to formally clip the regulators' wings by giving the Treasury a new 'public interest' power to intervene and get them to review rules – a role previously reserved for the FCA and the Bank of England. Supposedly, this power would be used only in 'exceptional circumstances', but it was difficult to see how this wouldn't undermine both institutions' authority and water down necessary rules. As Charles Randell, the outgoing chair of the FCA, warned in May 2022: 'There is always the risk that "exceptional circumstances" turn out to be surprisingly frequent, or that the mere existence of the power could bring pressure to bear on the FCA to change its priorities.'[18]

Although the Treasury eventually dropped this proposal (in November 2022), it persevered with another bad idea.[19] That was to reintroduce the need for regulators to facilitate the international competitiveness of the British economy and in particular of the City. True, this was to be a secondary rather than a main purpose; but that had also been the case with the FSA's ill-fated 'have regard' clause about Britain's 'competitive position'. In December 2021, Randell had told MPs on the Commons Treasury select committee that it could open the door to 'a large amount of lobbying input saying: "This rule does not exist in this country, that country or the other country and therefore you should not do it."[20]

All this was a long way from Carney's ambition that the City become a model of high standards and tough regulation. Lessons learned during the financial crisis were now being unlearned in a bid to drum up more business. A case in point was an intervention to facilitate a controversial way of bringing businesses on to the stock market through 'SPACs' (see box).

The readiness of the government to rewrite the rules in the City told its own story about a new deregulatory tilt. As did the removal of the cap on bankers' bonuses in October 2023, one of the few policies of the short-lived Truss and Kwarteng government to survive.

SPAC up and go

The traditional way for a private business to become publicly quoted was through an 'initial public offering' (IPO), in which it would raise capital from investors via the stock market. But a new method became wildly popular in America during 2020 and 2021. A shell company would raise money to be used to buy an operating business (as yet unspecified) with which it would merge. These special purpose acquisition companies (SPACs) were wiping the floor with traditional IPOs. This was one financial innovation that London could have done without. SPACs burgeoned in the US because they lacked regulatory safeguards applied to standard IPOs. They were a poor deal for ordinary investors.

But even as the US regulator, the redoubtable Securities and Exchange Commission, moved to restrict SPACs, the rules in Britain were *relaxed* to try to encourage them in the City. This followed a report about stock-market rules by Jonathan Hill (the former European commissioner) in March 2021 for the Treasury in which he recommended facilitating them. While acknowledging 'a number of reservations being expressed about SPACs', Hill glossed over the case against them.[21] Notably, that their management teams were doing rather too well out of them, which contributed to the fact that their performance in the US had in general been disappointing. His main concern appeared to be fear of the City missing out on business – 'the bottom line from a competitive point of view'. That was a line of argument often advanced before the financial crisis to encourage outré financial practices.

The FCA 'moved at pace', as one of its top officials later said, to remove the specific restriction that had made it difficult to issue SPACs in London. The regulator's readiness to do so was, to say the least, surprising given the ample evidence already available in the US about the flaws in these shell companies. In the event the unseemly rush was in vain. The first British SPAC to list under the new 'SPAC-friendly' rules was Hambro Perks Acquisition Company, in November 2021. In April 2023, it had to admit it couldn't find an appropriate target, blaming 'current market conditions' (the stock-market prices of smaller British firms had fallen sharply) and would be returning the funds it had raised to shareholders.[22]

The most extraordinary example of the government's move away from prioritising safety was the Treasury's backing for crypto. In early April 2022, Sunak set out his 'ambition to make the UK a global hub for crypto-asset technology'. For good measure, City minister John Glen, who was part of Sunak's Treasury team, said he wanted the UK to be 'the very best place in the world to start and scale crypto companies'.[23]

This was remarkable because both regulators had done their level best to keep crypto at bay – and with good reason. Andrew Bailey, the Bank of England governor, had highlighted the association between crypto and criminality.[24] Speaking at the Cambridge International Symposium on Economic Crime in September 2021, the FCA's Randell had set out the regulator's worry about the risks for individuals of holding crypto-currencies, which he described as 'purely speculative digital tokens'.[25]

The Treasury's rolling-out of the welcome mat could scarcely have been worse timed. Almost immediately afterwards in the spring of 2022 there was a massive decline in crypto valuations. One 'algorithmic stablecoin' called TerraUSD, which was supposedly anchored to the dollar through a sister token called Luna, became anything but stable, as both collapsed in May. Later that year came the spectacular implosion of the FTX exchange set up by Sam Bankman-Fried. The supposed good guy of the crypto world, feted for his philanthropy as well as his multi-billion-dollar wealth, was sentenced to 25 years in prison in March 2024 following his conviction for fraud by a New York court the previous year.[26]

Taken as a whole, the government's new approach to the City was short-sighted and ill-judged. Despite Brexit, London enjoyed the advantages of incumbency as a global hub. Memories of the crisis might have faded at the Treasury, but they remained as pertinent as before. The last thing we needed was a return to the light-touch regulation that had backfired so disastrously in

2008, let alone an embrace of crypto, the modern version of the alchemist's dream.

What has the City ever done for us?

Walk around the City of London and there are visible remnants close to Tower Hill of the Roman wall that used to surround it. A famous scene from Monty Python's *Life of Brian* asked: 'What have the Romans ever done for us?' We might ask the same question about the City. (A short answer would be that, unlike the Romans, the City didn't get many roads built.) In the early 2020s, that question was asked again with renewed force. Why was it that promising British companies were choosing to float initially in New York rather than London? Why had pension funds run down their investments in British equities? Why wasn't that capital staying at home to invest in new ventures?

The finger-pointing missed the point: as investment manager Schroders pointed out in 2023, 'Stop blaming everything on pension funds.'[27] Since companies had stopped offering final salary pension benefits to new members in the early 2000s their schemes were maturing, as the existing members retired or approached retirement. That meant a continuing portfolio shift among pension funds away from riskier equities – whether in Britain or overseas – to safer bonds, which were a better match for pension payments. The funds were also diversifying by putting money into alternative investments such as hedge funds and private equity.

More generally, investors were shunning London because of the disappointing record of British equities over the best part of a decade. New companies were tempted by Wall Street because they could get higher valuations. Essentially UK plc was trading at a steep discount to other economies, especially America with its sway over the higher-valued tech sector but also because of a Brexit markdown. The way to put the London stock exchange back on the map was for the economy itself to thrive again.

This imperative was recognised by City chiefs. It lay behind the attempts of Nicholas Lyons to assemble a public–private wealth fund while he was the City lord mayor in 2022-23 (see Chapter 3). Nigel Wilson, the boss of insurer Legal & General between 2012 and 2023, believed that the insurance industry should invest much more in British infrastructure, a strategy he himself pursued while at the helm of L&G.[28]

Lloyds, the most domestically oriented of the big banks, took an innovative step in July 2021 to back housing investment by moving into the private rental market through a new subsidiary called Citra Living. It would not only finance residential property developments but also rent them out as a landlord.[29] This was a promising development as private landlords were increasingly withdrawing from the buy-to-let rental market.

The best way the City could help the wider economy was to direct more funds to domestic businesses wanting to expand. By and large, bigger firms could look after themselves, raising the necessary finance in a variety of ways, such as issuing bonds as well as borrowing from banks. But for smaller and medium-sized enterprises Britain's big banks had long been the main source of funds.

Such lending is by its nature risky. Banks have to hold more capital against it than other loans such as mortgages. One way to encourage business lending would be to revisit ring-fencing, which had been introduced in the 2010s. This forced big British banks to put their domestic deposit-taking and payments services for both individuals and small businesses into separate subsidiaries with their own capital backing. The aim was to protect the core domestic financial system from any turbulence in the banks' international and investment banking activities.

Although ring-fencing had been the main proposal of an independent commission on banking in 2011, it was arguably regulatory overkill. Indeed, Britain was alone in taking such a step.[30] Once introduced, it had the undesirable side-effect of pumping yet more lending into an already overheated housing market, as HSBC, in particular, sought to make use of surplus retail deposits in its ring-fenced operation to build up its presence as a mortgage lender.[31]

Ring-fencing has only been fully in place since the start of 2019 and it is probably too early to reverse such a landmark reform still firmly backed by the Bank of England. Sam Woods, the feisty Bank executive in charge of prudential regulation, declared in January 2020 that he would defend ring-fencing to his 'last drop of blood'.[32] But an independent review of the reform that reported in March 2022 opened up the possibility of a future rethink.[33]

As well as getting banks to lend more, a City focused more on the domestic economy would mobilise long-term savings to help finance urgent infrastructure improvements. Owing to previous privatisations of utilities such as electricity about half of the work would have to be financed by private companies rather than the Treasury.

The need for more private funding was all the more urgent because of an under-publicised drawback to Brexit. Unlike most G7 members, Britain did not have a development bank to finance public works and infrastructure. In the aftermath of the Second World War, for example, West Germany had set up KfW to finance reconstruction and later small businesses. The British government did not follow suit.

However, when Britain joined the European club in 1973, it became a member of the European Investment Bank (EIB). Until it left the EU on 31 January 2020, Britain had benefited from EIB loans worth €119 billion helping to fund projects like the Channel tunnel and the renovation of the water industry in the 1990s. More recently the EIB had contributed to investments in offshore wind farms and London's new 'super sewer', the Thames Tideway

Tunnel, which aims to end overflows of untreated sewage into the Thames. In the pre-referendum year of 2015 alone, the EIB agreed loans worth £5.6 billion for forty British projects – roughly a third of total funding of UK infrastructure that year.[34]

Although the Treasury responded by setting up the UK Infrastructure Bank based in Leeds, in June 2021, it was a pale reflection of the EIB or indeed Germany's KfW. For one thing, it was under-resourced, with just £5 billion in equity, and a capacity to borrow up to £7 billion and to issue £10 billion in credit guarantees – a maximum financial capacity of a mere £22 billion. On a yearly basis the limits were just £1.5 billion for equity, the same for borrowing and £2.5 billion in credit guarantees.[35] Just as important, the UK bank lacked the skills and expertise that the European development bank had built up over more than sixty years.

Still, Britain did have a big insurance industry, especially life insurance, that could potentially step in and help. Insurers were keen to assist but argued that their ability to invest in infrastructure was curtailed by over-stringent 'Solvency II' rules introduced while Britain was in the EU. A Treasury overhaul of the rules ran into resistance by the Bank of England in its role as prudential regulator. However, on this occasion, the BoE didn't get its own way as regulator Sam Woods conceded when addressing the Association of British Insurers in February 2023.[36] The government pressed ahead with reforms that it hoped would release more long-term investment funding from the life insurers. This was not a Brexit dividend since the EU was heading in the same direction.

A new City?

Despite the setback of Brexit, it is possible to set out an optimistic vision for a new City. This would retain much of its existing role as a global hub, thanks to continuing strengths in bringing together the array of skills and technologies needed in international finance. The City was also spawning promising new 'fintech' ventures, which turned a mobile phone into a bank in your pocket and offered cheaper ways to make payments (see box).

The fintech revolution?

In the summer of 2021, Revolut was valued in a fund-raising round at £24 billion, making the British fintech firm founded in 2015 worth more than NatWest (as RBS had been renamed).[37] There were other notable digital start-ups, too, such as Monzo and Starling, which offered app-based banking for customers to use on their phones at any time of the day with no queues at branch counters. These also provided new services. For example, anyone banking with Starling could track their spending by category and enhance their saving by rounding up transactions to the nearest pound and allocating the difference to a saving pot.

Could these new digital contenders remake British banking, long dominated by the big four – HSBC, Lloyds, Barclays and NatWest? The snag was these heavyweights proved surprisingly agile in rolling out their own similar banking apps. They retained trad-itional strengths as safe places to park deposits and short-term savings. The big banks also offered a card-based system for everyday payments especially once contactless took off. Debit cards overtook cash as a means of payment for the first time in 2017; five years later they made up half of all payments compared with only 14 per cent using cash.[38]

A particular focus for the new fintech firms (and big tech) was payments, especially across borders where costs were high. As well as Revolut, another contender was Wise (formerly TransferWise). In June 2019, Facebook stunned the financial world with an audacious plan for a new international digital currency called libra but the project soon fell apart, not least owing to opposition from regulators.

The fintech revolution was given a helping hand by the FCA, which pioneered a 'regulatory sandbox' in 2016. This allowed financial firms, both start-ups and those already authorised, to try out innovations on actual customers on a small scale. The aim was to enable new ventures that proved their worth to get to the marketplace more quickly and at lower cost. The innovation proved a hit internationally as regulators in other countries followed suit.[39]

Outside the sandbox the fintech revolution was starting to look rather less revolutionary. Revolut's advantage over NatWest didn't last, as disclosures from investors in 2023 revealed cuts in the value of their stakes in the fintech firm of 40 and 46 per cent.[40]

As well as continuing to look out to the rest of the world and fostering fintech, the new City would do more to help rebuild Britain and its businesses. That change in focus would reflect the fact that the main virtue of a financial sector is not its size but its ability to foster growth in the rest of the economy. Getting the City to do more for the domestic economy was, however, easier said than done. Shortfalls in the provision of finance to small and medium-sized businesses were longstanding. Almost a century ago (in

1931), a committee of inquiry had identified the 'Macmillan gap' (named after its chair) in such funding. Despite post-war efforts to try to close the gap, the problem persisted. In November 2014 the state-owned British Business Bank was founded in a new bid to help smaller businesses. Based in Sheffield, the BBB sought to leverage its own limited resources by getting as much extra private money as possible into the projects that it backed.

Looking ahead, such public–private partnerships would be essential to get more finance into the domestic economy. The era of private equals good, public equals bad had ended definitively for finance in 2008 after it had demonstrated that private could be very bad indeed. A new City could win wider public support by working in collaboration with the state to finance Britain's future. As it happened, that was also the best way to maximise the depleted firepower of the Treasury.

Realising such a vision would require a coherent and consistent strategy by the government. That was notable by its absence in the early 2020s. Making regulators take account, once again, of the City's competitive position and Sunak's baffling ambition to make London a crypto hub sent out the wrong messages. A precondition for the City to do more for the domestic economy was to ensure financial stability and to avoid another crisis. That required high standards upheld and policed by independent regulators which, while imperfect, commanded more trust than their vacillating political masters.

Chapter 5

Whatever happened to 'Made in Britain'?

As the City tripped up in the financial crisis and was then caught in the crossfire of Brexit, attention turned to manufacturing. Making things that were actually useful to people had an obvious appeal compared with creating socially useless financial products. Starting with Peter Mandelson, who became Labour's business secretary at the height of the banking crisis, ministers started to blow warm rather than cold about having an industrial strategy.

If manufacturing were to step up, it would have to overturn a long history of decline. Since 1970 its share of GDP had shrunk from 27 per cent to 10 per cent ahead of the pandemic.[1] Industry, which in the national accounts includes the utilities such as energy providers, mining and oil and gas production as well as manufacturing, now made up only 14 per cent of the economy. In another bleak statistic, Britain had run a trade deficit on goods every year since 1983.[2] The pioneer of the industrial revolution had pioneered deindustrialisation. But if its glory days had gone, manufacturing hadn't disappeared. Even though Britain's financial sector hogged the limelight, its share of the economy – 8 per cent just ahead of the pandemic – was smaller than that of manufacturing. In international terms, Britain's manufacturing sector was no longer a heavyweight but it was still respectably sized, broadly similar to that of France.[3]

There were other reasons why British manufacturing remained important. It punched beyond its weight in trade, making up the great majority of goods exports. UK manufacturers accounted for two-fifths of business spending on research and development (R&D). The sector provided 2.6 million jobs, which on average were better paid than for the economy as a whole. Earnings in manufacturing averaged £36,500 in 2022, 9 per cent higher than the average of £33,400 across the economy.[4]

Even so, it was important not to get hung up on any one part of the economy, whether it was the City or manufacturing. What mattered was the overall health of business, including services as well as industry. And whether or not something was actually assembled in Britain was less important than where the real value resided – in the knowhow that lay behind the products.

As the idea of an industrial strategy came out of the post-Thatcher wilderness, it was vital to mould it for the business sector as a whole. For the Treasury, avoiding past mistakes, such as backing winners that turned out to be losers, was also essential. But given the need to foster growth while also moving towards a net-zero economy, the case for some form of overarching plan was becoming compelling.

The overdone declinist narrative

The world's workshop today is China: it accounts for an astonishing 30 per cent of global manufacturing output. However, the title was originally coined for Britain as the first industrial nation exporting the products of its new factories. The Great Exhibition of 1851 was a showcase for the extensive range of products made by domestic manufacturers. That heyday didn't last long. Within two or three decades, Germany and the US were stripping away that early British advantage in a 'second' industrial revolution based on new technologies in steelmaking and mass production. Even though it was inevitable that Britain would lose ground as other countries industrialised, the extent of its decline was arresting. British manufacturers appeared stuck in their ways, persisting with products such as textiles that were vulnerable to low-cost competition.

One influential explanation for this decline came to the fore in the early 1980s when Britain's post-war deindustrialisation was in full spate. The American historian Martin J. Wiener's book *English Culture and the Decline of the Industrial Spirit: 1850–1980* blamed the snobby values of an elite that looked down on industry and frowned on entrepreneurs.[5] Talent flowed into the more prestigious jobs provided by the professions and the civil service. That left manufacturing staffed and run by people who lacked the education and technical expertise needed for Britain to sustain its early lead as an industrial nation. This account helpfully let Thatcher off the hook for economic policies that were intensifying deindustrialisation: don't blame me, blame the elites. Indeed, her economic crusade could be depicted as an assault on a defeatist mindset held by Britain's ruling establishment. One of her key lieutenants, Keith Joseph, reportedly distributed copies of Wiener's book to every minister in her cabinet.[6] But was British industrial decline really so culturally deep-rooted?

An alternative narrative stressed the regeneration that occurred in the interwar period when new industries making cars and aircraft sprang up. In his 2005 book *Warfare State,* David Edgerton, an economic historian then at London's Imperial College, demonstrated how the British government backed an effective defence industry focused on modern military technologies able to defy Germany during the Second World War. In a more recent analysis, he pointed out that Britain after the war in the 1950s and 1960s was 'an exceptionally manufacturing-oriented economy'.[7]

The remaking of industry

But even if the declinist pessimism stretching back over a century was overdone, the scale of deindustrialisation after 1970 suggested underlying vulnerabilities. British firms had not been subjected to the same disciplines as European companies through the removal of tariffs within the customs union during the late 1950s and 1960s. That made joining the common market in 1973 more of a shock.

Overmanning was rife in industries old (shipbuilding) and new (commercial television) as powerful trade unions sought to protect their members through restrictive working practices such as rigid rules over what jobs each person could undertake. Sooner or later, there would have to be a shake-out across British industry, which was beset by poor productivity and chronic labour disputes, notably in car manufacturing. It came sooner in large measure owing to the impact of North Sea oil and gas production.

That was a benefit to the economy as a whole – and the Treasury. But already the downside had been illustrated in the Netherlands which experienced the so-called 'Dutch disease' after discovering abundant gas reserves. The snag in becoming a big producer of gas or oil was that it drove up the exchange rate, whether that was the Dutch guilder or British pound. That hit the part of the economy most exposed to international trade: manufacturing. What was good for the Netherlands or Britain as a whole would be bad for their industrial bases.

The shock was needlessly exacerbated in Britain by an overdose of monetarism at the start of the 1980s which drove up interest rates. However, the industry that did survive was undeniably leaner. Managers were able to push through changes to working practices that had previously been resisted. Manufacturing productivity rose sharply during the 1980s. Labour disputes were waning even before the humbling of the mighty National Union of Mineworkers in the bitter strike of 1984–85.

The car industry, in particular, which had come to represent all that was bad in British industrial relations, had a phoenix-style rebirth. Japanese car makers set up factories using 'just-in-time' production methods that did away with having to hold costly on-site inventories. In the 1980s, Nissan arrived in Sunderland and Honda in Swindon. In the early 1990s, Toyota's new car plant at Burnaston near Derby and its engine factory in North Wales started production. These plants were designed to export to the big European market and built up intricate supply chains. The Japanese influx was an endorsement of the changed business climate. With trade unions tamed through high unemployment and new laws constraining wildcat strikes, Britain looked a more attractive prospect. The new car plants were a world removed from the old ones beset by incorrigibly bad industrial relations.

It wasn't just Japanese car firms that were eyeing up Britain. Inflows of foreign direct investment (FDI), made by firms rather than financial investors, increased markedly as multinationals took advantage of Britain's open capital markets to build a presence in a large economy inside the EU. Even after Brexit, Britain had still the largest stock of inward FDI in Europe, just ahead of the Netherlands, at the end of 2022.[8] Attracting FDI boosted the economy, especially where it brought 'greenfield' investments such as new factories rather than the acquisition of stakes in existing British enterprises. Typically, the multinationals expanding their operations through FDI in Britain had high productivity. Indeed, on average foreign-owned businesses were twice as efficient as domestic firms focused on the home market.[9]

That remarkable gap reflected, in part, their exposure to

international trade and the discipline that competition brought to all exporters. It was also because of the expertise they brought and the capital with which they endowed their operations. Foreign-owned firms also stood out for the scale of their R&D in Britain. FDI had further positive impacts as the multinationals in Britain raised standards among their UK suppliers, improved products used by other firms and generally enhanced competition.

However, the increasing reliance on foreign firms had two downsides. First, command and control would remain abroad. That would leave the manufacturing sector – especially the car industry – vulnerable to the shock of Brexit. Investment in the industry collapsed in the wake of the vote and in 2021 Honda closed its Swindon plant. Second, a continuing strong inflow of FDI couldn't be taken for granted. Britain fell down the ranks from second place in 2016 among the OECD of thirty-plus mainly rich economies to fourth in 2019 and fifteenth in 2022.[10] British figures showed that following an exceptional high in 2016, inflows fell every year between 2017 and 2021.[11] A survey from consulting firm EY reported in June 2023 that Britain had slipped to third place in Europe for its attractiveness to FDI investors, behind Germany and France.[12]

At first sight, the picture for greenfield FDI, which was the most valuable for the economy, looked rather better. But much of these investments was in the renewables sector: for example, offshore wind farms. Stripping these out, greenfield FDI had been 'at best flat' since the financial crisis, according to a report for the Treasury in November 2023 by Tory peer Lord Harrington. Moreover, off-shore wind had 'limited potential for spillover benefits or crowding in of domestic investment'. Translated: it would do little to help the rest of the economy beyond providing a new source of energy.[13]

Foreign direct investment was, of course, a two-way process. British firms were also investing heavily overseas. In 2022, the cumulative value of outward FDI was $2.2 trillion, somewhat less than the stock of inward FDI, which was worth $2.7 trillion. That, in itself, was a big change since formerly the investments held abroad had exceeded those made in Britain; as recently as 2010 they had been $600 billion higher.

With or without FDI, the whole notion of something being made in any one place was becoming less clear-cut owing to the expansion of multinational supply chains designed to maximise profit. Such outsourcing took a great leap forward as China opened up to the global economy and became the world's workshop (see box).

How manufacturing denationalised itself

Identifying where things were made and sold used to be simple. British manufacturers, for example, would purchase raw materials from abroad. They would turn these into products in their factories and then either sell these final goods in the domestic market or export them. That was what 'Made in Britain' meant. Now it's much more complicated. For one thing, manufacturers in any one country don't just import raw materials but semi-made products and parts. For another, the final assembly may be done far away, typically in China. What matters is where the value is added in this production chain, which will mainly reflect knowhow and technology rather than physical manufacturing.

Supply chains aren't necessarily one way. A feature of Britain's car industry before Brexit was that parts would move seamlessly both in and out of UK-based factories, from and to plants in the EU. In 2017, the

Guardian featured 'a Mini part's incredible journey': a crankshaft from a French supplier would be drilled and milled at a BMW plant in Warwickshire, shipped to Munich to be inserted into the engine and then return to the Mini plant in Oxford.[14]

Figures from the OECD, which pinned down where value was added in British trade in 2018, while Britain was still in the single market, confirmed the car industry's reliance on such imports from the EU. They showed that 34 per cent of motor vehicle exports consisted of value added by foreign suppliers, almost twice as high as the overall 18 per cent foreign content of British exports.[15]

During and after the pandemic, supply chains came under unprecedented pressure. Bottlenecks at ports led to shortages that contributed to the international surge in inflation. Companies that had prioritised low costs when outsourcing production were taught a stern lesson about the risks involved. But even though there was a new focus on making supply chains more resilient, these international networks would remain a fact of manufacturing life.

Brain beats brawn

In or out of the EU, the only secure long-term footing for industry was innovation based on Britain's scientific and technological expertise. One flourishing sector was pharmaceuticals, where firms such as GSK, formed in its present shape through a merger in 2000 between Glaxo Wellcome and SmithKline Beecham, could hold their own internationally. Another, AstraZeneca, was an Anglo-Swedish multinational whose British component had been spun out of the chemicals giant ICI, long described as the 'bellwether' of the British economy, which was itself acquired by a Dutch company in 2008. The firm became a household name in 2020 developing, in collaboration with Oxford scientists, one of the first Covid vaccines.

The pharmaceuticals industry was 'highly productive and export focused', according to the government in 2017, highlighting the life sciences as a jewel in Britain's industrial crown. Two years later, just ahead of the pandemic, the sector had an annual turnover of over £80 billion and employed almost 260,000 scientists and staff in the UK.[16]

The choice of headquarters for the two big British pharmaceuticals companies was revealing. AstraZeneca's global base was in Cambridge, where it also had a big R&D facility. GSK was due to move from Brentford in west London to central London in 2024. Announcing the decision in December 2022, GSK said that the new location offered 'closer proximity' to the capital's 'fast-growing global Life Sciences hub, Knowledge Quarter and world-class academic institutions'.[17] GSK's R&D centre in Britain was in Stevenage, roughly in the middle of the 'golden triangle' between London and the university cities of Oxford and Cambridge.

The link between industrial success in an advanced economy and scientific advances was becoming ever tighter. Cambridge had led the way in 1970 when Trinity College started to build Britain's first science park. By the end of 2019, 60,000 people were working in the Cambridge 'ecosystem' of 4,700 knowledge-intensive businesses. The city had spawned big companies, notably Arm, which designs advanced microchips used in smartphones.[18] Other universities were quick to follow. An analysis of over 900 'spinout' companies – new business ventures based on university research – between 1998 and 2018 put Oxford in the lead, both for the number (15.8 per cent) and value (£6.4 billion). Cambridge came second for the number (11.5 per cent) and third equal with UCL for value (£2.6 billion). Imperial came second for value (£2.7 billion).[19]

The pay-off from the links between higher education and the economy was a thriving tech sector. In January 2023, a boosterish chancellor Jeremy Hunt said that the London-Oxford-Cambridge triangle had the largest number of tech businesses in the world outside San Francisco and New York. The chancellor boasted that Britain had created more 'unicorns' (start-up tech businesses valued at a billion dollars or more) than France and Germany combined.[20]

There were also notable strengths in advanced manufacturing, such as the aerospace industry, one of the largest in the world, and a big exporter. Britain specialised in the production of highly sophisticated parts, notably engines and wings. Rolls-Royce, based in Derby, made engines used by aircraft fleets around the world, while getting on for half the world's air passengers were flying on Airbus wings designed and manufactured in Britain.[21]

Britain's strength in aerospace was complemented by a big defence industry, spearheaded by BAE Systems. This reflected the country's continuing commitment to the armed forces after the Second World War. Even in the mid-1980s defence spending was still as high as 5 per cent of GDP.[22] That dropped in the era of détente that followed the collapse of the Soviet Union, but Britain remained one of the few NATO (North Atlantic Treaty Organisation) countries meeting the minimum 2 per cent of GDP target set in 2006 and reinforced at a summit held in Wales in 2014 when NATO members failing to comply promised to mend their ways within a decade. (Most still hadn't by 2023.)[23]

There were also some unexpected strengths in niche sectors. Britain made more Grand Prix cars than any other country and seven of the world's ten Formula 1 teams were based in Britain.[24] Entrepreneurs such as James Dyson developed world-beating companies. His 'cyclonic' vacuum cleaner was an innovation that revolutionised an industry previously synonymous with Hoover.

Impatient capital

Despite these heartening success stories, British manufacturing as a sector still had some underlying weaknesses. Overall productivity was dragged down by an unusually long 'tail' of underperformers.[25] Low investment was one reason. Fixed capital spending in Britain was persistently the lowest among the G7 economies, mainly because businesses were not doing enough though also reflecting insufficient public investment.[26]

Britain's SMEs – small and medium-sized enterprises, normally defined as firms with fewer than 250 employees – failed to pack the same punch as Germany's *Mittelstand*, a dense network of privately owned companies that underpinned German industry's continuing prowess. They lagged behind their counterparts in similar-sized advanced economies in their propensity to export. According to a report by Goldman Sachs in 2015, only 16 per cent of SMEs in Britain had more than a quarter of their customers abroad, compared with 22 per cent in France and 21 per cent in Germany.

British smaller firms were also lagging behind in innovation, whether in products or processes. Whereas more than 40 per cent of SMEs in countries such as Germany and the Netherlands had introduced such innovations, only 28 per cent of those in Britain had done so. According to the Goldman Sachs report, the two failings were related since research showed that 'the strongest boost to productivity growth occurs when exporting and innovation are undertaken together as part of a coherent strategy'.[27]

Owing to a continuing failure to provide top-grade vocational education, businesses large and small were let down by deficient skills. According to the OECD, just 18 per cent of twenty-five–sixty-four-year-olds in Britain had vocational qualifications in 2019. This was far below Germany's 53 per cent and considerably lower than the 33 per cent average among European countries.[28] This weakness was longstanding. The National Institute of Economic and Social Research (NIESR) laid bare in the early 1980s the disparities between Britain and Germany in equipping their workforces with skills. Thanks to their solid grounding through apprenticeship-based training, German workers were able to suggest and carry out improvements that raised efficiency. By contrast, British managers were often having to firefight problems daily because there were fewer workers technically equipped to prevent them in the first place – or deal with them when they did happen. Revisiting that pioneering research in 2018, the NIESR stressed the continuing salience of inadequate skills in holding down productivity in Britain.[29]

But it wasn't just British workers who came out badly in international comparisons. Managers, too, were found wanting. According to a long-running survey-based research project on 'Bossonomics' by Nicholas Bloom and John Van Reenen, the quality of British managers was worse than their counterparts in Sweden and Germany and even further behind those in the US.[30] This was particularly the case among family-owned businesses, which were often run in Britain by family members rather than more proficient external managers. This held back productivity. Indeed, the most recent analysis by Bloom and Van Reenen suggested that inferior management in Britain could explain as much as half of the difference between American and British productivity.[31]

That glum verdict, pithily summed up by *The Economist* as 'David Brent Ltd', was about existing outfits. What about start-ups and those trying to expand beyond that stage? Britain was good at setting up new enterprises; less so at getting them to a stage where they could punch at a heavier weight. Treasury analysis in 2017 found that Britain was 'lagging behind its potential in the longer-term process of scaling up successful start-ups'.[32]

One reason was what the Treasury called 'the UK's historically thin market for patient capital'. Venture capital funds release money for firms they are backing in stages. British companies found it harder to get later-stage funding (which is generally bigger than the first rounds). Whereas, on average, American firms would get almost four rounds until going to the market through an IPO (short for initial public offering, when a privately owned company first sells its shares on the stock market), in Britain it was only a bit above two. Although this was roughly similar to the rest of Europe, Britain was supposed to be the powerhouse in all matters financial. Instead, it was no better. This failing was on full display in 2021, a year when venture capital was abundant before being choked off by high interest rates. Britain did well in attracting 14 per cent of first round ('pre-seed', below $1 million) global venture-capital funding. However, its share fell to only 6 per cent for rounds raising between $15 million and $100 million.[33]

There was a broader lack of patience in an economy where the financial markets held sway. In one sense this was an indispensable discipline on companies. But there was an inherent tension between the short-term outlook of investors and the long-term horizon of manufacturing companies needing to make enduring investments. A prime example was the fate of electrical and defence conglomerate GEC, which businessman Arnold Weinstock had built into one of Britain's biggest companies. In the late 1990s, during the dotcom boom, a new team renamed the firm Marconi and chased higher returns by selling off the defence business (to what became BAE Systems) and buying new businesses in the form of American telecom-equipment makers. The City initially cheered on this corporate makeover; but the purchases turned out to be misjudged, mistimed and overpriced, wrecking a company once at the heart of British industry.[34] Weinstock had himself stitched GEC together through a series of mergers, but they had a broad industrial coherence. By contrast the Marconi team's failed strategy was narrowly financial.

Britain's unusually open market in corporate control had another downside. Promising companies such as the chip designer Arm were snapped up by foreign firms. Although they continued to operate from the UK, control now lay outside the country. AstraZeneca, which played such a big part in Britain's fight against the pandemic, had had to fight for its own life in 2014 when the American pharma giant Pfizer launched a takeover bid.

The British government subscribed to the prevailing market orthodoxy about companies existing only to provide value for their shareholders. But, in fact, shareholders didn't own companies in the way ownership is commonly understood. They couldn't turn up at the door and ask to use the facilities or to take a trip in the company jet. Certainly they had rights, but so too did managers and workers whose joint efforts were fundamentally what made firms tick.

Second thoughts on privatisation

By the early 2020s, flaws in the Thatcher reforms were becoming glaringly apparent. The initial benefits from privatisation came from eliminating inefficiencies in previously state-run industries and allowing more investment than a cash-strapped Treasury had been willing to allow. But these were one-off gains and further improvements required still higher investment. It wasn't forthcoming.

The water industry was a case in point. Initially, privatisation appeared to work, bringing higher capital expenditure than the Treasury had permitted when the dilapidated regional water boards were in state hands. The privatised firms were able to raise funds both in the private market and from lenders such as the

European Investment Bank. Britain started to shed its reputation as the dirty man of Europe. But the industry then developed in unanticipated ways. Private equity funds got involved in the sector and the water companies took on a lot of debt while paying out a lot of dividends to investors. An industry sold in 1989 with no debt at all had accumulated £60 billion debt by 2023 when Thames Water ran into trouble.[35] That, in turn, constrained its ability to finance new investment – the more so since the firms were under ministerial pressure mediated by the regulator to keep water bills down.

As a result, the industry failed to keep up with rising expectations for clean rivers and coastal seas. All too often, visits to the UK's beaches came with warnings against swimming amid untreated human waste – a symbol of national decline for a country that was one of the first to build a modern sewerage system in Victorian London. Analysis of the companies' accounts by the *Financial Times* in late 2021 showed how capital spending in the early 2020s had fallen back in real terms from its post-privatisation average in the 1990s, especially for wastewater and sewage networks. Meanwhile, dividends of £72 billion had been paid out.[36]

Or consider the electricity market. Following the 'dash for gas' in the 1990s, in which the newly privatised companies switched from coal to natural gas, there was a rush for wind in the 2010s. In little more than a decade, Britain became ringed by offshore wind farms, which together with onshore windmills were contributing over a quarter of total electricity being generated in 2022 – even more on days when it was especially windy.[37]

But Britain's privatised energy sector turned out to have an Achilles' heel. Despite the rapid development of renewable energy through all those wind turbines, electricity generation remained heavily dependent on gas. British gas production from the North Sea had peaked in 2000. Imports rose subsequently to make up around half of total gas used in the country. They came both from Norway via pipelines and from LNG (liquefied natural gas) brought in by tankers to three big terminals (two in south-west Wales and one on the Isle of Grain in the Thames estuary) where they were turned back into gas. The extensive use of gas both in home heating and in power production left an economy vulnerable to the price shock in 2022, the more so because of the failure to invest in storage. Britain wasn't directly affected by Russia ending its gas exports through pipelines to continental Europe. But it bought gas at the prices set in Europe and those, in turn, largely drove wholesale electricity prices.

One reason for the dependency was the neglect of nuclear power. Britain had been a nuclear pioneer when it opened the 'Magnox' reactor at Calder Hall in 1956. Several others of this first breed of reactors were soon dotted around the coastline. The unwary visitor to Berkeley in Gloucestershire, best known for its medieval castle where Edward II died in 1327 reputedly in a particularly unpleasant way, may stumble across a modern castle close by: the now closed Magnox nuclear plant.

However, the second generation of reactors proved to be an expensive mistake. Britain went its own way through its Advanced Gas-cooled Reactor (AGR) design rather than adopting what became globally the standard model of a Pressurised Water Reactor (PWR). After installing just one of the latter at Sizewell in Suffolk, which came on stream in 1995, the government became leery of nuclear power. It was one of those 'difficult' issues from which ministers shied away. By the time a decision was taken in 2013 to build a new nuclear power plant at Hinkley Point in Somerset, the government had to turn to a foreign provider: the French firm EDF. Financing was further outsourced to CGN, a state-owned Chinese company, through a controversial decision by David Cameron in 2015, which elevated Treasury tight-fistedness above strategic sense.[38] It brought home the extent to which Britain had squandered its early lead in nuclear power.

By the early 2020s the post-privatisation model of regulation was clearly failing. Ofwat had failed to keep tabs on the water companies. In the household energy market, Ofgem's policy during the 2010s of encouraging new entrants into the market had gone disastrously wrong. Many of the new firms were undercapitalised and folded when energy prices shot up. The cost of the rescue of otherwise stranded customers would fall on all energy consumers through higher bills as well as on the taxpayer in the case of Bulb, the energy company serving 1.5 million customers that had to be bailed out by the government in late 2021.[39]

Back to the future – and back again

The resurrection of industrial strategy that had started under Mandelson continued under the coalition government. In September 2012, his Lib Dem successor Vince Cable set out the rationale. Drawing on his experience in the oil industry, Cable said that Shell had planned much more than five years ahead, and that the government needed to do the same. That was why there should be partnerships with sectors of advanced manufacturing whose timescales stretched far into the future. 'Aerospace demands very long time horizons,' he said, 'and there are literally trillions of pounds worth of orders for civil aircraft alone over the next twenty years or so.'[40]

Other Cable objectives were supporting emerging technologies and creating a pipeline of skilled workers. But probably his biggest achievement was in dealing with another priority: access to finance. It was on his watch that the British Business Bank was founded, in 2014. Its main purpose was to tackle the 'real shortage of long-term, patient capital for businesses' that Cable had identified two years earlier – as well as providing more finance in general to smaller firms.

If taking the long-term perspective was central to industrial strategy, then that policy itself had to endure. But David Cameron's surprise outright victory in the general election of May 2015, largely at the expense of the Lib Dems (Cable lost his seat), ended the coalition government. Sajid Javid, a former financier at Deutsche Bank and a fan of libertarian writer Ayn Rand, was made business secretary. In an interview with the *Financial Times* in September that year, Javid confirmed that the policy had in effect been dumped: 'I don't particularly like the word strategy coupled with industrial.'[41]

That renewed rejection of industrial policy proved to be temporary. Following the Brexit referendum in June 2016, the new prime minister Theresa May decided she *did* like the word strategy coupled with industrial, so much so that she added it to the business department's name. Javid was moved elsewhere and Greg Clark became the new secretary of state. The industrial strategy Clark laid out in late 2017 seemed to be a turning point for a Conservative party so long in thrall to Thatcherite orthodoxies about the virtues of a small state. The new plan made clear that it was not trying to revive the failed post-war model: 'the role of the government is not to pick favourites and subsidise or protect them'. But, crucially, it adopted a hands-on rather than hands-off approach to the private sector.[42] As May herself wrote in a foreword to the white paper, the strategy epitomised her 'belief in a strong and strategic state that intervenes decisively wherever it can make a difference'. She said that a successful free market economy depended on 'firm foundations: the skills of its workers, the quality of the infrastructure, and a fair and predictable business environment. And where these are missing it takes energy and partnership between government and the private sector to address the problems.'

The strategy set out four 'grand challenges': artificial intelligence, clean growth, population ageing and changes in transport. This trendspotting was neither particularly insightful nor new.

The old Department of Trade and Industry had done something similar through its 'Foresight' panels back in the 1990s and early 2000s.

The substance of the plan, which covered business in general rather than manufacturing alone, lay in measures to try to raise productivity. One was a commitment to raise R&D investment as a share of GDP. There would be more infrastructure spending and extra funding to promote links between universities and business. Building on the aerospace partnership pioneered by Cable, the government would reach 'sector deals' to promote higher productivity within specific industries, starting with the life sciences, artificial intelligence, the car industry and construction. These deals involved mutual commitments. In the life sciences, for example, businesses pledged more investment while the government promised to do more in R&D while maintaining collaboration with the NHS.

Improving skills was a high priority and the plan boasted of establishing 'a technical education system that rivals the best in the world'. The claim was over the top. Achieving anything remotely close to that objective would be hard given that the plan also acknowledged, 'for too long, technical education has not had the same prestige that it has enjoyed in other countries'. Still, the steps announced – which included a planned new 'T-level', the technical-education equivalent of A-levels, to be supported by more resources to increase training hours for sixteen–nineteen-year-olds – were headed in the right direction.

Mindful of scepticism about just how long this latest attempt to do industrial policy would last, the government set up an independent industrial strategy council. The new body would assess how things were going and make recommendations to the government. As important, it would 'ensure our industrial strategy will endure', declared the white paper. Chaired by Andy Haldane, then chief economist at the Bank of England, the twenty-strong council held its first meeting in November 2018 at Number 10, joined by May, business minister Clark and the chancellor Philip Hammond. Clark asked the council to be 'challenging on how we evaluate our progress in preparing for the industries of the future, delivering increased productivity and high-quality jobs'.[43]

But the new council didn't have much chance to be 'challenging'. In the spring of 2021, with Boris Johnson now at Number 10, it was dismantled along with the industrial strategy itself. Writing to the council members in March 2021, Kwasi Kwarteng, the new business secretary, said the government had 'decided to mark a departure from the industrial strategy brand'.[44] So all that effort – during ten months of consultation there had been almost two thousand formal responses – had been no more than a branding exercise.

Instead of an industrial strategy came 'Build back better: our plan for growth'.[45] Crucially, this was the work of the Treasury rather than the business department. The plan had its merits – including a continuing stress on skills – but it focused heavily on encouraging innovation, something Britain was already good at doing. Yet as Haldane had pointed out in 2017, there was a strong case for prioritising improvements where Britain was performing badly.[46] But in a sense that no longer mattered because this was just the latest zig – or should it be zag, it was hard to keep count – in the government's view of its role in supporting the private economy. That showed no sign of relenting. Three more initiatives were announced by early 2023, taking the total since 2010 to eleven, according to the IPPR think tank's rather capacious definition.[47] The shortest-lived of all was the Truss growth plan, since labelled as 'archived' on the government website.

Jeremy Hunt pitched in with his own plan for growth at the start of 2023. It set out his '4Es of economic growth and prosperity': enterprise, education, employment and everywhere (the last of these shorthand for levelling up).[48] Arguably, that over-dignified the chancellor's speech since, according to Giles Wilkes of the Institute for Government think tank, it was 'policy-lite' and 'more of an aide-memoire than a vision'.[49]

Getting rid of the 2017 industrial strategy remained an act of policy vandalism. As the *Financial Times*'s Helen Thomas pointed out in November 2023, it was 'the last serious attempt at an overarching framework of priorities for the UK economy'.[50] The strategy had emerged after extensive consultation and envisaged continuing collaboration with business as well as the new council. Its abrupt termination smacked of Johnson's 'fuck business' mentality.

The chopping and changing had become a recurring pattern of government policy. Lord Harrington's review of FDI in late 2023 contained a barrage of criticism from businesses about Britain's chronic policy instability and the damage it was doing. They were frustrated that 'changes in ministers often resulted in policies being recast in their own vision at the expense of delivery'. The frequent changes in direction were 'an effective tax on their operations'. As a result they were 'withholding or underinvesting in the UK'.

What can aid thee?

The most controversial element of industrial policy had long been the use of public subsidy to promote individual companies. In 2017 Greg Clark had gone out of his way to stress that such support would not feature in his industrial strategy. Bit by bit though, state aid was making a comeback – notably in the car industry.

Under the post-Brexit trade deal negotiated by Boris Johnson, exporters now had to show that they met a threshold for the minimum value originating in Britain to the products they were exporting to the EU. These 'rules of origin' were a particular worry for British car manufacturers as the industry moved away from petrol and diesel vehicles to electric ones powered by rechargeable batteries, which make up a large part of their total value.

That made it essential for there to be large-scale battery manufacturing within Britain. For a time, hopes were unwisely pinned on Britishvolt, a start-up in the North-East whose ambitions to become a big battery producer proved wholly unrealistic. Following its all-too-predictable collapse, an alternative had to be found. Eventually, the Indian car maker Tata stepped up in July 2023. But the deal was clinched only with a substantial subsidy, reported by the *Financial Times* to amount to £500 million, towards the £4 billion cost of a gigafactory at Bridgwater in Somerset.[51] Business and trade minister Kemi Badenoch defended the decision by pointing to the context: Britain was 'competing with countries prepared to offer eye-watering sums to pry business away from our shores', she said, adding that 'we do recognise that the UK automotive sector needs certainty and targeted support'.

Later that year, Nissan announced a massive electric car expansion plan in Sunderland together with building a third battery factory at the site. This would also be supported by generous government funding, according to the *FT*.[52] In fact, there was nothing new about the Japanese car maker getting a helping hand. Even under Thatcher, under whose government the ideological anathema on subsidies had started, the Treasury contrived to ensure that Nissan's new Sunderland plant would retain a tax break abolished in the 1984 budget.[53]

Arguably the ideological rejection of subsidies had gone too far, especially as Britain grappled with the challenges of meeting the net-zero target by 2050. As Haldane pointed out in 2023, there was a legitimate place for subsidies where there are externalities, such as the climate crisis, that aren't being picked up in the marketplace.[54] Indeed, a good example was the rapid introduction of offshore wind in the 2010s, which had been kickstarted by subsidies – though the cost was ultimately picked up by consumers through their energy bills.

The world had changed. America was now pursuing Bidenomics – a resurrection of industrial policy designed to introduce green technologies and reduce reliance on China that was backed by ample public funding. In the early 1980s, Thatcher had taken the lead with Ronald Reagan in espousing free market economics. Now a rollback was under way, led by Joe Biden. This time Britain would have to follow suit, though with much less money to throw around than America – as Badenoch ruefully conceded.

Chapter 6

Battle hymn to public services

In September 2023, a cartoon in *The Times* summed up the country's frustration with public services marred by underinvestment and strikes.[1] Captioned 'Bright Future', it featured a couple of schoolchildren on a deserted railway platform, with one saying: 'We're waiting for a non-existent train to take us to our closed school (next to the hospital with no doctors . . .)'.

The deficiencies were most apparent in health: the waiting list for hospital treatments, around 2.5 million in 2010 and 4.6 million at the end of 2019 on the eve of the pandemic, rocketed to 7.8 million in England in autumn 2023.[2] However, the issues extended across the public realm including shamefully overcrowded prisons as well as unsafe school buildings. Even the one apparent bright spot – educational performance – flattered to deceive.

The public services were letting down those who relied on them. But their poor condition had wider consequences since they underpin the economy in a variety of crucial ways, ranging from transport infrastructure to upholding the law, and ensuring the population is healthy enough to work. Poor outcomes contribute to poor economic performance. There were also troubling fiscal implications. If they needed more money that would mean yet higher taxes – even though by the early 2020s the government's tax burden had risen close to a post-war high.

Why were public services in such a mess? Was this simply a lack of money following a decade of austerity? Or were they badly managed – especially the NHS? Could structural reforms be the answer?

One thing was clear: the default response of politicians like Boris Johnson – muddling through – was no longer a viable option. Although Johnson was rightly derided for his 'cakeist' approach, this was the policy that had long been pursued by governments of all persuasions. Every prime minister promised the public that it could have its cake (high-quality European-style services) while also eating it (paying comparatively lower, US-level taxes). But since the public was not prepared to accept the restricted menu of services provided by the American state, it would have to pay the full bill for the European version. Or else let the NHS – and much else besides – drift into disrepair.

Weighing Leviathan

The political philosopher Thomas Hobbes called his famous book advocating a strong sovereign state *Leviathan* – after the biblical Job's sea monster. But little could Hobbes have envisaged the scope of the modern state. The British government intrudes in our lives on a scale unimaginable in 1651, when *Leviathan* was published.

For centuries, the British government confined itself largely to providing security from war and domestic disorder through national defence and policing. But the era of the 'night-watchman state' is long past. In the twenty-first century, the state economically supports huge swathes of the country. Official figures showed 12.6 million people getting the state pension in 2023, while 9.2 million working-age people were receiving benefits, mainly through the 6.1 million on universal credit.[3] Although the government sloughed off nationalised industries in the 1980s and 1990s, it has since taken on many other responsibilities. The school leaving age, for example, has been pushed up from sixteen to eighteen. And even though money was tight in his 2023 budget, chancellor Jeremy Hunt announced an ambitious plan to expand taxpayer support for childcare for working parents: extending in stages the thirty hours a week free childcare for three-to-four-year-olds to cover younger children from the age of nine months.

The overall bill for government spending in the financial year between April 2023 and March 2024 was £1.2 trillion – 45 per cent of GDP. Two-thirds of this goes on the public services.[4] The rest mainly finances pensions and working-age benefits together with the now much higher debt interest bill (see Chapter 3). Setting out realistic plans for the huge amounts of money that the state spends is vital, but the current way that the Treasury goes about this leaves much to be desired (see box).

How the Treasury controls spending: high principle, low practice

When Gordon Brown became chancellor in 1997, he set up a new fiscal framework with supposedly binding rules for debt and borrowing. But a year later, he also introduced a new way of managing expenditure. Instead of setting budgets for the public services every year, they would get three-year settlements called DELs (departmental expenditure limits), which would give greater financial certainty to those running them. Other spending, such as on pensions and debt interest, would continue to be set annually.

The idea was a good one. But like Brown's fiscal

rules, which were discarded the moment they couldn't be met, it hasn't worn well. For one thing, chancellors haven't stuck to the multi-year DELs. In both 2019 and 2020 departmental budgets were set for the financial year ahead. Although 2020 was an exceptional year because of the pandemic, the one-year spending round announced by chancellor Sajid Javid in September 2019 was manifestly designed with an imminent election in mind. In addition, chancellors resort to top-ups between spending reviews. This has happened repeatedly for social care where temporary disbursements were needed to prop up a creaking system. But this hand-to-mouth existence – known as 'crisis-cash-repeat' – is hardly conducive to long-term planning.

Another snag is that the Treasury budgets in cash terms. For departments with multi-year spending limits that doesn't matter too much when inflation is low, as was the case during the 2010s. When inflation surged in the 2020s, it led to an unintended squeeze in real terms. A further weakness came to the fore ahead of the election in 2024. The spending review conducted by Rishi Sunak in late 2021 had set DELs for the three financial years starting in April 2022 and ending in March 2025. What would happen then? The Treasury was disinclined to disclose anything beyond broad totals based on assumptions that were quite unrealistic. Richard Hughes, chair of the OBR, vented his frustration to a House of Lords committee in January 2024 when he said the plans after the spring of 2025 were worse than a work of fiction.[5]

Public services are delivered by people working in offices, schools and hospitals that require a lot of investment to maintain and upgrade them. As well as doctors, nurses and teachers, these workers include civil servants such as the administrative staff at the DWP that deliver pensions and working-age benefits. In all, close to 6 million people work in the public sector – nearly a fifth of total employment. Many are highly qualified professionals: public service staff are generally more skilled than private sector workers, which is one reason why care has to be taken in comparing wages between the two sectors (another is the value of occupational pensions).[6]

The scale of the public sector is such that it makes a meaningful contribution to the overall efficiency of the economy. Unfortunately, it is an unfavourable one. Recent figures suggest that productivity in public services had grown by only 0.2 per cent a year on average between 1997 and 2019, efficiency gains that were disappointingly meagre.[7] That said, it is tricky to measure how well the public services are performing because they are largely provided without direct charges, whether that is patients getting treated in NHS hospitals or children attending state schools. Measuring quality improvements (or deterioration) isn't straightforward either.

Arguably, sluggish productivity goes with the turf. Unlike other professions that have economised using technology, public services are necessarily labour intensive: you need teachers and their assistants to be physically present in a classroom; hospital patients are attended to by nurses. The US economist William Baumol first diagnosed this phenomenon in the performing arts: a Schubert string quartet will always require four players and take roughly the same time to perform as in early nineteenth-century Vienna.

More importantly, the full value of the public services is not captured in conventional accounting. Teachers help build human capital. Doctors contribute to the health of the economy as well as of the nation. Increasing life expectancy extends working lives. Having an impartial civil service and an independent judiciary are crucial to economic success.

Jails breaking

Often the services generally receiving the least media attention were doing the worst. A prime example was prisons. If a country should be judged by the way it treats those behind bars, then Britain deserved a tough sentence. When Daniel Khalife, a terror suspect being held at Wandsworth jail while awaiting trial allegedly escaped in September 2023 – he denies all charges against him including that of escaping – there was a brief flurry of interest about conditions at the prison.[8]

A report by its Independent Monitoring Board covering the year to May 2023 was scathing. Staff shortages and a high turnover of officers were a way of life. The number of assaults was rising, including, on average, over ten a week on staff. 'Conditions remained inhumane,' said the report, with most men sharing cells designed for one person. At the end of May 2023, a prison with a capacity of 961 (without being crowded) was holding 1,584 inmates. It often had no heating or hot water in the winter months while cells were regularly flooded.[9]

Victorian jails such as Wandsworth should have been closed and replaced by modern structures that created better conditions. But while governments pursued a 'lock them up' policy that was catnip to the tabloids, they dodged the bill for modernising and expanding the buildings meant to house them. Instead, more and more prisoners were shoved into unfit jails. In mid-2023, 61 per cent of prisons in England and Wales were classified as overcrowded.[10]

A slap in the face for the reputation of Britain's prisons came from a court in Karlsruhe, Germany in 2023. The UK was trying to extradite an Albanian man accused of drug trafficking who had been living in Britain. On failing to receive assurances about the conditions he might encounter in detention, the court ruled his extradition 'currently inadmissible'.[11]

England and Wales had the biggest prison population per 100,000 inhabitants in western Europe (with Scotland hard on its heels). Only some countries in eastern and central Europe, such as Lithuania and the Czech Republic, had higher rates. The reoffending rate in England and Wales was also high: 37 per cent of adults released from prison between October and December 2021 committed another offence within a year.[12] For those behind bars for less than a year, the rate was even higher: 55 per cent. That was hardly surprising. Overstretched warders couldn't help prisoners go straight.

Quite apart from the social costs of continuing criminality, recidivism was a desperately bad return on investment. The annual direct cost per prisoner was £31,500 in 2021–22 in England and Wales while the overall cost was £47,400.

Care and care alike

Local authorities had borne some of the fiercest cuts during Osborne's austerity programme. One of their main responsibilities was adult social care – looking after elderly or vulnerable people – and even though they tried to protect the sector in favour of cutting other services like libraries, spending fell in real terms by around 10 per cent in the first half of the 2010s. A House of Lords select committee judged in 2017 that 'the funding crisis in adult social care is worsening to the point of imminent breakdown'.[13]

Inadequate social care has a knock-on effect on the NHS. Even before the pandemic, hospitals were struggling because of 'bed-blocking' by elderly patients ready to be discharged but with nowhere to go because councils couldn't find places in care homes or put together care packages to look after them in their own homes. That, in turn, prevented the admissions of other patients who needed urgent medical care.

The cascading impact of problems in social care highlighted the fact that local public services resembled a delicate ecosystem whose overall health can deteriorate if a few of its constituent parts weaken. Cutbacks in one particular service can generate problems elsewhere. For example, reductions in youth programmes could prove to be false economies if they result in more crime and greater demands being placed on the police.

For several years, the Institute for Government (IfG) has worked with the Chartered Institute of Public Finance and Accountancy (CIPFA) to produce an invaluable 'performance tracker' of public services. These surveys painted an increasingly depressing picture. The first, in early 2017, reported that services had initially coped well with austerity in part because of the preceding years of growth and investment under Labour. However, this original approach had 'run out of steam by 2015'. The authors warned that services such as adult social care and hospitals were being pushed 'to breaking point and, in the case of prisons, beyond it'.[14]

Even though a lot more money went into the public services from 2019, especially into the NHS, the assessment in late 2023 from the IfG and CIPFA was even gloomier: the government risked getting stuck in a 'doom loop' through 'the perpetual state of crisis burning out staff and preventing services from taking the best long-term decisions'.[15] The situation was 'particularly dire in prisons, hospitals, general practice and adult social care,' according to Rob Whiteman, CIPFA's chief executive. Services, he said, had been 'weakened by the loss of experienced staff and high turnover', resulting in 'a record number of vacancies in the NHS, adult social care, children's social care, and the highest prison-officer leaving rate on record'.

Nothing but facts

Eight of the nine public services covered by the performance tracker had got worse between 2009 and 2019. The exception was schools.

International comparisons cast England's schools in an increasingly favourable light. The results of the latest 'Progress in International Reading Literacy Study' (Pirls) for nine- and ten-year-olds ranked England fourth out of forty-three countries in 2021 – up from joint eighth in 2016, and exceeded only by Singapore, Hong Kong and Russia.[16] There was another positive finding in the OECD's programme for international student assessment (Pisa) taken by fifteen-year-olds in 2022.[17] This showed English children moving up the ranking for maths from seventeenth in 2018 to eleventh.

For education secretary Gillian Keegan these scores vindicated 'the government's unrelenting drive to raise school standards over the past thirteen years'. Citing the Pirls report as well, she said that England was 'now firmly cemented as one of the top performing countries for education in the western world'. What she didn't point out was that English schoolchildren had actually done *worse* in the Pisa maths test than in 2018 and hadn't improved in the Pirls reading test.[18] We only went up the rankings because other countries had fallen behind.

In England, the focus on exam results was increasingly reductive. The more that schools were judged by how they did in exams, the more they concentrated on doing well in the core subjects like English and maths. The result was steep falls in the number of pupils taking GCSEs in creative subjects such as music and drama.

The pressure on schools was unremitting because they were patrolled by Ofsted, the dreaded inspectorate. Its simplistic grades – ranging from 1 ('outstanding') to 4 ('inadequate') – were themselves inadequate given the complexity of what schools do. In

December 2023, a coroner ruled that an unfavourable inspection (based on just one aspect of the school's performance, specifically safeguarding concerns) had contributed to the suicide of Ruth Perry, a headteacher of a Reading primary school that had previously been considered 'outstanding'.[19]

In June 2022, an education commission set up by *The Times* passed a damning verdict: the system was 'failing on every measure'.[20] There was an over-reliance on exams and a failure to develop social and communication skills. Education had become 'more robotic'. One of the commissioners, Geoff Barton, general secretary of the Association of School and College Leaders, said: 'Let's stop defining young people ultimately as a grade.'[21]

Employers were also dissatisfied. A 2018 CBI report found one in four employers were unhappy about the standards of literacy and numeracy among young people applying for jobs; two in five about their aptitude and readiness for work.[22] A survey of businesses by PwC for the commission found that three-quarters had to give new recruits additional training in basic skills including literacy and numeracy.

The government's 'unrelenting drive to raise school standards' had, in fact, been an unrelentingly missed opportunity to reform education. Once the school leaving age (strictly speaking, the age until which it was compulsory to stay in education or training) rose to eighteen in England (from 2015) there was no longer the same need for GCSEs at sixteen. Rather, the focus should have been recasting A-levels to something more like the broader French baccalaureate.

Rishi Sunak proposed such a change at the Tory party conference in 2023 when he announced 'the new rigorous knowledge-rich Advanced British Standard' for post-sixteen-year-olds. But this was little more than a declaration of intent. Reshaping the curriculum to merge academic and technical education would be a decade-long policy needing buy-in from teachers. Sunak's parallel ambition for pupils to study maths until eighteen was laudably ambitious – but didn't add up while there was such a shortage of maths teachers.[23]

Overall, the government's approach was nostalgic. A 'knowledge-rich' education bore an uncanny resemblance to Mr Gradgrind's philosophy in *Hard Times*: 'Now, what I want is, Facts. Teach these boys and girls nothing but Facts.' But what mattered in the twenty-first century was not acquiring knowledge – now a mere Google search away – but the capacity to learn and relearn skills as well as to interact successfully with your fellow workers. This was a 'Fact' successive governments had studiously ignored.

The NHS in extremis

In the court of public opinion, however, the most ailing public service was the NHS. The public's despair was well founded. According to the IfG/CIPFA survey in late 2023, both hospitals and GP practices were much worse in the pre-pandemic year of 2019 than they had been a decade earlier. And they had deteriorated still further since then.[24]

One ailing vital sign was the waiting list for 'elective' (non-emergency) hospital treatments such as knee replacements and cataract surgery. The list soared after the pandemic even though there wasn't, in fact, the expected surge in demand from patients unable to access care during the lockdowns; rather, fewer treatments were being done than before the pandemic. Since some patients were waiting for more than one treatment, there were 6.5 million – over a tenth of England's population – on the list when it reached 7.8 million in September 2023.

It wasn't just electives. A longstanding standard was for at least 95 per cent of those attending A&E to be dealt with – admitted, transferred or discharged – within four hours. In late 2019, that was already being missed by a wide margin at 71 per cent in major hospital A&E departments. In late 2022 that had fallen to just 53 per cent. A year later it had barely improved, with 55 per cent of patients waiting less than four hours. The overall figure for A&E attendances including those at minor injury units stood at 70 per cent.

Then there was the struggle to see a family doctor. Getting a GP appointment had become extremely trying. In 2012, 81 per cent of patients found it easy to get through to their GP practice on the phone; by 2023, it was 50 per cent. Almost a quarter now found it 'not at all easy' (at the very least, it required patience, as in repeatedly being told 'you are number 8 in line'). One of the traditional strengths of Britain's GP system was continuity of care – being looked after by the same doctor. But this was increasingly the exception rather than the rule. In 2023, only a third of patients said they were generally able to speak to or see their preferred GP, down from two-thirds a decade earlier.

GPs themselves were unhappy. The rising demand from an ageing population wasn't helped by micromanaging targets, small premises and inadequate IT systems. Compared with their peers in nine other high-income countries, GPs reported the highest stress and lowest job satisfaction. It was becoming harder to retain young doctors who had joined practices.

The parlous state of primary healthcare was mirrored by hospitals. Britain entered the pandemic with only 2.5 beds per thousand inhabitants – among the lowest across advanced economies. This followed a decades-long decline. That was partly because more and more patients were treated through day surgery – an undoubted advance. But the drop in beds left the NHS perilously exposed before Covid.

International comparisons were troubling. Britain had higher mortality than most other advanced countries for 'treatable' diseases – mostly cardio-vascular, such as heart attacks, and cancers – among the under-seventy-fives. These deaths could mainly have been avoided through timely and effective healthcare interventions. Figures published by the OECD in 2023 showed Britain faring worse on this measure than its west European neighbours. Ironing out differences arising from variations in age profiles, the UK's rate of treatable mortality was seventy-one per 100,000, compared with thirty-nine (the lowest) in Switzerland and forty-eight in the Netherlands.[25]

Britain's infant mortality rate was also disquietingly high. The most recent figures showed four deaths per 1,000 live births for children under the age of one. By contrast, this was 1.6 in Finland (the lowest), and below two in Japan, Norway, Iceland and Slovenia. The failings in maternity care at the Shrewsbury and Telford Hospital NHS Trust were laid bare in a damning report in March 2022. It found that 'lessons were not learned, mistakes in care were repeated and the safety of mothers and babies was unnecessarily compromised as a result'.[26]

In principle, a state-funded and publicly run health service should be good at forward planning. In practice, the NHS was bad at it – especially when it came to anticipating staff requirements. Indeed, it was only in June 2023 that the health service issued its first long-term workforce plan, for the period to 2036.

The annual British Social Attitudes survey conducted a poll between 7 September and 30 October 2022 – before the wave of industrial action in the NHS had begun. It found that 51 per cent of the population were dissatisfied with the health service – the worst figure since the survey began in 1983. The satisfaction rate was at a record low of 29 per cent.[27] A year later it fell still further, to just 24 per cent. The opening ceremony of the 2012 London Olympics included a tribute to the NHS. At the time, that seemed over the top given that healthcare in Britain at the time was far from outstanding.[28] A decade later such a paean would have lacked any credibility.

Why had things gone so wrong?

Manifestly, the disruption caused by the pandemic had contributed to this sorry state of affairs. But that prompted the question: why had Britain's public services shown such a striking lack of resilience?

One reason was outdated buildings with inadequate equipment. In the spring of 2023, the think tank Resolution Foundation described Britain as 'an international laggard when it comes to public investment, consistently featuring in the weakest third of OECD countries'. If instead we had matched the OECD average in the past two decades, a 'truly transformational' extra £500 billion would have been invested this century.[29]

The reluctance to spend had a long history. The scandal of crumbling concrete (RAAC: short for reinforced autoclaved aerated concrete) in public buildings, which forced some to close in 2023, reflected short-sighted decisions taken as far back as the 1960s. As the IfG/CIPFA survey said: 'Governments have underinvested in capital across all public services for more than half a century, leaving GP surgeries, hospitals, schools, courts and prisons that are not fit for purpose.' There was also a massive maintenance backlog of close to £40 billion.

The NHS was especially hampered by defective buildings. Of the maintenance backlog, over a quarter – £11.6 billion – was in hospitals.[30] One example of this was St Mary's in Paddington, the major acute hospital for north-west London, beset by flooding including sewage coming out of the drains in the outpatient department. Several hospitals were also affected by the dodgy RAAC concrete.[31]

Inadequate investment also meant the NHS had a shortage of the MRI units and CT and PET scanners used to diagnose diseases such as cancer. These were much scarcer in Britain than in most other advanced economies, which held back hospitals in carrying out essential tests on patients.

Basic IT systems were also inadequate. During the second wave of the pandemic, in October 2020, 16,000 Covid cases went missing from the official count because Public Health England was recording them on an outdated version of Excel. This was in any case inappropriate for a database, Jon Crowcroft, a computer science specialist at Cambridge University told the BBC.[32] The lapse wasn't just embarrassing for health secretary Matt Hancock since it led to delays in tracing people who had been in contact with the missing cases.[33]

Austerity pursued for too long was clearly part of the problem. The cost of health services in advanced countries tends to rise faster than economy-wide inflation mainly because of expensive new technologies and drugs. That's why ringfencing the health budget from real-term cuts under the coalition government was actually harmful for the NHS since it needed spending to increase above the general rate of inflation. In practice, health expenditure did rise in the first half of the 2010s but by less than 1 per cent a year on average – well below its historic real-term growth rate of close to 4 per cent.[34] Yet the special treatment for the NHS made the cuts even tougher for unprotected departments like the justice ministry which had to cope with big reductions in spending on prisons and the courts.

Austerity meant a prolonged clampdown on public pay. There was a case for restraint in the early years of the coalition government: much of the higher spending on public services under Labour had gone into wages and salaries. But the squeeze went on for much too long, creating the discontent that came to the fore in the wave of strikes by public sector workers following the surge in inflation in 2022 and 2023.

It had become difficult to attract new teachers: in 2023, the number starting their training in secondary schools was half the government target.[35] Another problem was the loss of experienced staff. This should not have been a surprise to ministers. The public sector workforce was ageing towards the years when early retirement became financially feasible. In the NHS, senior doctors had an added incentive to quit to avoid breaching a cap on the value of their pensions – the 'lifetime allowance', beyond which they were exposed to hefty taxes on the excess. An expensive solution announced by Jeremy Hunt in the 2023 budget got rid of the lifetime allowance for everyone – but by then it had already prompted some doctors to quit.

The traditional package of pay and pensions for public sector workers no longer made sense. Although pay had failed to keep up with the private sector over the decade, public employees still had a better deal on their pensions. But for younger staff that was a long time in the future, whereas their inadequate pay was in the here and now. On the other hand, the high value of their pensions encouraged older staff to retire early. In 2022, the IFS said there was a 'strong case' for 'rebalancing public sector remuneration away from pensions and towards pay'.[36]

The loss of experienced staff in the NHS was the main reason why hospitals did so badly following the pandemic, even though there were rising numbers of doctors and nurses. As the IfG/CIPFA report pointed out: 'Replacing experienced staff with inexperienced staff is not a like-for-like exchange.' New staff took time 'to embed in the service' and needed more experienced colleagues to train them. 'The result – for now, at least – is a less productive workforce.'

Playing with trains

As public services teetered on the edge in the early 2020s, the Conservative government struck up a familiar tune. Reform rather than extra funding was needed to lick them into shape. Much the same message came from Labour: shadow health secretary Wes Streeting insisted that the NHS mend its ways rather than always putting out the hat.

Successive governments had blazoned reform on their banners. Acutely aware of the political danger of pumping lots of money into the public services, Blair and Brown had insisted on strictly monitoring their performance. This top-down regime was nicknamed 'targets and terror'.

The trouble with targets was that you could hit them while still missing the point. They could never encompass the full range of what was involved in delivering good public services. In straining to meet specific goals, other important aspects – especially their actual quality – were likely to be neglected.

Accompanying the target culture was a campaign to pull public service professionals down a peg. In the arresting analogy of Julian Le Grand, a health economist who advised Tony Blair, public sector professionals were once treated as selfless altruists – 'knights'. But from the 1980s, they were increasingly seen as self-interested 'knaves' to be treated with suspicion rather than reverence.[37]

That pendulum had swung too far. As Camilla Cavendish, a director of the Downing Street policy unit under David Cameron, noted in 2023 about the NHS, 'Speaking to professionals about why they have left or are thinking of leaving the service, all cite pay but most are also deeply upset about the lack of respect from their own employers.'[38] *The Times* education commission said that teachers were leaving the profession 'because they feel overworked and undervalued' and described Ofsted as a 'toxic brand'. Estonia, apparently, was getting things right. Their schools weren't even subject to regular inspections. 'We trust our teachers and our teachers have a lot of autonomy,' the Estonian education minister told the commission.

All too often, ministers mistook restructuring as genuine reform. A case in point was the full-throated backing for academies, state schools run by trusts and directly funded by Whitehall, which were displacing those controlled by local authorities. But even the government's own evidence on their effectiveness presented a mixed picture.[39] What really matters in schools is the quality and commitment of teachers, which is materially affected by salaries for both new recruits and existing staff.

Morale wasn't helped by endless structural tinkering. Under New Labour, the health service had devolved commissioning of hospital services to primary care trusts, or PCTs, which were also responsible for organising care provided by GPs. The coalition government took this a step further by getting rid of the PCTs and replacing them with GP-led commissioning groups. The reform (no more than hinted at in the Tory manifesto) was so big it could be seen from space, said David Nicholson, the then NHS chief executive with a flair for a striking turn of phrase. Quite apart from its cost and scale, the reorganisation put additional administrative strain on family doctors. Yet there was nothing new in ministers meddling in the internal structures of the NHS. Indeed, this process was dubbed 'redisorganisation' in the *British Medical Journal* in 2001 in response to Labour's planned shake-up of the health service.[40]

So it was no surprise that before long the reforms of 2012 started to be eroded. One of their few merits was the decision to make the NHS (in England) more autonomous. Under its new chief executive, Simon Stevens, who replaced Nicholson in 2014, the health service started to experiment with more collaborative structures, rather than pitting the commissioning groups against the hospitals. This, at least, helped in tackling actual problems. But NHS autonomy lasted only a decade. New legislation passed in 2022 sought to formalise this new 'integrated care' approach, which was welcome. But it also eroded the autonomy of the NHS in England by giving the health secretary more powers to intervene.[41] This shake-up followed a controversial move in August 2020 to replace Public Health England with a new agency, provoking Jeremy Farrar, who was then director of the Wellcome Trust, to tweet:

'Ill thought-through, short-term, reactive reforms.'[42] Nicholson had a point when he described the NHS as the 'biggest train set in Europe' for ministers to play with.[43]

Cuckoo in the nest

The unceasing resort to 'reform' was a futile attempt to square a circle. The NHS started to get a lot more funding from April 2019, with a five-year settlement announced by Theresa May the previous June intended to raise spending by 3.4 per cent a year in real terms.[44] But the extra money followed a decade of tight budgets. Research by the Health Foundation showed how health spending per person had lagged behind that in France and Germany.[45] That underfunding translated into worse outcomes for patients. In the quest to do more with less, successive governments ran hospitals 'hot', with little to no spare capacity – a crucial reason why during the pandemic the NHS cut back elective operations so much more than elsewhere in Europe.

Yet even though the NHS was underfunded by international standards, it was consistently the most successful at getting extra money from the British state. Indeed, the story of the public services in the past thirty or so years has been one of the NHS as cuckoo in the nest. Back in the late 1980s, the health and defence budgets were roughly comparable: each around 4 per cent of GDP.[46] Three decades later, defence's share had shrunk to 2 per cent while health's had swollen to 8 per cent – four times as high.

That shrinkage in the defence budget was showing. The army was only around 75,000 strong, half the number in the early 1990s and the smallest for two centuries. It also lacked enough modern equipment. In January 2023, Sky News reported that a senior American general had told defence secretary Ben Wallace that the British army was no longer considered a top-level fighting force.[47]

The navy's surface fleet of only around seventy vessels meant it was a shadow of its former strength.[48]

In November 2020, Johnson had announced a four-year boost for the armed forces: 'I have decided that the era of cutting our defence budget must end, and it ends now,' he declared imperiously. But higher inflation ate into the extra funding, which was (unsurprisingly) more modest than he had intimated.[49] Three years later, the *Wall Street Journal* published a leader entitled, 'God save the British military'.[50] This followed a report from the National Audit Office describing the Ministry of Defence's ten-year equipment plan as 'unaffordable', with forecast costs £17 billion higher than the available budget. In January 2024, a *Times* editorial said, 'Britain is ceasing to be a credible military power.'[51]

The fundamental problem was that the NHS was crowding out everything else. Britain seemed to be getting the worst of both worlds: a health service that was chronically underfunded but whose appetite for ever more money caused an unending squeeze on other departments. It was politically tempting to blame lacklustre efficiency and poor management rather than a lack of money. But that got things the wrong way round. As healthcare expert Chris Ham pointed out in November 2023, the NHS was both 'over-administered and undermanaged'.[52]

The continuing travails of the NHS, along with the pressure that its financial needs put on other public services, appeared to pose a bleak fiscal dilemma. Either there would have to be cuts in other areas, such as on the state pension, or taxes would have to rise still further. Neither choice was an appealing prospect.

Chapter 7

Is more immigration the answer?

As the outcome of the 2016 referendum hung in the balance, Leave campaigners played their trump card. Leaving the European Union, they claimed, was the only way to stop high immigration. Yet following the self-inflicted economic blow of Brexit, the question was turned on its head. Were even more migrants now needed to repair the damage? The answer depended on what kind of repair you were after. Was the goal to raise overall GDP or GDP per person? Relatedly, was immigration a way to deal with an ageing population by recruiting young foreign workers to replace retiring baby boomers? Or was it to deal with labour and skills shortages in a limited number of occupations?

To answer these questions, it was essential to consider timescale. In the short term, a big influx of young people keen to work would boost the economy and could be accommodated within the UK's existing infrastructure. That would make life easier for chancellors as the productive incomers added to tax revenues. But in the longer term these initial benefits would start to be offset by costs. Public services would come under greater pressure. Before long, more new homes would have to be built. The state would need to invest more in schools and hospitals and recruit extra staff to cope with the higher population.

There was a similar trade-off if immigration was used to meet staff shortages in low-wage sectors such as care homes. The immediate positive effect allowed businesses to survive. But continually resorting to immigrants acted as a disincentive to improve pay and conditions for British workers – or to invest in labour-saving equipment.

Overall, it is vital for Britain to remain open to new talent coming from abroad. But immigration isn't a miracle economic cure.

From *Auf Wiedersehen, Pet* to Polish plumbers

Economists generally treat Britain's demographics like the background of a film scene. The overall size and shape of the population is known while changes are generally predictable. What counts is what is going on in the foreground – output and inflation – which can vary from month to month.

Yet demographic change can spring surprises. One was the post-war baby boom, which followed a period when people were fretting about the population falling. In 1939, the Cambridge University economist Brian Reddaway predicted in *The Economics of a Declining Population* that in Britain 'each future generation is likely to be at least 20 per cent smaller than the one before'.[1] The baby bust of the 1970s was a further surprise, since for decades everyone had become used to high birth rates.

Another unexpected development has been the upsurge in migration in the first two decades of the twenty-first century. Until relatively recently, Britain had as many emigrants as immigrants. When unemployment was high in the 1980s, workers moved to Germany, inspiring the television series, *Auf Wiedersehen, Pet* in which Geordie construction workers find work in Düsseldorf. Overall net migration – immigrants less emigrants – was broadly in balance in the 1980s and early 1990s.[2] But then the picture changed – at first, with fairly small flows of net migration in the second half of the 1990s and then a surge during the 2000s and 2010s.

In May 2004, ten more countries joined the European Union, including eight in central and eastern Europe of which the most populous was Poland. Although freedom of movement was a defining characteristic of the EU, the terms of accession allowed for a phased opening of labour markets to migrants from new member states. Britain was one of only three countries (the other two were Ireland and Sweden) to unlock their doors from the outset. The ensuing inflow took everyone by surprise – not least the government, which had trusted a forecast that only between five thousand and thirteen thousand a year would come and stay.[3] Instead, many hundreds of thousands moved to find better-paid work. The population movement in the first two years was the biggest single wave of migration in British history, according to John Salt, director of the migration research unit at University College London in the summer of 2006 – though he pointed out that the arrival of the Huguenots from France in the late seventeenth century might have been bigger as a share of the population.[4]

The influx was undoubtedly a boon for the economy. Suddenly, there was a new source of willing hands prepared to do all manner of jobs in all manner of places. Unlike previous flows of immigration, which had tended to focus on London and the other big cities, the new migrants spread out more widely around the country meeting regional labour shortages. Because the new migrants were typically young adults, they provided a helpful boost to the Exchequer. Their initial demands on public services, especially the NHS, were limited. Most studies showed that on balance they contributed more in taxes than they cost in benefits and their use of public services.[5]

The 2021 census revealed the imprint of two decades of historically high immigration. In England and Wales, the total number of people who had been born abroad rose from 4.6 million in 2001 (9 per cent of the population) to 10 million (a 16.8 per cent share).

Of the total number of foreign-born, over a third – 3.6 million – lived in London. The capital's thriving economy was a poster child for the economic advantages of migration (see box).[6]

The middle bulge

Growth springs from two sources. The first and most fundamental is higher productivity: more output per worker. It is the sustained rise in productivity that has transformed living standards since the industrial revolution. But the second also matters in the short to medium term: more workers.

The main rationale for more immigrants is that they will increase the number of people in work, which will in turn raise GDP. Their presence will also help the public finances because bigger GDP means higher tax revenues. These positive outcomes will be enhanced if, as is often the case, the immigrants are entrepreneurial.

However, the positive effect on actual living standards of existing residents will be smaller. Migrants add to the population, so GDP per person won't increase by nearly as much as GDP overall. In general, the main gain of immigration goes to the migrants themselves: for the rest of the population the benefits are unevenly distributed. For those working in low-skilled jobs, the effect will be to hold their wages down. Often the worst affected are migrants from a previous generation being undercut by cheaper foreign labour. That in turn helps the better-off who purchase their services and the owners of businesses employing them. The highly skilled may also gain as the presence of migrants allows them to be

more productive and so earn more: having a cleaner,
for example, gives you more time to work. However, estimates of these effects suggest they are quite limited.[7]

Turning to demographics, bringing in young people
from overseas looks like a potential solution to an
ageing population. However, as an influential study by
the UN showed in 2000, it can't work without ever-
growing numbers of immigrants.[8] When the baby
boomers were at work, the age pyramid of Britain
bulged in the middle with relatively few older dependants at the top. But now the baby boomers are
themselves swelling the ranks of the elderly, very high
rates of immigration would be needed to restore the
former bulge. And as those immigrants themselves
eventually aged, a further multiple would be required.

Although the EU incomers were positive for the economy as a
whole, there were downsides. The migrants added to pressures on
public services in specific areas such as Boston in Lincolnshire,
which hadn't previously experienced much immigration. It took
time for the funding formulae the government used to distribute
public money across the country to catch up with the increased
demand. Migrants also pushed wages down among the low-skilled,
though various studies indicated the effect was small.[9]

The sudden increase in numbers was bound to put strain on an
infrastructure built for a smaller and more stable population. It
added to the need for new housing, especially in London and the
South-East, and contributed to the rise in house prices.[10]

Businesses, on the other hand, welcomed the new migrants
and, by and large, the economics profession agreed. However, the
House of Lords economic committee struck an early discordant

note in April 2008. It criticised the government for highlighting the positive effect on GDP, saying it was 'an irrelevant and misleading criterion'. If, instead, the focus was on income per head any benefit was modest. 'In the long run, the main economic effect of immigration is to enlarge the economy, with relatively small costs and benefits for the incomes of the resident population.'[11]

A weakness in the report was that it failed to acknowledge the importance of migrants' entrepreneurial vigour. In 2014, the Centre for Entrepreneurs reported that they were almost twice as likely to launch businesses: in all, 17 per cent of migrants had founded companies compared with 10 per cent among people born in Britain.[12] Almost a decade later, research published by *Forbes* magazine showed that 39 of Britain's 100 fastest-growing companies had a foreign-born founder.[13]

Giving back control

A crucial feature of the new migration was that it was driven mainly by people moving freely from the EU. This made the incomers especially responsive to the state of the economy as well as to the sectors that had the greatest need for additional workers. This sensitivity to the business cycle showed itself from the outset. The arrivals got under way in the mid-2000s when the economy had been expanding for over a decade. That meant reserves of spare labour supply were already drawn down: the unemployment rate was down to lows not seen since 1975. This made the new workers especially welcome and relatively easy to absorb.

When the good times ended with the 2008 financial crisis and the economy slumped into a severe recession, there was a corresponding fall in net migration from the EU, which picked up only as the economy itself recovered. Inflows were especially strong in the five years up to the 2016 referendum as the British economy outgrew the euro area, which was stuck in an economic rut owing to the sovereign debt crisis at the start of the decade. Indeed, Britain started to attract migrants from struggling economies such as Italy and Spain as well as eastern Europe. In the words of Denis MacShane, a former Labour minister for Europe, Britain became in effect the 'employer of last resort' for the EU.[14]

The sheer scale of immigration began to stoke a political backlash. The winning slogan of the Leave camp was 'Take back control'. No one entering the polling booths in June 2016 could be in any doubt that this meant control of immigration, which was adding (net of emigration) around 300,000 people a year to the population. It wasn't until the start of 2021 that Britain was able to introduce a new migration policy. However, many Europeans saw the way the wind was blowing and fewer came following the vote, while more of those already in Britain decided to up sticks. Even before the pandemic, the net inflows from the EU had fallen sharply and in 2021 they turned negative: more were leaving than arriving.

This highlighted another characteristic of the EU migration wave: more than other immigrants, many European incomers never intended to settle permanently. Rather, they wanted to spend time in a country where they could earn more than at home and improve their English. In economic terms, this was especially desirable since it added a pool of young people to the labour force that could wax and wane with overall demand while placing less long-term stress on infrastructure.

The government prepared for its long-awaited control over European as well as non-European migration with a 'points-based' policy, which was set out by home secretary Priti Patel in February 2020.[15] This applied equally to the EU and the rest of the world. The idea was to encourage skilled incomers while barring the unskilled. That was to operate through a points system in which the entry door swung open at the magic level of seventy. All applicants had to demonstrate that they had a job offer which was at least 'middle-skilled' (defined as one requiring at least A-Level education), and that they spoke English adequately. That earned fifty points. A salary of at least £25,600 won an additional twenty points, permitting entry. That salary threshold was higher in better-paid occupations and set at their 'going rate' (the pay level where a quarter of workers were earning less and three-quarters earning more). For those earning between the minimum salary of £20,480 and £25,600, immigration was still possible if they had the relevant qualifications or were in an occupation with staff shortages, such as nursing.

Although the policy was presented as if it was freshly minted, points had already been used for immigrants coming from outside the EU. Tony Blair's 'highly skilled migrant programme', introduced in 2002, was expanded in 2008 to cover workers sponsored by employers. And though that system was largely dropped by home secretary Theresa May in 2011, parts of it had survived in vestigial form.

In the 2019 election the Conservatives portrayed the approach as 'Australian-style'. But Australia's model admitted people on the basis of their personal characteristics including their age, qualifications and skilled work experience. By contrast, the British system required employer sponsorship. Furthermore, as Peter William Walsh of Oxford University's Migration Observatory pointed out in May 2021, the skill level was 'a property of the job, not the worker', who didn't necessarily have to have the qualifications defining a job.[16] All in all, the points were essentially a presentational device.

Two years after the new system had been introduced at the start of 2021, the slogan 'take back control' rang more hollow than ever. Throughout 2023, attention had been focused on the asylum seekers crossing the Channel – Rishi Sunak had made stopping the boats a hi-vis policy. But the number crossing – around forty-five thousand in 2022, falling to just under thirty thousand in 2023 – was as nothing compared with those coming with visas.[17]

Already in the year to June 2022, the total number of net migrants was extraordinarily high: 607,000.[18] That could, in part, be attributed to special dispensations for Hong Kong holders of British national overseas passports escaping China's crackdown and Ukrainians fleeing Russia's invasion. But in the year to June 2023, even though fewer were now coming from Hong Kong and Ukraine, net migration was even higher at 672,000. But the figure that really grabbed the attention was a revision to the previous estimate for the calendar year of 2022 (see box). The ONS, which had previously reckoned that figure to be 606,000, revised it up to 745,000 – far above the pre-referendum 303,000 in 2015. The 2022 figure would have been even higher but for a net outflow of 123,000 EU citizens.

Counting in and counting out

Working out how many people are immigrating and emigrating is far from simple. The figures of interest are for long-term migrants, defined as those changing their country of usual residence for at least a year. The key is separating them out from the vast flows crossing borders for much shorter periods, whether on holiday or business.

The upsurge in migration in the 2000s caught the bean counters on the hop. An ONS review in April 2014 owned up to an undercount of 350,000 during that decade. Many of the migrants coming from the EU from May 2004 had been missed by the international passenger survey used among other things (such as travel expenditure) to estimate migration flows. The survey was mainly conducted at transport hubs such as Heathrow, which meant that a large number of migrants arriving at regional airports including Luton and Stansted weren't picked up.

Since 2020, new ways have been introduced to count international migration. For migrants coming from outside the EU, the ONS relies heavily on Home Office data combining visas and travel information, which it adjusts for people leaving sooner than a year. It keeps tabs on EU migration mainly by using administrative data such as National Insurance numbers. Estimates of migration by British nationals are still based predominantly on the passenger survey.

Another crucial source for the ONS is the census. The 2011 count showed that the population was almost half a million bigger than expected, mainly because of unrecorded international migration. By contrast, the 2021 census showed the population was a quarter of a million people smaller than anticipated. Again, international migration was the main reason for the discrepancy. The ONS pinned down how this had happened in late 2023. Net migration from the EU was actually revised up by 745,000 over the ten years since the previous census. However, that was more than offset in roughly equal amounts by revisions that lowered net migration from the rest of the world and found more British nationals moving abroad.[19]

How had this post-2021 jump in migration happened? One reason was that the new points system was not exacting enough. In particular, the main salary threshold of at least £25,600 – subsequently raised to £26,200 – was too low, especially as wages rose sharply following the pandemic. Under the previous system for non-EU workers, the figure was set at £30,000. James Cleverly, who replaced Suella Braverman as home secretary in November 2023, pushed the threshold up to £38,700, starting in April 2024 (while also raising the going rates).[20] But more important was the loophole opened in early 2022 for employers to recruit social care workers, even though these were generally classified as low-skilled jobs.[21]

Another crucial factor was that far more people were coming to Britain to study. This was something universities welcomed with open arms because the foreign students paid much higher fees than British ones. Whether or not students should be counted in the overall immigration numbers was debatable given that their presence was supposed to be temporary. However, in practice, many students did stay on for longer than their original visas. The ONS estimated in 2021 that 35 per cent of those whose visas expired in 2018–19 got further ones that extended their stay.[22] That was made easier when the 'graduate route' was introduced in July 2021, allowing students completing their undergraduate or master's courses to stay and work in Britain for two years.

It was an open question whether the high number of incomers had come about through accident or design. Although the new immigration system undoubtedly made it harder for EU citizens to work in Britain, it loosened the previous tight controls on workers from the rest of the world, both by setting a lower salary threshold and opening access to middle-skilled rather than just highly skilled jobs. That was 'a notable liberalisation' according to the Migration Observatory's Peter William Walsh in 2021.

The outcome wasn't altogether surprising in a government led by Boris Johnson. As mayor of London, he had been an enthusiast for encouraging talent from abroad. In 2013 he described himself as 'probably the only politician I know of who is actually willing to stand up and say that he's pro-immigration'. In the closing stage of the Leave campaign, he qualified his position to: 'I'm pro-immigration, but above all I'm pro-controlled immigration.'[23]

When Patel, his home secretary, introduced the new immigration system, she claimed it would reduce overall numbers. But she failed to specify by how many. Her approach was more lenient than that of Theresa May, who had striven as home secretary to clamp down on immigration from outside the EU and who stuck to that tough stance as prime minister. May was a particular sceptic of the virtues of international students coming to British universities, regarding this as a disguised migration route for at least some of them.[24]

As for Cleverly's crackdown in late 2023, one of his measures had to be watered down within days of being announced in December. This was the stipulation that someone bringing in a family dependant would have to earn £38,700 from the spring of 2024 – up from £18,600, where it had stood since 2012. This was now to be phased in, rising only to £29,000 in April 2024. The new home secretary claimed that if his package of measures had been in place in the year to September 2023, inflows would have been around 300,000 lower, in a bid to show he was getting a grip on the numbers. The great majority of that reduction would come from stopping care workers and most students from bringing dependants with them.[25]

The use and abuse of immigration to tackle shortages

One of the most striking features of the influx in 2022 and 2023 was that it arose, in part, because of staff shortages in low-wage occupations. The labour market following the pandemic was markedly different from what it had been. Suddenly, as vacancies soared, workers were in short supply. Employers turned to foreign workers to plug the gaps and the new immigration system became accommodating. From the start there was an exemption for nurses, who could come to Britain even if their salaries were below the main salary threshold. Emerging from the pandemic, the government allowed in many more people to work in social care, which turned out to be a crucial driver of the increase in migration.

At the end of 2023, a wide range of other occupations were also included on the shortage list. They included highly skilled professionals such as civil engineers and software developers. Architects and laboratory technicians were also on the list, along with roofers and plasterers.[26] In all these occupations, employers could recruit from abroad paying 20 per cent less than the going rate. That wasn't the case for social care.[27] Nor did it apply to public sector jobs, such as in health and education, which had to follow national pay scales.

Providing a helping hand to understaffed sectors through migration could be defended in the short term as a way to keep them viable. But in the long term, this would simply maintain an over-reliance on foreign labour. The only way to properly deal with skills shortages was to pay higher wages. Instead, employers on the shortage occupation list could recruit immigrants at lower pay.[28] The Migration Advisory Committee (MAC) advised against introducing this feature of the new migration system in January 2020, saying there should be 'upward pressure on wages' in jobs where there weren't enough workers. Lower salary thresholds would be 'perverse' and have the 'effect of perpetuating or even exacerbating the shortages'.[29] But it was only following the uproar about the scale of immigration in late 2023 that the government said it would get rid of this economically illogical policy together with a review of the shortage list.

The most glaring offenders for shortages were publicly run or funded services. The NHS had long turned to overseas labour markets, for example recruiting doctors from India and Pakistan in the 1960s and 1970s to fill vacancies. As these immigrants started to retire from their jobs, mainly as GPs, thirty to forty years later, there were worries about who would take their place.[30] You might imagine that the NHS would have endeavoured to avoid such crises by looking a decade or more ahead and training enough doctors and nurses to meet impending shortfalls. But until the long-term workforce plan of June 2023, that hadn't happened. When shortages emerged it was cheaper and quicker to recruit if necessary from abroad. This was a risky strategy at a time when there was increasing international demand for medical staff, as the workforce plan itself acknowledged.[31]

The plight of social care was a familiar one. By failing to square with the electorate the true cost in taxes required for this essential service, the government had to scrimp and save. Since local authorities, which were responsible for social care, lacked the money to pay the full cost, wages were held down at rates too low to attract enough British workers.

Research by the Resolution Foundation in January 2023 spelled out the problem. The typical hourly wage for frontline care workers in the spring of 2022 was £10.90, less than that for low-paid jobs in offices, call centres, transport and the NHS. The pay advantage that social care had previously commanded in low-paid sectors including retail, hospitality and cleaning had fallen from 5 per cent in 2011 to 1 per cent in 2021.[32] No wonder it had to recruit from abroad and that the government allowed it to do so.

In an illuminating interview with the *Financial Times* in March 2023, Alan Manning, a labour economist at the LSE and former chair of the MAC, delivered some home truths to sectors complaining of labour shortages. 'If we had a firm that says, "I'm struggling to sell my product," we'd be inclined to say, "Well, perhaps your product is priced wrongly. Or it's not a very good product." But somehow when employers complain that "nobody wants to take my jobs", they expect us to say, "Oh well, we'll provide you with some workers who will do it under the terms and conditions you view as appropriate."' If that concession was made, he said, 'You will cause that sector to become totally dependent on that source of labour.'[33]

How many points for the new points-based system?

When announcing the government's post-Brexit policy in February 2020, Patel made two central claims. First, the new immigration system 'will bring overall migration numbers down'. And second, 'We will attract the brightest and the best from around the globe, boosting the economy and our communities, and unleash this country's full potential.'

Manifestly, the new system had failed to bring overall migration numbers down. Indeed, in January 2024, the ONS raised its long-term projection for net migration from 245,000 a year to 315,000.[34] As for Patel's second claim, in principle, it made a lot of sense. But there was nothing new about wanting to attract skilled and talented workers to come to Britain. The Blair government's attempt to do this had used the same language about the 'brightest and the best'.

What did employers make of the new system? A report in May 2023 from the Chartered Institute of Personnel and Development was broadly supportive. The CIPD's polling of employers revealed that over half found it effective in meeting skills and labour shortages; a third found it ineffective. The main snags were the time and cost of hiring. Similar concerns put off employers from using it at all.[35]

The massive influx of students undeniably boosted the economy. According to the HEPI think tank, which specialises in the higher education sector, the overall value generated by foreign students (net of the costs of using public services) was £37 billion – around 1.5 per cent of GDP – in the 2021–22 academic year.[36]

Yet the broader picture was less favourable. In particular, the new immigration system was less effective than the previous one (through which Britain controlled only immigrants from outside the EU) in converting migrants into workers. Census figures revealed that four-fifths of EU migrants from Eastern and Central

Europe (including Bulgaria and Romania) were either employed or self-employed.[37] In the year to June 2023, a third of the immigrants from outside the EU came in on work-related visas. Of these 322,000 just over half, 169,000, had jobs with the remainder comprising dependants – partners and children. Although dependants could work, the Home Office estimated that only a quarter of them did.[38] Furthermore, there was a net loss of 67,000 EU workers over the same period as 117,000 left while only 50,000 arrived.[39]

If the purpose of encouraging immigration was to pump-prime growth, the plan wasn't working. The economy flatlined from the start of 2022 through to mid-2023 (the end date for the migration figures published later that year). Undoubtedly, it would have done worse but for the foreign workers and students who helped to bail out care homes and universities. But the absence of any growth in GDP suggested that even historically high levels of immigration could not rescue an economy suffering from stagnant productivity and reeling from the burst of inflation and jump in interest rates.

GDP might not be growing but the population of England and Wales rose by 1 per cent in the year to mid-2022, largely because of international migration – the highest since a similar rate of increase in 1962 driven by the baby boom.[40] In part, this reflected a bounce back from the exceptional circumstances of the pandemic, which had suppressed migration. Yet high population growth seemed likely to continue, meaning that for any rate of GDP growth, that for GDP per head would be considerably lower.

It was, of course, still early days for Britain's new immigration policy, not least because the new measures to cut numbers came into force in early 2024. The overall figures had, for a while, been distorted by refugees coming from Ukraine. Net migration was, in any case, set to fall, according to research published by the Migration Observatory in late 2023. This was mainly because 'high immigration leads to high emigration', as many of the incomers, especially students, would subsequently leave.[41]

The missing British workers: ill or idle?

When Patel marketed her new immigration system in 2020, she said she wanted to mobilise labour resources from within the existing population. She had some reason for optimism. Although much went wrong with the economy in the 2010s, the labour market went from strength to strength, and not just because of the continuing flow of EU workers. In 2019, the unemployment rate fell below 4 per cent of the workforce, reaching its lowest since the early 1970s.

Specifically, Patel focused on one group: 'There are over 8 million people, that's 20 per cent of the workforce, aged between sixteen and sixty-four in the UK who are economically inactive.'[42] Here, the home secretary got her figures in a muddle, because the workforce actually comprises the employed plus the unemployed who are looking for jobs (the latter being around 1.3 million in 2019). What she meant was that there were more than eight million working-age people in Britain who were neither working nor looking for work. These made up a fifth of sixteen–sixty-four-year-olds. Many of these, it has to be said, were not able to work because they were full-time students or looking after their family.

The inactivity rate – the economically inactive as a share of the working-age population – had steadily fallen during the previous decade, from around 23.5 per cent in 2010 to 20.5 per cent by the end of 2019, the lowest on records going back to 1971. As was the case in most other G7 economies, inactivity unsurprisingly rose during the pandemic. But rates then generally fell back below where they had been in late 2019, reflecting a sharp increase in demand for labour which was quickly supplied.[43] By contrast, in Britain the rate remained stubbornly higher even though there was the same labour shortage. Signs that things were improving were dashed by revised official figures in February 2024. These showed that total inactivity had been higher than previously estimated and that by late 2023 it had reverted to the previous high in the summer of 2022 of 9.3 million. Likewise, the inactivity rate had gone back up to 22 per cent.[44]

With or without the revisions, the explanation at first sight appeared to be straightforward: the long-run impact of the pandemic in causing ill health. Indeed, by the end of 2023 there were 2.8 million people who weren't working owing to sickness, making up 30 per cent of the total number who were inactive. They reported a wide range of health problems, with musculoskeletal conditions prominent but many also saying they suffered from depression, bad nerves or anxiety.[45]

But if more British people weren't working because of ill health arising from the pandemic, why wasn't this happening in other countries? A case in point was Italy, where the eventual toll of Covid judged by excess mortality had been slightly above Britain's, yet whose inactivity rate had fallen.[46] Could the swollen NHS waiting list for elective treatments be to blame? It was a reasonable hypothesis but as more evidence emerged it didn't stand up. Only a quarter of the sixteen- to sixty-four-year-olds who were inactive owing to sickness were on the waiting list in 2022. The OBR estimated in July 2023 that halving the waiting list over five years would cut working-age inactivity by only around 25,000.[47]

An alternative culprit was the welfare system. Incapacity benefits were more generous and subject to less harsh conditions than ordinary ones. That created an incentive to claim them. Assessments of eligibility became more lenient: four-fifths or more of new claims were approved from mid-2019 compared with just over half in 2016.[48]

In an effort to solve the problem, the government came up with a 'back to work plan' in November 2023. The chancellor Jeremy Hunt and work and pensions minister Mel Stride described this as 'a package of employment-focused support that will help people stay healthy, get off benefits and move into work'. This included expansion of those eligible for health programmes such as the NHS 'Talking Therapies' to help those with depression and other mental health conditions stay in or find work.[49] However, past experience suggested it would be tough to get people back to work. When Labour was seeking to curb the number of people on incapacity benefits in the late 2000s, the figures were stark: once someone had been claiming for a year, on average, that person would do so for eight years. Research also showed that once people had been off sick for six months, 80 per cent would be off for five years.[50]

If some were shirking rather than sick, that had a lot to do with so many low-wage jobs being at best soulless and at worst arduous and stressful. Maybe that was, in part, because ready access to immigrants had let too many businesses get away with poor working conditions. As the *FT*'s Sarah O'Connor wrote in late 2022 of the road-haulage sector: 'For many years migration from the EU helped employers to limp on with an employment model based on relatively low pay for antisocial hours and a lot of responsibility.'[51]

The limitations of immigration

When, in early December 2020, Margaret Keenan, a ninety-year-old grandmother, became the first person in the world to get the Pfizer Covid vaccination outside a clinical trial, Matt Hancock couldn't resist the temptation to dub the occasion 'V-day'.[52] The health secretary's flag-waving remark was particularly inappropriate because the vaccine had been developed by Pfizer's German partner, BioNTech, whose founders, Uğur Şahin and his wife Özlem Türeci, were both the children of Turkish immigrants to Germany.[53]

Their story exemplified the enterprise and drive that often characterises immigrants and their children. It also showed that some of the most positive impacts of immigration can be a generation or more in the making. Closer to home, another example was none other than Rishi Sunak, whose parents of Indian descent had immigrated to Britain from East Africa.[54] Addressing global investors in late 2023, Sunak was indeed keen to emphasise the extent to which the British economy benefited from entrepreneurial immigrants.[55] And, he might have added, their children.

Such benefits have to be borne in mind when considering the very long-term impact of migration. Eventually, the original migrants grow old and retire, becoming burdens on the Exchequer. But by then, their children will be contributing to tax revenues. Working out with any confidence the overall balance of advantages and disadvantages of immigration at this timescale is well-nigh impossible.

In the here and now, an open economy such as Britain's requires a continuing flow of migrants, bringing fresh talent and people who would roll up their sleeves. But using immigration to foster GDP growth, as opposed to GDP per person, was the wrong objective according to the LSE's Alan Manning (in that same *FT* interview): 'The growth we should be aiming for is growth in GDP per capita. Just growth by having more people is not what we should be aiming for. And then it's much more debatable whether immigration does or does not improve GDP per capita.'

Prosperity in the long run comes from higher productivity rather than a bigger population. If Britain was to kick its low-growth habit, it needed to recognise the economic limitations of immigration, as well as the political limits, which came to the fore again in late 2023. Those political limits also mattered. What the economy needed was a relatively stable net inflow of migrants. Instead, policy veered between extremes, creating uncertainty among businesses and undermining its political sustainability. Boom and bust was no more welcome in immigration policy than it was in the economy.

Chapter 8

Levelling up – or down?

There is nothing new about a regional divide between northern and southern England. Over a century and a half ago, the underrated Victorian author Elizabeth Gaskell explored the contrast in her novel, *North and South*. But in the past decade or so, that divide has become a central political and economic concern.

The politics of regional inequality became increasingly toxic in the 2010s. Support for leaving the EU was especially high in the Midlands and north of England. That revealed deeper discontent: these regions reckoned they were getting the worst part of the national bargain. There was a widespread feeling that the country was run in the capital, for the capital.

Naturally, the view down south was rather different. A long-standing complaint in London was that a big chunk of the taxes raised there were shipped up north. Now injury was added to insult through the Brexit vote which would make Londoners, who had backed staying in the EU, worse off.

The economics of the divide were also becoming increasingly salient. Taken by itself, London and the South-East was among the most prosperous parts of Europe. If the lagging regions could do better, the whole of Britain would do better. An economy suffering from sluggish growth needed to work harder at getting all its engines firing.

Even so, for Britain to reverse decades of increasing regional disparities was a tall order. It would require clear analysis of the problem. Was the divide just between North and South? Or was it more fundamentally about cities and smaller towns, in particular, the disappointing performance of big cities outside London?

Any serious analysis would also seek international insights from countries facing similar divides. Why had Germany managed to revive the East after reunification whereas Italy remained stuck with its struggling *mezzogiorno* of the south? How important was extra public money to kickstart flagging regions?

Instead, what the nation got was a slogan – 'levelling up' – from the sloganeer-in-chief Boris Johnson. It was a memorable (if ugly and much mocked) phrase: but what did it mean in practice? That was a question apparently vexing Downing Street as the pandemic subsided in 2021 and attention switched back to Johnson's promised agenda. The PM turned to Michael Gove to find the answer.

But it was far from clear that the lengthy 'to-do' list Gove eventually presented would work, still less so once Johnson was defenestrated as prime minister in 2022. Maybe the only way to level up would be to level London down – by moving the political capital, or at least part of it, to Manchester or Leeds?

Divide and rule

The day after the Conservatives' landslide victory in the general election of December 2019, Boris Johnson set out his defining mission beyond Brexit. Speaking at Number 10, he declared: 'If you ask yourselves what is this new government going to do, what is he going to do with his extraordinary majority, I will tell you that is what we are going to do: we are going to unite and level up.' Johnson spoke of 'unleashing the potential of the whole country delivering opportunity across the entire nation'.[1]

Less than a week later, the Office for National Statistics published new figures that set out the scale of Britain's regional disparities.[2] London was not only the country's political centre, it was also economically dominant. Its output made up almost a quarter of the economy, an outsized share by any reckoning. Combined with the South-East's 15 per cent, the two regions produced almost two-fifths of national output with just over a quarter of the population.

Even more remarkable was how much the gap between the capital and the rest of the country had widened in the previous two decades. London's share of total output had risen dramatically from 20 per cent in 1998 to 24 per cent in 2018. None of the UK's other eleven regions had increased their share over that period. Declines were particularly marked in northern and central England. More recent figures published in the spring of 2023 told a similar story.

The North–South divide had long been regarded as one of northern decline. The new wealth being generated by factory owners in the North, which Gaskell portrayed in her novel, proved less resilient than the longer-established wealth of the South. The new industries of the nineteenth century, such as textiles and shipbuilding, became the old ones of the twentieth century, condemning northern workers to mass unemployment in the 1930s and prompting the Jarrow crusade of 1936. Although the North–South divide narrowed during and after World War II, it then started to widen again as a result of deindustrialisation during the 1970s and 1980s.

But what these twenty-first-century figures from the ONS showed was a divide opening up yet further because of London's success. That dynamism came out of the blue. For decades after the Second World War the city's population fell. From a pre-war high of 8.6 million in 1939, it dropped to 6.8 million in the 1980s.[3] The London of the late 1970s was a very different place from today's bustling and congested metropolis. You could still easily drive into the centre to shop or even to work.

The turnaround in London's fortunes was helped by the

re-emergence of the City as a financial hub. But it was also part of a broader international phenomenon. Research by McKinsey published in late 2022 found that an astonishing half of global growth since 2000 had been powered by big cities – such as Delhi in India and Dallas in the United States – that collectively accounted for a quarter of the world's population.[4]

Metropolises like London and Paris were at the forefront of the international exchanges that accompanied increasing world trade. Served by airports such as Heathrow and Charles de Gaulle, they were the first points of contact for globetrotting business executives building overseas relationships. They provided the array of commercial services that multinationals needed. And by virtue of their rich heritage, whether in museums or in famous sites such as the Tower of London or the Eiffel Tower, they became essential venues on tourist itineraries – even more so as the appetite for short city breaks increased.

Generational change also contributed to London's revival. The children of the suburbs wanted to live where the action was: close to the centre. Indeed, the inner boroughs of London are now almost as densely populated as they were in 1951. Changing work patterns were another factor. Young professionals no longer did nine-to-five commuting hours, which put an additional premium on living closer to the centre.

The capital's growing population diverged from the rest of the country in its age profile. Figures for mid-2022 showed that in London the median age (which divides the population into two equal sizes) was 36 compared with the UK's 41.[5] In some inner London boroughs such as Hackney and Lambeth, it was 33. That reflected both internal and international migration of young people to the capital.

London not only had a relatively youthful population; it was also much better qualified. The capital was a magnet for new graduates and did particularly well in attracting those with good degrees.[6] This mattered. According to the Treasury in early 2021, the distribution of high skills among workers explained up to 90 per cent of wage disparities between different areas.[7]

While London basked in a virtuous circle, the lagging regions were stuck in a vicious cycle. Young people with skills tended to leave for the capital, attracted by the higher salaries. This left populations which were older and less qualified. That, in turn, meant businesses were less likely to locate there.

Productivity gaps lay at the crux of the divide. Figures published by the ONS in 2023 showed that output per hour worked was a third higher in London than the whole of the UK. The only other region above the national average was the South-East, where it was 10 per cent above the national average. Productivity was 9 per cent below average in the North-West and 13 per cent lower in the East and West Midlands. The worst performer of all was the North-East, where it was 17 per cent less than the national average.[8]

One oddity was that the usual mechanism by which growth spills out from a vanguard region seemed to be jammed. There was a compelling reason for businesses to locate activities out of London wherever possible: costs were lower. Furthermore, advances in information technology were making it easier and easier to operate from virtually anywhere. And indeed some businesses did do precisely that. First Direct set up its telephone banking service in Leeds at the end of the 1980s. The choice had been between the Yorkshire city and Swindon in the southern county of Wiltshire. Leeds prevailed because it would cost less.[9] Leeds became a favoured spot for financial services outside London while also building up a formidable presence as a legal centre.

For people, too, there were good reasons to want to leave the capital. One was congestion. Another was the cost of housing. London's exceptionally high property prices contributed to regional rancour especially as websites like Zoopla enabled instant comparisons to be made with a capital whose houses, if not streets, appeared to be paved with gold. The flipside for Londoners, of course, was higher housing costs, whether in rents or increasingly large mortgages.

Taking those higher costs into account together with the transfers of taxpayer money being made from south to north, the regional divide in living standards or poverty was less marked than that for output or productivity. Indeed, disposable incomes for a typical (median) household in London – which were highest – sank, after taking into account housing costs, to fifth among the UK's twelve regions. On that basis, the poverty rate in the capital was among the worst in the country.[10]

Despite these drawbacks, the pull factors of London outweighed the forces pushing activity away. Though some businesses and people did leave for cheaper locations, they were replaced by others eager to take advantage of the skills and connections packed into a world city. But Britain's regional divide was not just a simple matter of the gap between London and the rest of the country. Delving down to more local levels a more variegated pattern of success and failure emerged, which suggested that having an overweening capital was not the only issue (see box).

Drilling deeper

Disparities were manifest not just between the UK's twelve main regions, but between the forty-one sub-regions corresponding to counties such as Essex, groups of counties such as Dorset and Somerset, and five subdivisions of London. Analysis by the Industrial Strategy Council (ISC) in early 2020 revealed that only a dozen of these sub-regions, headed by Inner London West, had productivity that was at or above the national average. Of these high performers just four were outside London and parts of the South-East: Eastern Scotland, including the Scottish capital Edinburgh; north-eastern Scotland including the oil city Aberdeen; Cheshire, a genteel county in the North-West; and Bristol with its hinterland stretching out along the M4 to Swindon.[11]

All the remaining twenty-nine sub-regions had below-average productivity. The worst performer of all was not in the North but Cornwall. For all its beauty and attractions for rich Londoners in resorts such as Rock on the north coast and St Mawes on the south coast, the county whose natural beauty made it the unspoken star of the *Poldark* television series was held back by its reliance upon agriculture and tourism.

Drilling even further down to over 170 smaller local-ities it emerged that several cities outside London were also forging ahead. These included ones in the orbit of the capital's economy such as Milton Keynes. Beyond London's gravitational pull, Derby and Edinburgh were thriving. Elsewhere in the country, however, towns such as Swansea and Wolverhampton were faring less well.

The places doing worst of all were often coastal towns. Blackpool, for example, was stuck in a down-ward spiral. Its bucket-and-spade glory days as a seaside resort have been long usurped by package holidays in Spain, and it has even been deserted by the political parties that for so long had held their autumn conferences there. As the *FT*'s Sarah O'Connor re-ported in 2017: 'Blackpool exports healthy skilled people and imports the unskilled, the unemployed and the unwell.'[12]

Scanning wider: international perspectives

How did Britain's regional disparities compare with other countries? Not well. Richard Prothero of the ONS in 2018 compared productivity — output per worker — in British regions with those of five other big European economies: France, Italy, Germany, the Netherlands and Spain. In all, there were fifty-two regions across the six countries. Britain stood out for having one economically pre-eminent region and several lagging ones. London was second only to the greater Paris region (Île-de-France). But Britain also had eight of the fifteen lowest-ranked regions (the other seven were in eastern Germany and southern Italy).[13]

The 2020 ISC report painted a similarly dispiriting picture when comparing the disparities between the forty-one sub-regions in Britain with those among similar areas in eighteen European countries. Specifically, it measured the productivity gap in each country between the best- and the worst-performing sub-regions. Only Romania and Poland had bigger gaps.

A particular weakness intensifying Britain's regional divide was the poor performance of big cities other than London. Examining eleven such 'second-tier' cities (Belfast, Birmingham, Bristol, Cardiff, Glasgow, Leeds, Liverpool, Manchester, Newcastle, Nottingham and Sheffield) – seven of which were in the Midlands and the North – the OECD found that their productivity was almost 15 per cent below the national average. By contrast, second-tier cities in other comparable countries tended to be as or more productive. Since the eleven cities in the UK contributed close to a quarter of overall output, this was holding back the whole economy.[14]

The Centre for Cities think tank pointed out that looking at France, Germany and the US, the larger the city the more productive its workers tended to be. But that wasn't the case in Britain outside London. Indeed, productivity in Glasgow, Birmingham and Manchester was 'well below what is expected of cities of their scale'. They weren't playing 'the role that cities such as Lyon, Munich and Cologne do'. It was 'the underperformance of our big cities that affects the largest number of people and has the biggest drag on the national economy', said the researchers.[15]

A more recent analysis published by the Harvard Kennedy School was even bleaker.[16] The researchers, who included Ed Balls, a former Labour minister, presented evidence showing that the divide between London and the South-East and the rest of the country was even wider than the gaps in Italy or Germany, which had to cope with rebuilding the poor East after 1990.

Italy's divide between the economically lagging south and prosperous northern regions such as Lombardy dated back to Italian unification in 1861. This suggested that regional gaps can be intractable. A report by German researchers in 2021 found that 'limited employment and business opportunities continue to cause out-migration and demographic decline' in the *mezzogiorno*. The researchers spoke of the 'depth' and 'persistence' of regional dis-parities. Indeed the divide had widened in the 2010s as the South made a feebler recovery than the North from the economic blows inflicted by the financial and euro crises.[17]

If the stubbornly enduring plight of the *mezzogiorno* was a counsel for despair, the reviving fortunes of Eastern Germany following reunification brought a message of hope. Still, much of the advance occurred in the early 1990s after which progress slowed.[18] Furthermore, it required massive financial help from the federal government. Another favourable factor was that the East contained a big metropolis, Berlin, which became the capital of reunified Germany.

The economic reintegration of Germany's eastern states was an exceptional episode with limited relevance for Britain. But the ex-perience of another part of Germany, the Ruhr in the north-west, was highly pertinent. This previous engine of the German economy, fired by coal-mining and steelmaking, had been hit hard by deindustrialisation. But it had made a better job than Britain's former industrial heartlands in reorienting itself to a more promising future.

Research by the ISC in January 2021, shortly before it was wound up (see Chapter 5), pinpointed a number of factors that had helped the Ruhr and its population of five million reinvent themselves.[19] One was maintaining investment in urban redevelopment and cleaning up the environment. Another was collaboration between the various political bodies. Setting up three new universities – in Bochum, Duisberg and Essen – also helped. So, too, did a big effort to make the Ruhr an attractive place to live: there was a wealth of cultural venues including 120 theatres, 200 museums and 250 festivals.

(If) only connect

If nothing else, these international comparisons suggested that Johnson was quite right to prioritise tackling Britain's regional divide. It was in no one's interest for the gap to be the worst among advanced economies. If the North could start to catch up with the South, the whole country would benefit. But could the win–winism of the levelling-up slogan – the North improving but not at the cost of the South – turn into reality?

All agreed that something needed to be done about transport. But there the consensus ended. Should the priority be bringing the North closer into London's orbit through high-speed rail? Or should it be to improve transport links within the Midlands and the North?

A high-speed North–South rail link had been the choice since 2009. The brainchild of Andrew Adonis, transport secretary in Gordon Brown's government, this had obvious political sex appeal. It was a *grand projet* that would bring Britain, or at least England, into line with other countries that had invested in high-speed rail links. HS2 as originally conceived would run from London to Birmingham and then become Y-shaped, with one branch going to Manchester and the other to Leeds. It was also a logical extension of HS1 which went from London to the Channel tunnel.

But whether Britain really had to emulate geographically bigger countries such as France and Spain was more questionable. In December 2006, a comprehensive independent survey of the transport system by Rod Eddington, a former boss of British Airways, sounded a cautionary note about brand-new high-speed rail. He backed improving key 'inter-urban corridors' but was sceptical about whether that should entail a high-speed link, noting factors such as Britain's compact economic geography, the environmental impact and unfavourable ratio of benefits to costs.[20]

Top of Eddington's to-do list was 'supporting the UK's successful, agglomerated urban areas and their catchments'. That was about to happen in London through the east–west Crossrail project, renamed the Elizabeth line, which opened in 2022, but there was a clear case for pushing resources to the North for similar city-centred projects. Instead what happened was that HS2 became the main focus of transport policy and a big drain on the transport budget.

Eddington's scepticism about the potential snags of building high-speed rail in a small country was vindicated as HS2 costs rose and rose – in large measure to address environmental concerns – while the project was delayed and delayed. Johnson missed the last opportunity to cancel the runaway railway before construction formally got under way early in his new government. An independent review put the cost at maybe as much as £106 billion – far above the 2012 estimate of £33 billion.[21] Making matters worse, it might not be completed until 2040 rather than the previously envisaged 2033.

But Johnson failed to grasp the nettle. At the end of January 2020, he dropped a broad hint, telling a children's current affairs TV programme that 'in a hole the size of HS2, the only thing to do is keep digging'.[22] That was a perfect example of the sunk-cost fallacy, in which previous spending mistakes dictate what to do next. When the prime minister formally confirmed the government's continuing support for the project, he addressed MPs in glossy-brochure speak: 'Let us bring about a future where high-speed trains glide between our great cities.'[23]

As costs continued to escalate, though, that prospect started to fade. First, it turned out that Leeds would not be one of those great cities: the north-eastern arm of the 'Y' was lopped off in November 2021.[24] Then, almost two years later, Rishi Sunak dropped the link between Birmingham and Manchester. The trains would glide at high speed only between London and Birmingham. The prime minister claimed that the £36 billion savings would be used on other transport projects.

This was the worst possible outcome. On a narrow value-for-money basis, mainly measuring direct benefits such as shorter travel times against costs, HS2 made more sense running all the way up to the North rather than just to the Midlands. In early 2024, the Public Accounts Committee said, 'HS2 now offers very poor value for money to the taxpayer.'[25] And, in any case, this method of appraisal could not capture the potential for trans-formational economic gains from a strategic investment which would knit the central and northern regions more closely with the prosperous South. Six years earlier, May's government had cited HS2 as 'an example of an infrastructure project that can deliver the wider ambitions of our Industrial Strategy', pointing to the op-portunity it would bring 'in making Manchester a more attractive business location'.[26]

Whatever its cost, HS2 had at least been carefully planned and prepared. That could not be said for the other transport projects into which the £36 billion would supposedly be shunted. The suspicion was that a good chunk would end up in the Treasury's back pocket and never be invested at all. And, unlike the northern leg linking Birmingham and Manchester, the money would not be reserved for central and northern regions. Sunak's pledge to reinvest 'every single penny' of the £36 billion specified 'hundreds of transport projects in the North, the Midlands, and across the country'.[27]

More investment was certainly needed both within and between northern cities. They had been starved of public investment in comparison with London. Research by the IPPR North think tank found that on average during the 2010s capital spending on transport per person in London was more than double that in the North.[28] The shortfall was harming the region's big cities and there wasn't nearly enough urgency about transport improvements that would bind them closer together (see box).

The travails of northern travellers

Inadequate networks meant that far fewer people used public transport to commute to work than in comparable European cities, according to the Centre for Cities in November 2023. For example, 33 per cent of people used bus, tram or train to get to work in Lyon; 44 per cent in Munich. That compared with 16 per cent in Manchester and 22 per cent in Newcastle. This held back local economies by restricting the range and scale of their labour markets.[29]

But links between cities in the west such as Liverpool and Manchester and those in the east such as Leeds and Sheffield were also notoriously poor. Indeed, Britain's Infrastructure Commission had said in December 2020 that 'prioritising regional links, for example from Manchester to Liverpool and Leeds or Birmingham to Nottingham and Derby, has the potential to deliver the highest benefits for cities in the Midlands and the North'. This was the most effective way for transport investment to raise their productivity, especially in Liverpool and Manchester.[30]

However, the upgrade of the Transpennine rail link between Manchester in the west and Leeds and York in the east had made little progress since 2011 when the plan was first announced. The case for it remained compelling despite the general reduction in use of railways following the pandemic. Travellers were subject to so many delays and cancellations that TransPennine Express, one of the two main operators on the route, had to be taken under government control in May 2023, joining the other (Northern) that was already in public hands.[31]

This infrastructure project – so crucial to increase passenger capacity, reduce journey times and improve punctuality – would not be completed until the late 2030s, according to the National Audit Office in 2022. Parliament's public spending watchdog tore a strip off the transport department for its handling of the upgrade, saying it had 'repeatedly altered the scope of the programme to meet differing ministerial priorities and budget constraints'.[32]

Yet better transport in the region was vital to realise the vision of a 'northern powerhouse'. Whether or not you liked the phrase, which chancellor George Osborne introduced into the national vocabulary in a speech at the Power Hall of Manchester's Museum of Science and Industry in June 2014, it embodied a compelling economic rationale.[33] The idea was that size and integration mattered increasingly in spurring regional success. Accordingly, the northern powerhouse was 'not one city, but a collection of northern cities – sufficiently close to each other that combined they can take on the world'. Osborne spoke of an area centred on Manchester that included Liverpool, Leeds and Sheffield where ten million people lived – more than in London. Such a northern super-conurbation could potentially create a counterweight to the southern powerhouse. But as things stood, Osborne said, 'the whole is less than the sum of its parts'. For the northern power-house to thrive, it had to be much better integrated.

For that, better connectivity was crucial. Quite simply, people needed to be able to get around more readily and faster, both within and between the North's city regions. Ten years after Osborne had set out his vision, far too little had been done to tackle the North's substandard transport system. As well as being unfair to people living in the North this was a quite unnecessary economic own goal.

Brain drains and brain gains

Sorting out the North's transport deficiencies was at least attain-able through more investment – even if it cost a lot of money. But the bigger problem undermining Britain's lagging regions was human rather than physical capital. They had fewer highly qualified people of working age with degrees than those available to employers in the South.[34] This applied to the central as well as northern regions, which since 2017 had become part of the 'midlands engine', a version of the northern powerhouse stretching from Shropshire in the west to Lincolnshire in the east.

Inadequate workforce skills lay at the heart of the vicious circle that beset Britain's lagging regions. Businesses requiring superior expertise tended to locate elsewhere. That, in turn, meant that those who were better qualified left the regions to secure higher earnings, which in turn reinforced the reluctance of firms to set up there. The drift from north to south in the 1970s and 1980s involved 'mainly young adults coming from professional and managerial families and destined for occupations similar to those of their parents' according to research published in 1998.[35]

Though this persistent brain drain had long been the case the expansion of higher education brought an opportunity to remedy the situation. Both the Midlands and the North hosted highly regarded universities: ten out of the Russell Group's twenty-four. These included Durham, one of England's oldest, as well as York, one of the new universities set up in the 1960s. The other five northern universities in the Russell Group were Leeds, Liverpool, Manchester, Newcastle and Sheffield. The Midlands had three: Birmingham, Nottingham and Warwick. Every year, these and other universities in central and northern England received brain gains through their new students. If more of these students could be tempted to stay rather than to leave after getting their degrees, it could transform regional economies.

One direct way for the universities to stimulate local growth was through their research, attracting companies wanting to exploit it. Already there were signs this was beginning to happen. Manchester and Leeds were among the ten universities producing the most spinouts (those new business ventures based on academic research – see Chapter 5) between 1998 and 2018 – Manchester with a share of 4.6 per cent, Leeds with 3.1 per cent.[36] To put those figures in perspective, only Oxford and Cambridge had shares in double digits – 15.8 and 11.5 per cent respectively.

Northern and central regions also needed to improve their cultural and social offer. Part of the attraction of London to talented young people was after all the overall vibe. It made sense for the big central and northern cities to enhance their attractiveness to artists, musicians and filmmakers. In modern economies, culture was no longer just an aesthetic add-on. When Liverpool was chosen to host the Eurovision song contest (on behalf of Ukraine), it was as much a tribute to the city's place in the history of pop music – thanks to the Beatles – as to its many other attractions. The event held in May 2023 boosted the city region's economy by over £54 million, according to an evaluation published later that year. Over 300,000 visitors came to Liverpool and 175,000 hotel rooms were booked that May.[37]

Investing in modern housing that fitted the needs of younger people was another must for the regions. Building new apartments in city centres served a double purpose. They revitalised rundown areas and tempted students to stay on rather than leave once they had completed their university courses.

As well as retaining more of their brain gains, Britain's lagging regions needed to equip their own populations with better skills. Further education in colleges mattered as much as higher education in universities. This was a national as well as a regional priority. But it was more urgent outside London and the South-East for two reasons. First, fewer school leavers in the Midlands and the North attended universities. The contrast in England was starkest between London, where 50 per cent of 18-year-olds were off to university in 2023, and the North East, where only 30 per cent were heading there.[38] And second, the sectoral mix of their economies with a higher manufacturing share of employment meant that vocational skills were particularly important.

Tackling the weaknesses of vocational education required the public sector to work with businesses in their areas, since they would provide the hands-on training that formed part of college courses. There was also scope for more general cooperation, in particular in helping to build economic clusters, such as the 'motorsport valley' in the Midlands, where most racing cars were built in Britain.[39]

Local leadership was vital in all this. Michael Heseltine knew a thing or two about regenerating declining regions. As the 'minister for Merseyside' in Thatcher's government he led Liverpool's economic fightback in the early 1980s. Speaking on Channel 4 News in late May 2020, as Britain was starting to emerge from the first Covid lockdown, the veteran Tory politician said that in his view 'most major economies are driven by local people who know how to maximise their local assets and advantages'.[40] But for visionary local leaders to emerge they had to have the elbow room to make a difference.

The Westminster power-grab

When Birmingham City Council declared itself in effect bankrupt in September 2023, it was commonly described as the largest local authority in Europe.[41] That might well have been the case, but it certainly wasn't the most powerful. Like all councils in England, it had been subject to ever-increasing control from central government. The council's imposing headquarters hinted at a more glorious past. Built in the 1870s, the Council House in Victoria Square was a declaration of municipal power and independence. Above the main entrance was a pediment showing Britannia receiving local manufacturers.

Indeed, Birmingham was the powerbase of Joseph Chamberlain, who as mayor in the 1870s extended the remit of the council to provide basic services such as gas, water and lighting, as well as championing free education for all children. He led the campaign to set up Birmingham University, which was founded in 1900.

Chamberlain was not alone in espousing municipal reform, but according to Matt Cole, a historian at the university, 'the pace, scale and impact of his project earned Birmingham the epithet "the best-governed city in the world"'.[42]

Where Chamberlain had shown what could happen through local initiative, energy and resources, the plight of his 2023 successors showed what happened when local authorities were stripped of authority. Yes, Birmingham City Council might well have made budgetary mistakes, but it was held on so tight a financial leash by the centre that it couldn't sort them out itself. A relentless power grab by Westminster had reduced local authorities to a shadow of their former selves – subject to more and more central control over taxation and even tighter curbs on borrowing.

Starting in the late 1990s Westminster had devolved sweeping powers to Scotland and, to a lesser extent, Wales. Northern Ireland had long enjoyed considerable autonomy. But England, with more than four-fifths of the British population, was one of the most fiscally centralised states in Europe, and much more so than other big economies such as Germany and Spain.[43]

If nothing else, the levelling-up agenda drew attention to this chronic overcentralisation. Local initiatives were essential to breathe new economic life into the Midlands and the North. This had to happen at a bigger scale than local councils, which have administrative rather than economic boundaries.

The development of metro mayors appeared to offer an answer. Directly elected, they ran regions that were broader than local councils. These combined authorities now cover much of northern and central England. According to the Centre for Cities, a third of the population of England would have metro mayors following the local elections of May 2024 (a half, including the London mayor).[44]

But this constitutional innovation fell far short of what was needed to restore local autonomy. Metro mayors such as Andy Burnham in Greater Manchester (population: 2.8 million) certainly had name recognition and were effective tribunes for their areas. But no more than the local councils beneath them did they enjoy real power – for example, through controlling regional taxation. If they were to be handed that power, though, more problems could ensue: would it be wise to give tax-raising abilities to mayors whose objectives might differ radically from the councils within their bailiwick? Arguably, true devolution means trusting local authorities more rather than building another impotent political layer on top of them.

A plan is born

Conscious that levelling up remained a slogan in search of a policy, Johnson turned once more to the ever-useful Michael Gove. Appointed in September 2021, sacked less than a year later in the dying throes of Johnson's premiership and reappointed to the same role in October 2022 by Rishi Sunak, Gove was the secretary of state for levelling up, housing and communities, a cumbersome title that hinted at the difficulties of the task.

Gove set out the government's thinking in February 2022.[45] His ministry's white paper on Britain's regional disparities took an expansive perspective, even citing Jericho, whose walls famously came down millennia ago, as the world's first supercity. There was name checking, too, of the city states of Renaissance Italy such as Florence, as well as a nod to the 'contemporary Medici model' of urban success. All that set the tone for a plan which would bring a 'system change' and 'transform the UK by spreading opportunity and prosperity to all parts of it'. But the ambition was easier to declare than it would be to deliver.

The plan set out twelve 'bold' missions to be achieved by 2030. The first tackled the heart of the problem: pay, employment and productivity would rise by 2030 across the country, with the gap between the top-performing and other areas closing. But the means offered were already well rehearsed from reports and policy initiatives past: improving education outcomes, skills and transport networks. Indeed, several of the missions were ancillary targets: reducing crime especially in the worst-affected areas, and reducing the number of poor-quality ('non-decent') rented homes with the biggest improvement, once again, in the worst-performing areas. Some were essentially aspirations such as improving well-being and increasing satisfaction with local town centres.

The government claimed that all twelve missions were quantifiable and would be monitored by 'a suite of supporting metrics'. There would be annual reports tracking performance. However, subsequent analysis by the Institute for Government (IfG) found that five weren't ambitious enough while three were unrealistic.[46]

A new levelling-up advisory council was to be set up. If that had a depressingly familiar ring, it was because in November 2017, just four years earlier, the government's industrial strategy with a strong regional dimension also had what turned out to be a short-lived advisory council. Moreover, the new outfit didn't have the clear remit of its predecessor to mark the government's homework.

The most radical-sounding mission was the twelfth: decentralising power. By 2030, every part of England wanting a devolution deal could get one 'with powers at or approaching the highest level of devolution and a simplified, long-term funding settlement'. But that promise of 'London-style' mayors was less impressive than it appeared. Even in London, the mayor could raise money from taxpayers only through an extra charge added to the council tax. Moreover, no one could seriously claim that having a mayor had made the slightest difference to the capital's outperformance of the rest of the nation. What the position had offered was a political platform for Johnson to fast-forward his political career. His successor Sadiq Khan was lower-key but not shy of standing his own ground, such as in pressing ahead with a controversial plan to limit vehicle emissions. Moreover, metro mayors were already established in the city regions where they were most needed: Liverpool and Manchester, South and West Yorkshire on the other side of the Pennines and the West Midlands. The first nine areas invited to get such a devolution deal included Norfolk and Suffolk in the East of England, one of the country's more prosperous regions.

Gove's plan lacked strategic focus. Apart from the twelve missions there were five 'mutually reinforcing' pillars, not to mention six different types of capital ranging from the physical stuff to fluffier (though worthwhile) notions such as 'social capital', defined as 'the strength of communities, relationships and trust'. The first mission should really have been the only one. Everything else should have served as a means to raise productivity in the lagging regions closer to that achieved in the South. It didn't help that both Johnson and Gove repeated the standard levelling-up trope that talent was evenly distributed across the country. That was true at birth – but at the heart of the regional divide was the uneven distribution of highly qualified and skilled adults. Manifestly, improving skills in lagging regions was essential. But as the IfG pointed out in a follow-up report, the target of 200,000 more people a year successfully completing high-quality skills courses by 2030 would still leave them below the level of the mid-2010s.[47]

The levelling-up strategy embodied Johnson's trademark 'cakeist' philosophy. Instead of grappling with hard choices and accepting that the policy could make the South marginally less well off, it sought to offer something for everyone. But with limited resources that meant less for those initiatives that were most promising.

Sprinkling public money across towns large and small was the wrong approach. Instead those resources should be used to drive forward the big city regions. The IfG researchers called for 'focusing big economic investments on cities such as Birmingham and Manchester, which have the biggest capacity to attract highly skilled workers and jobs but which underperform economically'. As these did better, they would pull in their wake smaller towns in their surrounding regions through 'ripple effects'.

A modest proposal

As Gove's white paper recognised, there had been 'no shortage of attempts to tackle geographical disparities in the UK over the past century'. There is also nothing new about such policy being reinvented every few years – again, the white paper admitted that 'these efforts have tended to be short-term'.

Naturally, Gove promised to do better. His missions were 'rolling decade-long endeavours' that would provide 'consistency' and 'serve as an anchor for policy across government'. And just as naturally, that pledge of stability did not survive long. Two prime ministers later, levelling up was patently no longer a prime objective for Rishi Sunak. Cancelling the HS2 link to Manchester was a slap in the face of the very metro mayors – not just Labour's Andy Burnham in Manchester but also the Conservatives' Andy Street in the West Midlands – whom the government claimed it wanted to promote.

If levelling up was already suffering the same fate as previous policies was there another way – to level down, if not London, then Westminster? About six decades ago, Norman Macrae, a journalist at *The Economist* with a flair for thinking outside the box, suggested moving the capital to the North. *Prospect* resurrected the idea two decades ago. Imagine that fantasy had become reality. There would certainly have been no question of stopping HS2 at Birmingham. Indeed, the line would have started at Britain's political capital: Manchester.

In early 2020, Johnson floated the idea of moving the House of Lords to York.[48] But that would have split parliament and made it harder for the upper house to review legislation brought in the Commons. Instead, the government made tokenistic gestures such as the Treasury setting up an 'economic campus' in Darlington. Just as it made no sense to spread the levelling-up effort widely rather than concentrating it in a few places, so too with these attempts to disperse civil servants to various random locations.

There is, however, a workable alternative to either piecemeal or wholesale changes: moving ministries out of London with their secretaries of state. Virtual technology could mean that the ministers could remain accountable to parliament and vote. To maximise the effect, the departments should be set up in one city − Leeds, perhaps, or Manchester. You could even brand them a 'political cluster'. Furthermore, there is what Johnson might have called an 'oven-ready' recipe for such a reform. Following German reunification, the new Bundestag voted narrowly to make Berlin the political capital rather than the old West German capital Bonn. However, Bonn retained the status of 'Federal City' (Bundesstadt) and six federal ministries would be primarily based there covering education, health, defence, overseas development, food and agriculture, and the environment. Roughly 30 per cent of civil servants in the federal ministries currently work in Bonn.[49]

If Germany has made it work, why not Britain? Two obvious candidates for relocation were education and health since these are already devolved responsibilities outside England. Likewise, the environment department, which also covers food and rural affairs, lends itself to a regional location. The department for work and pensions is another candidate, as is the culture, media and sport ministry whose staff could look forward to enjoying English National Opera's performances in its new Manchester base. And the sixth ministry? What better choice than the levelling-up department itself − or whatever it is renamed in the future?

Chapter 9

Boosters and gloomsters: could Britain bounce back?

As the trauma of Britain's brief experiment with Trussonomics receded during 2023, Rishi Sunak and Jeremy Hunt were no longer satisfied with having restored some sanity to the public finances. The first and second lords of the Treasury turned into optimistic cheerleaders for a comatose British economy.

Lifting the gloom was a struggle. Addressing the grandiosely named 'global investment summit' at Hampton Court Palace in November 2023, an event organised by the government, Sunak sought to soothe his audience of international investors: 'My argument today is that the UK is a modern, dynamic, thriving economy.'[1] Manifestly, the British economy wasn't thriving, but was it even as 'modern' and 'dynamic' as the prime minister claimed?

In fact, there were some underlying and under-appreciated British strengths. All advanced economies were becoming more knowledge-based. That was a breaking wave that Britain was well placed to surf, with some of the world's leading universities and acknowledged scientific excellence especially in the life sciences.

Another economic shift occurring across the developed world was away from goods and towards services. This also played to

Britain's advantage: it was second only to America as an exporter of services, and was especially strong not just in finance but a variety of other activities, such as the creative sector. Unlike trade in goods, which year upon year was in deficit (more imports than exports), trade in services was consistently in surplus (more exports than imports).

Yet given the economy's dismal track record over the previous fifteen years, such strengths were not enough. For one thing, Britain needed to sustain its (somewhat overblown) scientific standing. For another, universities were under threat from a funding crisis of the government's making.

As well as building on strengths, Britain also needed to overcome its longstanding economic weaknesses. Prominent among these was a continuing shortfall in investment in both the public and private sectors that left capital stock too low and meant workers were less productive. A lack of skills was another brake on businesses as well as the public services.

Britain also needed to build more homes to meet the aspirations of young people and accommodate a growing population. But the notion that this could be achieved simply by curbing planning regulations – endorsed by Keir Starmer when he promised to 'bulldoze' through 'our restrictive planning system' in order to build more homes – was simplistic.[2] Even if life was made easier for construction firms, they would still need more skilled workers. And, in any case, the problem with planning was as much about a shortage of the planners needed to approve the new houses as the rules themselves.

A temptation following the introduction of ChatGPT in late 2022 was to imagine that AI could be a get-out-of-jail card. Whatever the potential of advances in artificial intelligence, though, it would not obviate the need to renew national infrastructure, provide workers with modern equipment and upgrade skills.

Cheerleading from the top wasn't nearly enough to combat the doom and gloom around the British economy. Nor was pushing a narrative that simply focused on where Britain was already doing well. Tackling the negatives was vital, too, even if that made for a less upbeat message.

A science superpower?

For over a century, Nobel prizes have been awarded to minds who have provided 'the greatest benefit to mankind'. In all, there were one thousand winners by 2023, two-thirds of which were for scientific achievements.[3] It said something about Britain's intellectual prowess that it was second only to America in the overall number of laureates – a point that Sunak wasn't shy of mentioning in his Hampton Court speech.

By their nature, Nobel prizes reflect past accomplishments. One guide to current performance is the number of research publications and citations. On that basis, Britain was also doing well. In 2020 it ranked third in the world – behind China and the US – for its share of publications, which made up 6.3 per cent of the global total. It was also third in its share of citations. Another welcome finding was that Britain accounted for 13 per cent of the world's most cited articles (the top 1 per cent).[4]

Britain's high standing in academic research was related to the excellence of its universities. They consistently appeared either at or close to the top of the international rankings. For example, three were in the top ten of the *Times Higher Education* list in 2024. The league table covered nearly two thousand universities around the world, ranking them on teaching, research, knowledge transfer and international outlook. Oxford came first, Cambridge fifth and Imperial eighth. In all, seven British universities featured in the top fifty compared with three in Germany, one in France and none in Italy.[5]

Did this add up to us being on the path to becoming a 'science superpower', as first Johnson and then Sunak claimed? When brandishing this ambition, both framed this as 'cementing' that role. Handily, this suggested that Britain just needed to firm things up. Sunak's take in March 2023, when the government announced new measures to support science, was that 'trailblazing science and innovation have been in our DNA for decades'. Even so he backed 'a bold new plan to cement our place as a global science and technology superpower by 2030'.[6]

The 'cementing' strategy made sense if Britain was already a scientific powerhouse, as the punching-beyond-its-weight record in citations suggested. But Paul Nightingale of Sussex University's science policy research unit and James Phillips, a former science adviser at Number 10 to Boris Johnson, queried the relevance of that evidence. They pointed out that in practice, relatively few of even the top 1 per cent of cited papers, which they put at 18,000 a year, 'really shift the dial'. Looking instead at the top one hundred papers in each of three areas designated as government priorities – artificial intelligence, synthetic biology and quantum computing – Britain's performance was underwhelming. 'Is the UK a world leader in science?' they asked. Their dispiriting answer was: 'Whilst we do well, we are not outstanding.'[7]

In fact, the notion of aspiring to be a 'science superpower' owed more to post-Brexit politics than to economics. International collaboration is more than ever vital in science. That's why scientists and universities were up in arms when it appeared that Britain wouldn't participate as an associate member in the EU's 'Horizon Europe' programme funding scientific research between 2021 and 2027. When Britain eventually struck a deal to join Horizon Europe there was a sigh of relief among British scientists. Welcoming the announcement in September 2023, Michelle Mitchell, chief executive of Cancer Research UK, said that 'nearly three quarters of respondents to our survey of cancer researchers cited funding from the EU as important for their work'.[8]

However, damage had been done through joining so late and the uncertainty that created. In the summer of 2023, when Britain's membership of Horizon Europe still remained uncertain, Fiona Lettice, a specialist in research and innovation at the University of East Anglia, spelled out the effects of staying out of the EU programme: 'In the last couple of years, the UK has led far fewer international research projects.' She added: 'The longer-term effect of this is that we import fewer ideas and new approaches into the UK.'[9]

In any case, becoming a science superpower would not necessarily support national growth. As IMF economists noted in 2021, 'Basic research is not tied to a particular product or country and can be combined in unpredictable ways and used in different fields.'[10] What mattered for the economy was having abundant scientific expertise at hand, providing the ability to interpret research findings wherever they are made and to assist firms in making use of them.

Innovation nation? Yes and no

Important though academic research and pure science is for society, it is the translation of breakthroughs into new products and smart processes that enables businesses to create new markets and conquer existing ones by driving down costs. Scientific discoveries count for the common good; innovation for the national economy. In his sales pitch at Hampton Court, Sunak highlighted innovation as 'the golden thread running through the British economy'. Was he right?

One undeniable golden part of the economy was the life sciences. Despite the overall failings of the government's response to Covid in 2020, British scientists and doctors did come up with the first effective treatment for the sickest patients in the form of a cheap steroid called dexamethasone. The collaboration between Oxford scientists and the Anglo-Swedish firm AstraZeneca produced one of the first vaccines against Covid, which helped to curb the epidemic, even though it got a bad press because of a very rare but potentially fatal side-effect.[11]

Britain was also doing well in producing promising new businesses based on IT. As Sunak pointed out, the number of 'unicorns' (those start-ups valued at a billion dollars or more), was surpassed only by the US and China. 'Not that I'm in any way competitive,' Sunak added with a rare attempt at wit.

Innovation could also be found in unexpected places – such as the English countryside. Walkers in southern England began to stumble across the unfamiliar sight of vines growing. Those who had previously scoffed at the very notion of English wine were now scoffing the stuff down: English sparkling wine, in particular, won a reputation for excellence (see box).

Fizzy business: the unexpected rise of English wine

Although there were English vineyards in medieval times, Britain's status as a wine importer had long been taken for granted. Indeed, the exchange of English cloth for Portuguese wine was the classic example used in the early nineteenth century by political economist David Ricardo in his famous principle of comparative advantage in trade – whereby countries benefit through trade by specialising in the products they are better at making.

However, over the past two decades, the warmer summers associated with climate change have helped the rise of English wine, especially in Sussex, Kent and Hampshire. By 2022, vineyards covered almost four thousand hectares of land, a figure expected to rise to 7,600 by 2032.[12]

Investment in vineyards and wineries amounted to almost £500 million in the five years between 2018 and 2022, according to Nick Watson, head of viticulture at estate agency Strutt & Parker. 'It is an investment that requires deep pockets,' he pointed out in a 2023 report. 'The upfront costs of establishing a vineyard are significant and it takes five years before the vines reach full productivity.'[13]

Just over twelve million bottles were produced in 2022, a figure expected to reach around twenty million in 2023 following a record autumn grape harvest. The quality of English wine was acknowledged at the annual Decanter international wine-tasting competition. In 2020, Roebuck Estates in West Sussex won a 'best in show' for a sparkling white with flavours of 'baked apple, buttered toast and layered citrus fruits'.[14]

Although the proportion of English wine that was exported was still fairly low, at 7 per cent in 2022, domestic production was also substituting for foreign imports. The rise of English wine showed that a traditionally conservative sector of the economy could grasp new opportunities.

Innovations are spurred by research and development mostly financed by the private sector. For a long time, brows were furrowed over why Britain did so little of it. When Greg Clark's industrial strategy was published in 2017, for example, it highlighted figures showing that two years earlier R&D made up 1.7 per cent of GDP – well below America's 2.8 and Germany's 2.9 per cent. The plan's ambition was to raise Britain's share to 2.4 per cent by 2027. That goal was retained when the strategy was replaced by the Treasury's growth plan in 2021.[15]

Meeting that target proved to be much easier than expected: revisions by the official numbercrunchers in late 2022 did the job. One was finding a £5 billion undercount of R&D in higher education. Second and more important, the rising amount of R&D being done by smaller to medium-sized firms had been underestimated by about £15 billion. Taking that previously missed activity into account, the ONS reckoned that total R&D in 2020 was £62 billion, or 2.9 per cent of GDP.[16]

But, in a way, that only deepened the mystery about Britain's disappointing growth record. Insufficient spending on R&D had been a prime suspect. Now it turned out that British R&D was much higher than previously estimated – even though it still lagged behind America (3.5 per cent), Sweden (3.4 per cent) and South Korea (4.9 per cent).[17]

The new figures chimed with other evidence suggesting a more than respectable track record on innovation. For example, the UN's global innovation index ranked Britain fourth – behind only Switzerland, Sweden and the United States – among 132 economies in 2023.[18] In fact, the UK had been in the top five (at times second) in the previous ten years and fourth since 2020. That consistency of performance was all the more surprising given the shock of Brexit. The eighty individual indicators making up the index offered telling insights into Britain's performance in innovation. As one might imagine, universities and original research were particular strengths. Beyond these, Britain also scored highly for software spending and use of ICT.

But doing well in an index is one thing – actually coming up with innovative industries quite another. Despite Britain's decent record in unicorns, breaking through to the premier league remained elusive. For all the buzz about fintech firms, those new digital contenders in the City (see Chapter 4), none had made it to the big time.

A services superpower

Britain might not be on the path to becoming a superpower in science. But it was already one in tradable services. That was a position worth having, since trade in services was growing as a share of total world trade including goods. Between 2012 and 2019 that share rose from 20 per cent to almost 25 per cent. The pandemic caused a relapse when travel collapsed; but by 2022 it had rebounded to 23 per cent.[19] According to Richard Baldwin, an economic leading light on globalisation, the future of world trade lay in services.[20]

Britain's strength in services was vital for an economy with a consistent deficit in goods. Figures from the World Trade Organisation showed that in 2022, it ranked only fifteenth as an exporter of merchandise but sixth as an importer. By contrast, it was second as an exporter of commercial services and fifth as an importer.[21]

The entire service sector had largely been ignored in Johnson's trade deal with the EU, even though it was the part of the economy that was most successful. When the deal came into force at the start of 2021, it affected everything from City-based banks no longer able to provide services to the EU to musicians finding that tours in Europe were no longer commercially feasible. This made it all the more remarkable that exports of services – unlike goods – held up in the three years after Britain left the single market and customs union. That didn't mean Brexit was pain-free. As John Springford of the Centre for European Reform pointed out, exports of services would have done even better if Britain had stayed inside the single market. Financial services, in particular, underperformed outside the EU.[22]

One reason for the relative resilience of British services exports, though, was that they were less reliant on trade with the EU. In the referendum year of 2016, 37 per cent of services exports went to the EU compared with 48 per cent of goods exports.[23] Another was the diversity of what Britain offered. As well as the traditional strength of the City, Britain did well in a wide range of professional and business services, such as accountancy, management consultancy, legal advice, recruitment and advertising. Together these were bigger than the financial sector as a share of the economy and had long run hefty trading surpluses.[24] These firms were helped by London's position as an international hub. They also benefited from Britain's highly regarded professional institutions and the reputation of the English legal system. The sector had been identified by the government in 2013 as one outperforming since 2000, with the potential to carry on doing that.[25]

Thanks to foreign students, British universities were also big exporters – their fees together with their spending while in Britain were counted as exports. Altogether that came to £22 billion in 2021, roughly split in half between tuition fees and personal spending.[26] This was lower than the £37.5 billion estimate worked out by HEPI (see Chapter 7), which used a 'multiplier' to capture the overall impact on the economy of foreign students through a chain reaction of spending and re-spending.

A less conventional *forte* was the cultural sector. Long regarded as an economic irrelevance, the 'creative industries' – including some goods as well as services and encompassing everything from films and television shows, to book publishing and video games – had flourished in the past two decades. Indeed, creative and cultural services exports were one of Britain's particular strengths identified by the global innovation index.

The rise of the 'creative industries' owed at least something to labelling. When the Beatles became a global phenomenon in the 1960s their success wasn't recorded under that heading. Indeed, as former Labour culture minister turned vice-chancellor of the University of the Arts London, James Purnell, pointed out in early 2024, it took some persuading in Whitehall to take the sector seriously during the early years of the Blair government. Yet he also noted that the sector made up over 5 per cent of GDP in 2021, having outgrown the economy in the previous decade: 'Fashion houses and design studios are of no less importance to economic growth than labs and factories,' he wrote in the *Financial Times*.[27]

However, these success stories couldn't be taken for granted. As Purnell also pointed out, Brexit and inadequate research funding meant there were worries about the competitiveness of the cultural sector. Another concern was the drop of more than 40 per cent in the number of students taking arts GCSEs since 2010, as schools responded to government pressure to concentrate on 'core subjects'.

In higher education, the increasing presence of foreign students was driven by the growing shortfall in domestic funding. The ramping-up of tuition fees financed by student loans from just over £3,000 a year to £9,000 in 2012 had brought in a gush of new money. But the failure to uprate that amount with inflation – it was raised only once, in 2017, to £9,250 – meant that it fell in real terms, especially following the post-pandemic surge in inflation. By 2023 it was worth just £6,600 in 2012 prices – a fall of more than a quarter.[28] International students paying much higher fees were in effect subsidising loss-making domestic ones.

Announcing his retirement as chancellor of Oxford University in early 2024, Chris Patten was scathing about the funding system, calling it a 'pseudo-market mechanism' which was 'now threatened by complete collapse'. The former Conservative minister said that higher education needed 'root and branch reform'.[29]

Such a reform would have to wean universities off becoming

over-dependent on foreign students. What would happen if students from China, say, permanently stopped coming to the UK owing to geopolitical tensions?[30] Unpopular as it might be politically, the freeze on tuition fees had to end: they needed to rise with inflation. Over and above that, the Treasury would need to provide extra funding to cover more of the cost of home students and to support research. From any long-term fiscal perspective this made sense: a better-qualified British workforce would pay higher taxes.

Turning negatives positive

Despite these undoubted strengths in science, innovation and tradable services, relying on them was like saying a car's internal combustion engine could work on two cylinders rather than four. It would condemn Britain to continue with a growth model dominated by London and the South-East with strength in exports of services offset by weakness in exports of goods.

The bleak reality was that productivity was still mediocre across much of the country and among most businesses: too many firms were under-firing. Britain's lacklustre performance boiled down to two big minuses: insufficient capital and inadequate skills, both among managers and in the workforce.

Cracking these problems wasn't rocket science. There was broad agreement among policy experts about what to do. Moreover, dealing with the negatives offered a potential upside by reducing their drag on productivity. But rather than countering these deficiencies through a comprehensive strategy pursued consistently over time, public policy was exacerbating these weaknesses through a series of half-baked initiatives. The only constant in policy was inconstancy.

A prime example was the Treasury's record in using the tax system to foster business investment. In his Hampton Court speech, Sunak claimed that Britain offered international businesses a 'competitive tax system'. This followed Hunt's decision in his autumn statement to make the 'full expensing' of investments a permanent rather than a temporary three-year concession. This would allow companies to offset upfront, as opposed to gradually, the full cost of any capital spending against corporation tax.

The new 'full expensing' policy announced by the chancellor made some sense. But then the previous approach of cutting the rate of corporation tax had also appeared to make some sense, not least to George Osborne, who said in 2016, 'all the evidence shows it's one of the most distortive and unproductive taxes there is'.[31] When running against Johnson in the race to become Tory leader in 2019, Hunt backed lowering the corporate tax rate even further, to 12.5 per cent.[32] How could businesses have any faith that this latest policy would last?

The same lack of consistency was found in public investment: the HS2 fiasco was a glaring example of an endemic stop–go cycle. (See Chapter 8.) At the start of the 2020s there had appeared to be a sea change in government thinking, with a commitment to raise capital budgets over the coming five years. But by November 2023 the Treasury was planning real reductions beyond 2025.[33] This was the triumph of a pernicious short-termism. Because chancellors repeatedly resort to cutting public investment when in fiscal trouble, it would be foolish for construction firms to plan on any boost to capital spending being anything other than temporary. That means they are reluctant to invest in a bigger and better-trained workforce.

Crucially then, a sustained effort to boost investment had to include human as well as physical capital. In his Hampton Court speech, Sunak had put a positive spin on what Britain had to offer, declaring that 'we're delivering a world-class education system' and that 'we've already got one of the most highly qualified workforces in Europe'. However, the global innovation index told a more depressing story. Britain was well down the league table for its pupil–teacher ratio in secondary schools. And it stood out for the relatively low proportion of students graduating with STEM degrees (in science, technology, engineering and maths).

Sunak's rosy picture was carefully framed to leave out a lot that mattered. Britain does have a higher share of the adult population with degrees than the European average among members of the OECD. But it is below average for vocational qualifications. And it is also weak in basic literacy and especially numeracy skills.[34] That is why it is essential to improve vocational education, for so long eclipsed in the public mind by schools and universities.

In the autumn of 2020, Boris Johnson gave a speech in Exeter which set out a new path for the education sector.[35] The prime minister announced a 'lifetime skills guarantee', which he claimed would transform further education in England by helping people 'to train and retrain at any stage in their lives'. But a catchy pledge did not translate into a practical policy. Johnson made no mention of the 14 per cent real terms fall in spending (per student) for sixteen–eighteen-year-olds in further education (FE) colleges during the 2010s.[36] Nor did he mention all the previous failed attempts to try to improve vocational education. These had been documented by the Institute for Government in 2017. The think tank portrayed a picture of continual upheaval in the FE sector: since the early 1980s there had been twenty-eight major pieces of legislation and forty-eight secretaries of state in charge. The IfG authors highlighted 'the sheer scale of churn' – and its damaging consequences.[37]

Tellingly, the worst performance of all in the global innovation index was in Britain's institutional standing – covering, among other things, whether there was stability for business, and rating government policies towards entrepreneurs. But that wasn't something Sunak chose to acknowledge in his sales pitch to global investors.

Britain can't build: who's to blame?

'Let's kill all the lawyers' calls out Dick the Butcher in Shakespeare's *Henry VI, Part II*. The modern version could be 'Let's kill all the planners'. Or, if not them directly, then at least the planning restrictions that were increasingly singled out as the reason why Britain wasn't building enough houses or infrastructure. Keir Starmer's pledge to 'bulldoze' his way through planning restrictions underpinned his promise to build 1.5 million new dwellings in England – 300,000 a year, a target made familiar by the number of times it has been missed.

But were planners really responsible for the persistent failure to build enough homes? In early 2021, the Local Government Association disclosed that in England between 2010–11 and 2019–20, almost 2.8 million homes were granted planning permission. However, only 1.6 million were built.[38] This suggested other factors were at work, including the lack of skilled construction workers and the fact that Britain's builders also sought to dodge the busts that followed booms by building at a more regular pace. Another reason – usually ignored in the handwringing – was that councils had dropped out of the equation. The last time that 300,000 dwellings a year were built in England was in the 1960s. During that decade, local authorities contributed an average of 120,000 a year. In the 1970s, they delivered 100,000 out of an average of 260,000 a year. Many were poor quality, unfortunately, but in recent decades scarcely any council homes of any quality have been built and housing associations have been unable to make up the shortfall.[39]

Inveighing against restrictive planning rules largely misses the point. More housing should be allowed on parts of the green belt that don't deserve the name, as *The Economist* rightly argued in September 2022.[40] But the main reason why not enough homes are being built is that the state has largely withdrawn from getting affordable ones built.

In early 2024, the Competition and Markets Authority (CMA) blamed the shortage of new homes mainly on a complex and unpredictable planning system. But a revealing chart in its report also showed a widening gap during the 2010s in England between the rising number of planning permissions and the lower number of new dwellings. The CMA itself noted: 'Looking at the history of this market, it is notable that housebuilding has only reached the levels that are currently being targeted in periods where significant supply was provided via local authority building.'[41]

For bigger infrastructure developments, planning hold-ups are undoubtedly a pressing problem. In 2023, the Infrastructure Commission reported that it was taking four years on average to get planning consent on major projects, up from about two and a half years a decade earlier.[42] One crucial reason was a shortage of planners. When austerity bit in the first half of the 2010s at local authorities, planning departments felt the pinch. According to a report from the Royal Town Planning Institute, the number of planners working in the public sector fell by a quarter between 2009 and 2020.[43] There was no mystery why. Real earnings fell sharply over that period as councils economised on how much they paid their planning staff. Over time this led to a chronic shortage. The *Local Government Chronicle* found in May 2023 that only one in ten council planning departments were fully staffed in 2022 while a quarter of them had staff turnover rates of 20 per cent or more.[44]

Yes, speedy decision making was vital to speed up big infra-structure developments. It was absurd that in early 2024 the Lower Thames Crossing to the east of London, a project first identified as a national priority in 2011, had yet to get the final go-ahead, having already totted up 359,000 pages of planning applications.[45] But for the less ambitious but still apparently unattainable goal of building more new homes, extra government funding was essen-tial, not least to recruit more of those reviled planners.

Could AI be a gamechanger?

In the breaking waves of technological change, ChatGPT was one of the 'big ones' that surfers dream of. Artificial intelligence had long been talked about. Now, apparently, it had arrived through a new application of machine learning. This 'trains' computers to find patterns and relationships in reams of data, which in turn can be used to make predictions based on new data. ChatGPT is a language-based model that serves up answers based on this method. There is no real intelligence engaging with the question; rather it is a statistical model that sometimes gets things wrong.

ChatGPT certainly excited Wall Street. Its release pushed up tech share prices with analysts queuing up to estimate the potential for productivity gains in anything from basic legal documents to job applications. The application could also help academic researchers by, for example, collating relevant work from a variety of sources. In March 2023, Goldman Sachs predicted that 'generative' AI systems such as ChatGPT could lead to the automation of a quarter of work done in America and the eurozone while, in the process, raising global GDP by 7 per cent over a decade.[46]

But would it really be so transformative? In the late 1990s and early 2000s, advances in IT certainly spurred higher growth, especially in America. Intuitively, that made sense. The internet changed the way everyone shopped, travelled and interacted. It's far from clear that AI has the same potential to transform commerce. And it's worth noting that even the previous online fillip to productivity growth didn't endure.

Indeed, it was impossible to avoid a sense of déjà vu. There was for example a burst of optimism during the pandemic that the shift to working from home made possible by Zoom would boost productivity. This turned out to be a false dawn.[47] In the middle of the previous decade, there was a similar unwarranted frenzy about robots taking our jobs. According to widely cited research by Carl Benedikt Frey and Michael Osborne of Oxford University, getting on for half of American jobs were at high risk of being automated. As many as fifteen million British jobs were at risk, according to estimates by the Bank of England in 2015.[48] However, research by Mannheim University's Centre for European Economic Research suggested that these estimates were wide of the mark. That was because they assumed whole occupations would be displaced rather than specific tasks within them. Focusing on tasks, the Mannheim team worked out that only about a tenth of jobs in America and Britain were especially vulnerable to automation.[49]

Among the occupations supposedly at risk from driverless vehicles was trucking. But as America and Britain emerged from the pandemic, both countries were instead grappling with a shortage of truckers. Widespread deployment of self-driving vehicles remained elusive. Nor was there any noticeable impact from the new wave of automation on growth. In America, for example, GDP expanded by 2.6 per cent a year between 2017 and 2019. Even though the economy had a helping hand from Donald Trump's big tax cuts, that performance was little better than the preceding four years, 2013–16, when it had averaged 2.4 per cent.

A survey in 2022 by the Bank of England revealed that nearly three quarters of British financial firms, particularly in the banking and insurance sectors, were using or developing machine-learning applications.[50] These were especially helpful in countering fraud and money laundering, as well as increasing operational efficiency. But overall the financial firms considered the benefits to be small.

A problem with machine learning is that its predictions emerge from a 'black box'. Even if they are right, they may be counterintuitive and difficult to explain. This limits the applicability for decision-makers whether in firms or among regulators. One alarming aspect of ChatGPT is its tendency to 'hallucinate', giving faulty answers and citing false sources. Noting that shortcoming, Richard Waters, an *FT* journalist following tech in San Francisco, wrote at the end of 2023 that 'even as the buzz around the technology has intensified, serious doubts about its practical usefulness have surfaced'.[51]

AI does offer some hope that the next fifteen years or so may be rather better than the past. But for the economy to extract the full benefit from this and other technologies depended on Britain tackling the hindrances that have already been holding back productivity for so long.

Could AI save the NHS?
Not on past form

There appeared to be great potential for AI in the health service – it could help, for example, radiologists interpret the results of screening tests, speeding up and improving the process. Less ambitiously, more effective use of existing information technology in the NHS offered the prospect of greater efficiencies. This was the central proposal of a *Times* commission of inquiry into health. In February 2024, its 'prescription for health' essentially amounted to a heavy dose of IT. Concluding that 'technology has the power to transform healthcare', the panel of experts called for 'digital health accounts for patients, called patient passports, accessed through the NHS app, to book appointments, order prescriptions, view records, test results or referral letters and contact clinicians'. Who could argue with that?[52]

Except that we have been here before. The idea of digital medical records has been around for decades. In 2002 Tony Blair's government launched the National Programme for IT in the NHS, which had exactly the same objective. Everyone would have their own electronic patient record, making the coordination of medical care between GPs and hospitals far easier. The project was initially supposed to cost £6 billion. But when abandoned in the early 2010s the bill had mounted to £10 billion – with less than £4 billion in realised benefits.[53]

A more recent example was the attempt during the pandemic in 2020 to develop a bespoke contact tracing app. There were high hopes for the project, which started to be tested in the Isle of Wight in early May.[54] Announcing the trial, the health department said the app had been 'developed by NHSX, the technology arm of the health service, and a team of world-leading scientists and doctors'. The app was abandoned a few weeks later. Like Germany and Italy, Britain had to adopt the alternative model supported by Apple and Google.

The failure of the National Programme for IT highlighted a more general lesson. IT specialists emphasise that it isn't enough simply to introduce new technologies. You have to take staff with you through a broader 'change-management' reform. That was particularly difficult in the health service because the institution was so vast and sprawling. Whether the NHS would ever be truly capable of learning and applying that lesson was open to doubt.

Physician, heal yourself

With so much gloom and doom around, it was important for Sunak to point out that Britain retained some underlying strengths, even if his government too often tended to undermine rather than bolster them. It was also politically attractive to associate yourself with success rather than facing up to failure. But focusing on the glamorous part of the economy was a strategic mistake. The areas in which Britain excelled would probably do so regardless of what the government did. The big surpluses in financial and business services revealed a longstanding comparative advantage. So, too, did the rise of the creative industries.

This wasn't enough. However well the successful sectors were doing, their boost to growth would be curtailed if the drab underbelly continued to drag down overall performance. It was vital to counter these negatives. Welcoming the Treasury's 2021 plan for growth, then business secretary Kwasi Kwarteng said the industrial strategy that it replaced was 'a pudding without a theme'.[55] In fact the two had more in common than he chose to admit. But if there was a theme to the new plan it was on fostering innovation. By contrast the 'pudding' policy was more even-handed, seeking as much to address weaknesses as to build up strengths.

But that policy roundabout illustrated a bigger point: government had necessarily to play an active role. Only public money could build more affordable homes, modernise the transport system and plot the path to net zero. Only the government could tackle Britain's educational weaknesses. For that to happen, however, Britain needed policies that grasped what actually had to be done and carried it out. Instead, it had a dysfunctional state. The route to greater prosperity passed through a junction blocked by chronic misgovernment. More than ever, it was apparent that reforming the way Britain was governed was vital to restore growth.

Chapter 10

A ten-point plan to
save the economy

At times the British government has shown that it *can* sort out difficult long-term problems. A prime example was pension reform in the 2000s. The pension system had long relied on employers providing a second pillar to supplement the meagre state pension. But companies were closing their schemes to new entrants. What was to be done?

The government set up a three-strong pensions commission headed by Adair Turner, a former CBI boss who had previously worked at management consultants McKinsey. After weighing the evidence, they came up with a workable and innovative solution. A main recommendation was to set up a new private pillar based on 'auto-enrolment' of employees into a scheme in which they, the employer and the government (through tax relief) would all contribute. Workers could opt out but the onus was on them to do so.

Auto-enrolment worked remarkably well in practice with an opt-out rate of only around 10 per cent among newly enrolled employees in the early 2020s.[1] The policy was based on the discoveries of behavioural economics, for which Chicago University economist Richard Thaler won a Nobel prize in 2017. Thaler showed how people routinely behave in ways that aren't wholly rational and which hurt their long-term interests – such as procrastinating over when to start saving for a pension – a weakness that programmes like auto-enrolment sought to address.

Politicians embraced the idea because it appeared to offer big wins at small cost. As prime minister, David Cameron set up a behavioural insights team advised by Thaler to explore the wider potential of this approach in getting people to take better long-term decisions. But the 'nudge unit', as it was nicknamed, would have been better directed towards ministers. Far more than any individual citizen, the state can take the long view. Yet time and again it doesn't do so. Instead of the analytically rigorous approach of the Turner commission, there is ill-thought-through policy-making across the board. Difficult decisions are postponed (such as renewing nuclear power in the 2000s) while others are rushed through with little forethought (such as the 'triple lock' introduced by the coalition government, a win-win policy for pensioners but not the public finances).

Behavioural economics can't provide a blueprint for how to get Britain going again. But there is plenty of scope for the government to improve the way it behaves – and in so doing to regenerate the economy – without taxing and spending more. Providing a more stable political environment for business lies in the hands of ministers. So does divesting more power to local and regional authorities, if that's what's necessary to galvanise their economies. Similarly, a revamp of Britain's creaking constitution would be the bargain of the century if it prevented a rerun of the chaos of the past few years.

Even so, hard times call for hard choices. An overriding question in coming years is how to pay for better public services. Jeremy Hunt's spring budget in 2024 failed to answer it. Instead, the chancellor banked on big productivity gains in the public sector that would obviate the need for expenditure higher than the meagre extra amount pencilled in by the Treasury – an average increase in real day-to-day spending of just 1 per cent a year from April 2025 to March 2029.[2]

The budget claimed that the government was 'reimagining how it delivers public services' through its effort to boost public sector productivity. But this was a form of magical thinking. Rather than a genuine leap forward in efficiency a further deterioration in already unsatisfactory services was more likely. Cash-strapped public providers would shed staff and prioritise price over quality when procuring from the private sector. Moreover, there was nothing new about striving to make the public sector more efficient. Two decades before, an independent review for the Labour government by Peter Gershon, a businessman who had headed a Treasury office set up by Labour to get better value for public money and scrapped by the coalition government, suggested ways of doing just that with the aim of 'releasing resources to the front line'.[3]

Presenting his budget, Hunt made much of an extra £3.4 billion that the NHS would get to modernise its IT systems 'so they are as good as the best in the world'. But was it that easy? After all, as health secretary in 2013, Hunt had set a goal for the NHS to be paperless by 2018.

The harsh reality of the public finances midway through the 2020s is that taxation will have to rise even more than is currently planned if Britain is to have high-quality public services while keeping a cap on already onerous debt. The tax take in Britain may be high by historical standards, but it is still below that of other European economies that perform better across the board.

So, what should be done? There is a wide variety of proposals on the table from think tanks such as the Institute for Government, Productivity Institute and Resolution Foundation. Here are my ten personal suggestions.

1. Lay the building blocks for growth – but don't set targets

Since a faster-growing economy is the goal, it might seem obvious to set a numerical target. Obvious, but wrong. Take the target that Gordon Brown's Treasury set itself in the early 2000s – raising the trend rate of growth in the economy above 2.5 per cent a year.[4] But this was just for overall GDP, even though (as we have seen in Chapter 1) it is GDP per person that really matters. And though the goal appeared to have been met for a while, it turned out to be anything other than a long-term trend.

Or consider the first of Keir Starmer's five 'missions' proclaimed in early 2023, when he promised to deliver the highest sustained growth in the G7 by the end of the first term of a Labour government.[5] This made even less sense than Brown's objective because Britain had no control at all over how the other six economies would fare.

Setting a growth target pays no attention to the longstanding imperfections in using GDP as a gauge of living standards. As Robert Kennedy memorably pointed out more than half a century ago, 'it measures everything in short except that which makes life worthwhile'. A decade and a half ago, a commission backed by the French government and chaired by Nobel laureate Joseph Stiglitz called for more emphasis on a broader set of measures covering 'well-being'.

That call to arms was right. Indeed, the UN is currently orchestrating a drive to go 'beyond GDP'. Worries about what constitutes GDP, which, for example, includes a host of carbon-intensive activities, have become more relevant as the world strives to move towards net zero and to protect biodiversity. The quality as well as the quantity of growth matters. Lower, cleaner growth is better than higher, dirtier growth.

Top-down targets offer politicians gratifying soundbites, but often turn out to have perverse outcomes. A notable example was health secretary Matt Hancock's pledge at the start of April 2020 to increase Covid tests to 100,000 a day by the end of the month. That target was met only by including testing kits that had been sent out but not yet used and returned as well as tests actually processed in labs. As important, the target prioritised the number of tests rather than whether they were being deployed in the most effective way to contain the pandemic.[6]

Instead of simplistic growth targets, the priority should be to ensure that the building blocks for high-quality growth are in place: higher investment, both private and public, and better skills. Achieving these two objectives requires perseverance. It would be better, for example, to set a lower goal for public investment that can be maintained year after year rather than one that is higher but is later abandoned.

High standards are also essential. Too often in the past, quality has been sacrificed, as in the RAAC building scandal. The lowest bid is not necessarily the best one. There should also be a sufficient margin to cope with unexpected increases in demand. It's troubling that the plan to build new hospitals in England based on a standardised design trendily called Hospital 2.0 is founded on what the House of Commons Public Accounts Committee has called 'unrealistic assumptions' such as shorter stays and very high bed occupancy. The MPs highlighted the risk that the design 'will result in future hospitals being too small, which could lead to significantly greater expenditure and disruption in the long run'.[7] Which would naturally come as a great surprise when it happened.

There are also ways to bolster growth that don't require more public money. Taxes can be reformed to make the economy work better without a loss of revenue. Stamp duties snarl up the housing market, reduce labour mobility and contribute to the property shortage by discouraging older people from downsizing. They should be slashed – and the lost revenues made up by reforming council tax so that it falls more heavily on people living in more expensive homes. Another revenue-neutral tax reform would be to replace most road fuel duties with road pricing, a change that will have to happen anyway as cars go electric. This would bring big benefits by curbing congestion and carbon emissions – as Rod Eddington pointed out almost two decades ago in his advice to the government based on his transport report (see Chapter 8).

Reforms along these lines have been gathering dust since a comprehensive review of the tax system headed by Nobel prize-winner James Mirrlees over a decade ago.[8] That's because politicians know that losers always shout louder than winners in tax shake-ups. But these kinds of policies are more likely to boost growth than any explicit target.

In his 2010 book *Obliquity*, the economist John Kay identified what he called the 'profit-seeking paradox'.[9] The companies that focus single-mindedly on profits often do worse than those whose overriding objective is to deliver outstanding products and services. Much the same applies to government in what you could call the 'growth-seeking paradox'. Growth emerges from the right policies – not by making it the be-all and end-all of public endeavour. Indeed, as Kay points out, many goals are more likely to be attained when pursued indirectly.

2. Stop the policy churn

Names can tell a story. The DTI (Department of Trade and Industry) was for many years the ministry that handled business matters and many other relevant tasks. But in 2007, it lost innovation and science when becoming BERR, responsible for business, enterprise and regulatory reform. A year later it also shed energy. In 2009 the department made a big comeback as BIS, in charge of business, innovation and skills, regaining science as well and also acquiring universities. With Theresa May at Number 10, BIS metamorphosed into BEIS, reincorporating energy and adding industrial strategy but shedding skills and universities as well as trade. That was unpicked by Sunak in 2023, as the department lost energy again and the now defunct industrial strategy but regained trade. Science and innovation were moved to a new ministry. The new DBT (Department for Business and Trade) was strikingly similar to the core responsibilities of the old DTI.[10]

Kemi Badenoch, the new business secretary appointed in 2023, was the seventh in less than four years. There was a similar ferment at other ministries. Indeed, the reshuffle in February 2023 that elevated Badenoch also brought the fifteenth housing minister since the 2010 election and the fifth in just the previous year.[11] Increasingly, Whitehall seemed to have succumbed to an internal mergers and acquisitions frenzy, as ministers came and went, departments acquired new functions and lost others. Yet that was even more pointless in government than in the private sector where takeovers all too often don't pay off for the acquiring company.

The way to tackle issues straddling departmental boundaries wasn't to reconstruct ministries but to get ministers to work collaboratively across dividing lines. Forget the labelling, what mattered for the private sector was consistency and reliability of government. Instead they got the exact opposite.

A case in point was a shake-up in the way that financial institutions were regulated through the 'consumer duty' imposed by the Financial Conduct Authority in 2023. This was a set of rules designed to enhance protection for financial customers. That sounded like a good idea. But the FCA itself had pointed out in 2018 that existing rules largely covered the same ground. In a follow-up statement in 2019, it said: 'There is unlikely to be a one-size-fits-all solution to any deficiencies in consumer protection.' The regulator's hand was forced by a last-minute government amendment to a financial services bill in 2021 that was supposed to be a post-Brexit tidying-up exercise.[12]

This was an extraordinary way to adopt a sweeping new set of rules costing financial firms an initial sum of up to £2.4 billion to ensure compliance with subsequent ongoing expenses of up to £175 million a year. These costs would in all likelihood be passed on to consumers in one way or another. Tony Danker, former head of the CBI, said it was switching responsibility at least in part from buyer to seller – moving away from the time-honoured *caveat emptor*.[13] This was the type of change, you might think, that deserved careful consideration rather than a policy swerve during a 'ping-pong' session between the two houses of parliament.

Stopping the policy churn is vital. For every major new initiative there should be a published audit of previous ones, explaining why they haven't worked. Departments should employ historians to provide context for officials and ministers now that they come and go so quickly. Consultation should be meaningful rather than box-ticking exercises. Expertise outside government should be fully tapped.

If Whitehall can put its own house in order, that will do more to improve the environment for growth than setting unrealistic and poorly specified targets. In short, the government needs to take back control of itself.

3. Build a business strategy

There was no place for an industrial strategy in the new economic policy model introduced in the 1980s. The idea that government could straddle the strict divide between the private and public sectors was anathema. Britain's economic success in the fifteen or so good years up to the financial crisis appeared to vindicate this decision. But, in fact, much was lost by the government abandoning the field and thus losing the ability to tell what works in practice and what doesn't. According to Cambridge University economists Diane Coyle and Adam Muhtar, that lack of information feedback is a crucial deficiency in British industrial policymaking, leading to 'the UK being locked in a constant cycle of premature policy changes'.[14]

Now that manufacturing is a smaller share of the economy, it probably makes more sense to talk about a business rather than an industrial strategy. What is the case for such an approach? A minimalist argument in favour is that it simply recognises reality. The government already intervenes in business in manifold ways. To name just a few: corporate taxation, competition policy, the remit of regulators, trade credit support for exporters, labour and market regulations, immigration rules. It is only sensible to coordinate all these separate interventions in the round just as a conductor keeps all the various members of an orchestra in time.

A more activist case has been made in the past fifteen years by three business secretaries from different parties. For Peter Mandelson, in charge during the closing years of the Labour government, there were three main arguments in favour.[15] First, the economy needed to become less reliant on the City. Second, left to its own devices the private sector would underdeliver. Exploiting new technologies, he said in early 2010, would not happen with 'government simply standing on the sidelines'. Third, the state should intervene to plug financing gaps for start-ups and expanding SMEs.

For the Lib Dem Vince Cable, in the business hot seat between 2010 and 2015, the main argument for an industrial policy was timescale. When investing, private firms had to think strategically. Similarly, the government should adopt a longer-term framework for its decisions. The British Business Bank introduced on his watch has since more than shown its worth in getting more finance to smaller firms, amounting to £12 billion for almost 100,000 businesses at the end of March 2022.[16]

For the Conservative Greg Clark, business secretary under Theresa May, the point of an industrial strategy was to improve the supply side of the economy in ways that only the state could deliver. Raising productivity was the chief goal. He recognised that it wasn't enough simply to foster the sectors that were already doing well; it was also vital to tackle longstanding weaknesses holding back the economy.

Over and above these arguments, the role for a business strategy is clearer than ever as Britain strives to become a net-zero economy by 2050. Hitting that goal will require an overarching plan and a continuing dialogue and collaboration with the businesses that will actually make it happen.

Worries about a business strategy degenerating into handouts to individual firms are overstated. For one thing, the priority should be to build the underlying conditions that facilitate business success. For another, having such a framework helps determine where public money is best directed. In any case, Britain has less of a free hand since America embarked on its own industrial policy of supporting green growth with public money – though trying to match American largesse would be folly.

4. Bring back the nanny state

The health of nations matters just as much as the wealth of nations. That is one thing we have learned since Adam Smith wrote his classic economic work two and a half centuries ago. Since then, there have been extraordinary advances in health and therefore life expectancy.

Naturally, people put a high value on living longer, healthier lives. However, this is not picked up in conventional economic measurements. At the turn of the millennium, William Nordhaus, an economist at Yale, estimated that the value of the increase in

US life expectancy between 1975 and 1995 was almost as great as the entire increase in American consumer expenditure over the period.[17]

Not only does health matter in its own right: it is also crucial for the economy. Businesses need a physically fit and mentally well workforce. Attempts during the pandemic to prioritise GDP over fighting Covid were misguided. Restoring a healthy nation was vital to restoring a healthy economy.

Emerging from the pandemic, national output has been held back by the growing number of sick people not working. That followed a decade in which improvements to life expectancy have largely stalled. As with the economy, Britain wasn't alone in experiencing this slowdown, but it was more pronounced.[18]

One imperative is to tackle obesity. Britain has one of the fattest populations in Europe. A health survey for England in 2018 found that almost two-thirds of adults and nearly 30 per cent of children were overweight or obese. Obesity is linked to increased risk of a variety of diseases notably diabetes.[19]

It was the state that intervened to arrest smoking through higher tobacco taxes, health warnings on packets and the ban in enclosed public places introduced in 2007. In October 2023, Sunak went a step further by proposing to prevent younger generations from ever smoking by raising the age at which people can be legally sold cigarettes and tobacco – currently eighteen – by one year every year.[20] You don't have to be libertarian to question this gimmicky idea (unveiled at the Tory party conference), which will be difficult to enforce. Prohibition seldom works and unlike the ban on smoking in public places, this measure can't be justified by the interests of non-smokers.

What is beyond doubt is that the state should now do much more to promote a healthier diet and to encourage more exercise. The 'sugar tax', a levy on the soft-drinks industry for products containing excessive amounts of added sugar, which George Osborne announced in his last budget, in spring 2016, should be just the beginning.[21]

Politicians shy away from telling people what to eat and drink. Boris Johnson appeared to see the light after his near-death experience with Covid in the spring of 2020. In July that year, the government announced a 'world-leading' plan to slim the nation. But implementation was half-hearted. One crucial measure – a 9pm watershed for television adverts of unhealthy foods – was put off until October 2025.[22]

That political reluctance to interfere in people's life choices is understandable. But actually it is just what the doctor should prescribe for all of us who find it difficult to resist the moreish blandishments of the junk-food industry. More than ever, we need a return to the nanny state – though one that cajoles and nags rather than resorting to outright prohibition.

5. Widen the curriculum and sort out vocational education

What will Britain be like in 2050? No one can say precisely. But assuming that geopolitical and environmental catastrophes can be avoided, one thing is certain: economic success will depend upon having a well-educated and highly skilled workforce. And even though that date might appear distant, decisions taken now will be decisive in preparing the children born in the near future for their mid-century lives.

Increasing human capital is more vital than ever. The state has a crucial part to play, from infant and primary schools through to further and higher education. In schools, one priority is for children not simply to acquire knowledge but to learn how to communicate and to work together, skills that have become more and more vital in the workplace. Another priority is to emancipate the curriculum from the grip that universities still have over it, which has for too long enforced too early specialisation for sixteen–eighteen-year-olds.

The funding of higher education needs a thorough rethink and will require the state to provide considerably more financial support. But the biggest challenge of all is vocational education. For far too long, this has been neglected. Teachers in the sector have suffered big falls in their pay, which was almost a fifth lower in real terms in 2022 than in 2010 – a sharper decline than for schoolteachers.[23] Various attempts to dragoon firms into contributing more have backfired. Rather than yet another initiative that on past form will quickly be torn up, a commission similar to the one headed by Turner on pensions should work out a comprehensive and lasting solution. As well as taking evidence from employers and vocational colleges, it must conduct a searching investigation into why so many previous policies have failed.

One lesson will surely be that you can't rely on employers. Left to their own devices some will poach young people who have been trained elsewhere – which puts off other willing companies from offering training. Those that do offer training naturally focus on the specific skills they require. But what young people going down the vocational route need is as wide a set of skills as possible, allowing them to switch occupations and thus adjust to the changing mix of the economy in their longer working lives. At worst, some schemes short-change apprentices by in effect using them as a source of cheap labour.[24]

Instead, you have to put further education colleges in the driving seat, as Geoffrey Holland, a former top civil servant with vast experience of these issues, argued in a programme for the BBC as far back as 1995.[25] Pursuing that policy now will involve undoing decades of neglect.

Vocational courses must vary according to the needs of regional economies, so it would be better to come up with local solutions.

In Cornwall, for example, there will be a greater emphasis on agriculture than in the Midlands, where there will be more of a focus on manufacturing. Also, there are more incentives for employers to collaborate locally because of a common interest in the strength of the local economy and a shared labour force.

After one failure after another, it is understandable to despair about whether Britain can ever get vocational education right. But we can't afford to be defeatist. It is possible to envisage a future in which there are fulfilling opportunities outside higher education for students, young and old.

6. Think the unthinkable on the NHS

Right now, the public services are in the worst of all possible states. The NHS has historically been underfunded compared with what other countries spend, and our healthcare is accordingly worse. Yet its seemingly insatiable appetite for more money starves all the other public services.

The only realistic way out of the dilemma is to raise taxation. But how can the British public be persuaded to pay more when there seems to be so little link between what you pay and what you get?

One drastic solution would be to switch NHS funding away from general taxation to social insurance contributions paid to health funds that are largely independent of government. This is how it works in European countries such as Germany.[26] Such contributions are still taxes but because there is a clear benefit attached – the provision of treatment if you fall ill – this could allow more revenue to be raised.

In 2006 the Netherlands created a framework for 'managed competition' in healthcare.[27] Everyone signs up with health insurers, paying a flat-rate premium for basic healthcare. Employers pitch in a lot, too, and the state picks up the bill through general taxation for children and assisting poorer people. The insurers – private but almost all not-for-profit – have to accept all applicants regardless of their age or medical condition. The funding they receive takes into account the health of the patients they are covering. The full costs of treatment are covered subject to a small annual deductible (which does not apply to GP services and maternity care). But people have the choice to select among insurers and providers.

The Dutch healthcare system gets plaudits in international comparisons, more so than the NHS.[28] It brings genuine competitive pressures to bear on medical providers. This is something that Tony Blair sought to achieve through an internal market, which was taken a step further with the GP-led commissioning groups introduced by the coalition government. But the lesson is that these pseudomarkets just don't work.

On the other hand, switching systems would undeniably be a reorganisation to beat all others. It's far from clear that ditching the taxation-based funding model is feasible in a country where, as Nigel Lawson said, the NHS was 'the closest thing the English have to a religion'.[29] The King's Fund, a health policy think tank, argued in 2023 that countries should improve what they have rather than import a different model.[30]

Given the malaise of the NHS, there should nonetheless be serious and open-minded consideration about whether Britain should introduce a version of the Dutch model. Intrinsically, it is superior to the NHS. For one thing, it removes health care out of the direct control of politicians. For another, it brings competitive pressures to bear on providers, just as Blair sought to achieve with his reforms.

But if that is too much to contemplate, a second-best alternative would be a special NHS tax with the revenues earmarked for the health service. The advantage of such a 'hypothecated' tax is that people would be more prepared to foot the bill. The health service could thus get the increase in revenues needed, which in turn would reduce pressure on other public services. Two decades ago, health economist Julian Le Grand made the case for a hypothecated health tax as a way of avoiding the NHS being the cuckoo in the nest.[31]

Hypothecated taxes, though, have an unhappy history. In the 1920s, the revenue from vehicle licences was supposed to fund solely road building, but that ended in the mid-1930s when it was subsumed in general taxation. Moreover, the Treasury would worry that the NHS would still come knocking on the door if it ran into financial trouble.

Arguably, the most workable solution is the one suggested in 2018 by a former Treasury permanent secretary Nicholas Macpherson: an incremental NHS tax.[32] Boris Johnson announced a version of this – the health and social care levy – in September 2021, which was introduced the following spring through raising National Insurance rates. A few months later, it was abolished by Kwasi Kwarteng, the main measure in his mini-budget to survive.[33]

This idea could be revived, but in the shape that Macpherson favoured. Instead of raising NI rates, which are levied only on the working population, the NHS tax should take the form of additional income tax (the same tax favoured by Le Grand), payable on all income and by the old as well as workers, with the extra money going only to the NHS. If more fundamental reform through going Dutch is politically impossible, this may be the most feasible way to sort out the finances of the health service – and in so doing relieve the pressures on other public services.

7. Bring the Treasury down a peg (but not two)

Chancellors are second only to prime ministers in the power that they wield. The turf war between Gordon Brown and Tony Blair damaged the effectiveness of the Labour government in the 2000s. Tellingly, Brown tried (unsuccessfully) to sabotage the Turner pensions commission and the recommendations for reform that it made.[34]

The Treasury rules the roost in Whitehall through its tax and spending decisions. And it combines that role with running economic policy across the board, though operating monetary policy has been delegated to the Bank of England. There is an obvious risk in clipping the wings of the Treasury, not least to Britain's credibility in the markets. It is an indispensable shield to incessant departmental demands for more and more money. Someone has to say no on behalf of taxpayers and ensure that the public finances are on a sustainable footing.

Furthermore, there has already been a failed experiment in creating a rival department. Under Harold Wilson's Labour government following the 1964 election, a new ministry was created to conduct economic policy under George Brown, the party's deputy leader.[35] The Department of Economic Affairs was supposed to mastermind higher growth (complete with ambitious targets) through a national plan. But the plan was hijacked by the fragility of the pound. When sterling was eventually devalued in 1967, the Treasury took the decisions that mattered. Far from being a rival, the DEA turned out to be an embarrassing flop.

Even so, there is a strong case for reducing the dominance of Britain's finance ministry. A report from the Institute for Government in January 2024 worried about an 'imbalance of power in government that leads to bad outcomes in policy and spending'. The prime minister lacked 'the firepower, intellectual support or control of the levers to set and drive strategy, leaving the Treasury to fill the resulting vacuum'. It argued that 'short-termism is clearly a damaging outcome of the Treasury's public finance processes'.[36] An admittedly inexact analogy is a big company where the finance director calls the shots. A concern for the bottom line has its merits but why should one expect a corporate treasurer to have a strategic vision, to understand customers and inspire the workforce?

In March 2024, the IfG suggested reforms that would strengthen the position of the prime minister, reducing the sway of the chancellor.[37] However, Andy Haldane, former chief economist at the Bank of England, wants to go much further. In January 2024, he proposed setting up a new economy ministry with a growth mission given 'equal billing' to fiscal sustainability for which the Treasury would remain responsible.[38]

Given the unhappy experience of setting up a rival ministry in the 1960s, a more workable reform would be to strip the Treasury from overseeing the supply side of the economy. In many ways, it is quite unsuited to this role, which may be why Gordon Brown's many worthy initiatives to try to boost productivity came to nothing. As Turkish-American economist Dani Rodrik told the *FT* in early 2024, 'industrial policy cannot be formulated and implemented in a top-down, arm's length manner'.[39] Rather, improving the way the economy works requires dialogue and collaboration with a host of stakeholders. Or, as Rodrik put it, 'You need to base policy on input, information, iteration and learning.'

Another worthwhile reform would be to return to having just one budget a year. The autumn statement has, in effect, been turned into a second fiscal set piece. (Theresa May's chancellor Philip Hammond reverted to a single budget but that was too sensible to last.) At the same time, the antiquated financial year, which for historical reasons starts in April, should be aligned with the calendar year. Maybe it's too much to ask, but it would also help if chancellors desisted from their beloved attention-seeking announcements. The Treasury, for its part, could put an end to conniving in the fiscal illusionism that has ultimately been counter-productive.

The Treasury should keep its core functions as a finance

ministry that controls and allocates spending, as well as being responsible for the tax system. Overall macroeconomic policy must also remain its domain in partnership with the Bank of England. But supply-side policies should be set by the business department whose role would be complementary rather than adversarial.

8. Decentralise power – really

In 1962 the American statesman Dean Acheson famously remarked that Britain had lost an empire and had yet to find a new role. But Whitehall did find a new role for itself: establishing a new empire within England.

Cambridge University historian Simon Szreter has argued that a 'new "civic gospel" of municipal pride and ambitious improvements' rippling out from Birmingham transformed late Victorian Britain for the good. Essential services, such as providing clean water, brought death rates down.[40] This continued through the first half of the twentieth century when as Allan Cochrane of the Open University noted, local authorities 'took the initiative in developing welfare services across the board, from housing to education, health to children's services'.[41] That included the building of hospitals subsequently taken over by the NHS in 1948. It was during this heyday of local government that there were record gains in life expectancy, rising by around twenty years between 1900 and 1950.[42]

But councils have since proved easy game for the predations of politicians in Westminster largely because they have so little fiscal autonomy. Local authorities are tightly circumscribed in how much they can raise in council tax. They lost control over business rates as part of the poll tax fiasco of the early 1990s. In the past decade they have kept half the revenue raised locally through business rates, but they still remain in financial thrall to Whitehall.[43]

This degree of centralisation has become counterproductive. The 'levelling-up' agenda, for example, requires local initiative rather than top-down directives.

An in-depth survey of over ninety experts involved in regional development, published by Harvard Kennedy School in late 2023, found that most of them believed that 'the UK's unusually central-ised governance has hampered economic growth across the English regions'.[44] Yet the survey also reported 'a continuing Whitehall scepticism about local capabilities', especially in education. That disparaging view 'stifled local initiative and dynamism', and led to 'the patchy implementation of national objectives'.

Out of the rubble of one failed policy after another – a familiar theme in this book – some green shoots have been appearing. An underlying problem in local government is that the physical areas covered by councils are much smaller than economic regions. A solution in predominantly urban areas is to have an overarching metropolitan authority such as in Greater Manchester, which spans ten local authorities. These bodies can drive through vital changes such as integrating transport services.

Whether these combined authorities also require the magic sauce of directly elected metro mayors – figures like Andy Burnham in Greater Manchester – is more open to question. The idea that city bosses get things done is an American import. It certainly hands a powerful political platform to the incumbent, which Johnson exploited as London mayor. But it fits uneasily with the way councils choose their own leaders, through a vote by elected councillors.

Still, combined authorities do offer a way forward in the big conurbations. This approach has more democratic legitimacy than, for example, the failed experiment with regional development agencies introduced in 1999 by Labour and abolished in 2012 by the coalition government. But more generally there has to be a reversal of at least some of the centralisation.

There are two areas where local leadership is vital. The first is housing. If Britain is to get more homes, then councils have once again to build affordable ones. The second is skills, a policy area where according to the Harvard Kennedy School study the case for decentralisation was clearest.

For vocational education to deliver, links with local businesses and public sector bodies are vital. Councils, which originally fostered further education colleges, need to drive change on the ground. A recent step in the right direction is that funding for adult vocational education has been devolved to combined authorities like Greater Manchester.[45] But that's just the start of the return journey, in which regional voices should be amplified instead of being ignored.

9. Get Brexit undone

When Theresa May said 'Brexit means Brexit', she was perhaps more insightful than she intended. Brexit did indeed mean whatever version of Brexit was chosen. It didn't have to be the barebones trade deal that Boris Johnson eventually negotiated. Instead, it might have been the Brexit May eventually plumped for with her 2018 Chequers white paper, which envisaged as close a relationship with the EU as possible while still honouring the result of the referendum.

So why should Johnson's bad Brexit deal dictate Britain's fortunes for years to come? Granted, there is no appetite among the public for a total reversal of Brexit any time soon. Rejoining the EU is a distant prospect, not least because the bloc would need confidence that Britain would be signing up for good. But softer gradations of life outside the EU are still possible. That has already been demonstrated through Britain belatedly rejoining the Horizon science funding programme. Another has been in the government's retreat from actively seeking regulatory divergence from the bloc. Since the EU will remain a regulatory superpower, it makes sense for Britain to stay close to European rules rather than vainly to set its own.

Maybe there could be a scheme where under-thirties were allowed to live and work freely for a couple of years in Britain and the EU? Or to find a way for musicians to tour without the hassle that has disrupted their activity? It helps that these are objectives shared by the EU, which would also like Britain to rejoin the Erasmus student exchange programme.[46]

More generally, there is plenty of room to intensify cooperation on defence and security. Indeed, that goal was set out in the October 2019 political declaration that accompanied the withdrawal agreement setting out the terms for the UK's exit from the EU. This envisaged 'a broad, comprehensive and balanced security partnership' as well as Britain being invited to informal EU ministerial meetings. Ditched by Johnson in May 2020, that agenda should be revived.

All this could pave the way to a bigger step: rejoining the customs union. This lay at the heart of the European club that Britain joined in 1973. It was a good idea then and it remains a good idea now. As Charles Grant of the Centre for European Reform wrote in late 2023, it would be 'of huge benefit to many industries, including cars, chemicals and pharmaceuticals, which would face greatly reduced bureaucracy at the border. It would at a stroke solve the problem of rules of origin – which are not controlled within a customs union.'[47]

Rejoining the customs union would mean sacrificing an independent trade policy for goods, but Britain has already learned how tough it is to negotiate deals outside the EU and how nugatory are the economic benefits that they yield. Trade negotiators notoriously don't do sentiment, as the government found out when striking a poor bargain with Australia in 2021. In January 2024 talks with Canada broke down, leaving Britain in a worse position than before it left the EU.[48]

If Britain is to adopt a softer Brexit, it is vital to treat European states as partners rather than adversaries. When Johnson spoke about 'our European friends', there was a Godfather ring to it. By contrast May genuinely wanted to build a 'partnership'. She was right.

10. Defend and rebuild institutions

Institutions matter. The success of the private economy depends upon a partnership with a strong state with an independent judiciary and a civil service unafraid to speak truth to ministers. Until recently, this could be taken for granted in Britain. Indeed, in some respects things had improved through reforms such as delegating control over interest rates to the Bank of England and the creation of the Office for Budget Responsibility.

But in the past ten years, underlying weaknesses have been exposed. Johnson had no respect for the unwritten conventions that act as a crucial safeguard of the constitution. He introduced legislation in September 2020 that contravened the treaty with the EU that he himself had signed at the start of the year. One minister was unexpectedly frank when he confessed it would 'break international law in a very specific and limited way'.[49] Although the offending clauses were removed later that year, Johnson then renewed the threat to rip up the treaty in the Northern Ireland Protocol bill introduced in June 2022 shortly before his downfall. This was dropped only when Sunak negotiated the Windsor Framework in early 2023.[50]

The nadir was reached under Liz Truss when her government ousted Tom Scholar from his job as the head of the Treasury and bypassed the OBR before the disastrous 'mini-budget'. What followed was an object lesson in why institutions and conventions matter. It should not have been left to investors and traders to bring the prime minister into line.

You might have expected some serious soul searching in the wake of these constitutional outrages. We should recall that but for the misfortune of a pandemic and the partygate scandal, Johnson's premiership might have lasted for the best part of the 2020s. Instead, there has been a reversion to the complacency and indifference about the constitution that allowed such misgovernment to happen in the first place.

At the very least we must overhaul how referendums are held in Britain. Setting the hurdle at 50 per cent is the norm among democracies. But other countries add safeguards. In Australia, for example, a proposed change to the constitution requires majorities in at least four of the six federal states as well as a national majority.[51] For the UK there would have to be majorities in at least three of the four nations – something that wasn't achieved in 2016 since both Northern Ireland and Scotland backed Remain.

Another approach is to stipulate that the winning side also achieves a minimum level of support in the electorate as a whole, including those who don't turn out to vote. That was the case in the Scottish referendum on devolution in 1979 when the bar was set at 40 per cent of the electorate for those voting in favour. That proved fatal to the cause of devolution, which had to wait another two decades.[52] If this had been applied in 2016, it would also have scuppered the Leave victory since Brexit was supported by only 37 per cent of the electorate. (Feebly, David Cameron hoped that backbench MPs might press for the referendum to include such a threshold, which didn't happen.)[53] There should also be an agreed framework for how referendums are conducted to ensure campaigners can't bandy about false claims.

Should we change the electoral system from first past the post to proportional representation? The argument in favour of first past the post used to be that it created strong governments – self-evidently not the case in the past few years. Even so, making such a change would be disruptive and could have unintended consequences.

A more feasible reform would alter the way that the party leaders are selected. Allowing party members to determine who runs the country or is leader of the opposition hands extraordinary power to small and unrepresentative groups of people. That was in full display during the Tory contests to replace May in 2019 and then Johnson in 2022. Similarly, Labour party members saddled the country with Jeremy Corbyn as their leader, which in effect ruled the main opposition party out of contention in the 2017 and 2019 elections.

As Meg Russell of the UCL Constitution Unit argued in February 2020, 'membership ballots undermine parliamentary accountability, weaken parliamentary parties and cast leaders' legitimacy into doubt'. She called for a more radical approach: 'to accept the logic of a parliamentary system and return the choice of parliamentary leader to MPs'.[54] William Hague, who introduced the current Tory system in 1998, handing the final say to members, now regrets the change. 'Where we have tried something and it hasn't worked,' he has said, 'it would be very strange indeed if we didn't correct it.'[55]

Britain's political system has become increasingly presidential. That makes it all the more vital that MPs decide who leads them – and thus who is the leader of the opposition and prime minister. Constitutional issues are usually dismissed with a yawn or deferred for someone else to tackle. But as much as anything restoring Britain's economic fortunes requires a fundamental overhaul of the way we are governed.

Notes

Introduction: Forty-nine days of madness

1. IFS Mini-budget response, ifs.org.uk, 23 Sep 2022
   The NI reversal had been announced the day before.
2. Kwasi Kwarteng sacks top Treasury civil servant, ft.com, 8 Sep 2022
3. Kwarteng defends tax cuts, saying there is 'more to come', bbc.co.uk/news, 25 Sep 2022; Sterling falls to record low of $1.035 against the dollar, ft.com, 26 Sep 2022
4. How Kwasi Kwarteng's mini-budget broke the UK bond market, ft.com, 28 Sep 2022
5. Chancellor statement 17 October 2022, gov.uk, 17 Oct 2022
6. Liz Truss regime's 'moron premium' still looms over UK economy, ft.com, 29 Dec 2022
7. It is time for the UK to think like an emerging market, ft.com, 23 Jun 2023
8. OBR, Economic and fiscal outlook (EFO), p. 15, obr.uk, 17 Nov 2022
9. OBR, EFO, pp. 44–45, 6 Mar 2024
10. Factsheet 2022–23, trusselltrust.org
11. What is happening to life expectancy in England?, kingsfund.org.uk, 9 Aug 2022
12. Comparisons of all-cause mortality between European countries and regions, spreadsheet 14, cumulative excess mortality by end May 2020, ons.gov.uk, 25 Sep 2023

13. OECD, Health at a glance: Europe 2022, pp. 70–71, oecd-ilibrary.org, 5 Dec 2022
14. OBR, EFO, p. 59, obr.uk, 15 Mar 2023; Centrica bolsters UK's energy security by doubling Rough storage capacity, centrica.com, 30 Jun 2023

Chapter 1: From hero to zero: a brief (recent) history of the British economy

1. What have two decades of British economic reform delivered?, p. 29, davidcard.berkeley.edu/papers, 2004
2. OECD, Annual GDP per capita, at PPP exchange rates relative to OECD, multilateral index; at constant prices. Source for this and other such comparisons. Accessed 10 Feb 2024
3. GDP, chained volume, recession measured between 1979 Q2 and 1981 Q1. Also source for subsequent references
4. ONS, unemployment rate and level for all aged 16 and over, time series MGSX and MGSC. Also source for subsequent references
5. Brown's historical boasts have little weight, ft.com, 12 Apr 2005
6. As measured by the retail prices index (RPI), which was the official measure at that time, ons.gov.uk
7. Average weekly earnings in Great Britain, ons.gov.uk, 13 Feb 2024. Real earnings series uses CPI
8. The US productivity slowdown: an economy-wide and industry-level analysis, bls.gov, Apr 2021, Figure 1. Note: this is based on output per hour worked
9. OECD, GDP per person employed, accessed 12 Feb 2024. Figures cited are for period between 1992 and 2007
10. CPI, Annual rate, ons.gov.uk, 14 Feb 2024
11. IFS Green Budget, chapter 3, pp. 39–43, ifs.org.uk, 31 Jan 2007
12. The man who would make you rich, economist.com, 21 Jun 2001

13. Births in England and Wales: summary tables 2022 Edition, table 1, column G, ons.gov.uk, 23 Feb 2024

14. Cohort effects in the age structure of the population, obr.uk. Shows population pyramids for England and Wales in 1951, 1981 and 2011

15. Workforce ageing, consequences and policy responses, 1998, Chart 4.3, p. 133, oecd.org

16. Freeman, Richard, The great doubling: the challenge of the new global labour market, eml.berkeley.edu, Aug 2006

17. The Growth Effects of EU Membership for the UK: Review of the evidence, smf.co.uk, Apr 2016

18. Mervyn King speech, Bank of England, bankofengland.co.uk, 14 Oct 2003

19. The industrial analyses, Table 2.3, ons.gov.uk, 31 Oct 2023

20. HMT, Budget 2002, Apr 2002, Annex B, pp. 181, 190–191; Pre-budget Report, Nov 2001, p. 149; Pre-budget report, Dec 2006, pp. 191–193

21. Sources for box:
ONS, 15 Feb 2024: GDP and GDP per head: ABMI and mid-year UK population estimates released 21 Dec 2022 and 26 Mar 2024
Labour productivity: output per worker A4YM and output per hour LZVB
OECD, data extracted Feb 2024, GDP, national currency at constant prices; GDP per person employed and per hour worked; constant prices, 2015 PPPs, comparing growth rates between 1992 and 2007; and 2007 and 2022; note: at constant prices (PPPs of 2015), France's GDP per person was a bit lower than Britain's, at current prices in 2022, just higher

22. Speeches by Andrew Haldane: Productivity puzzles, 20 Mar 2017 (Table 2, p. 28) and The UK's productivity problem, 28 Jun 2018 (p. 6), bankofengland.co.uk

23. The impact of workforce aging on European productivity, imf.org, Dec 2016

24. Charting Globalization's Turn to Slowbalization After Global Financial Crisis, imf.org, 8 Feb 2023

25. Why Joe Biden is the heir to Trump, ft.com, 7 Aug 2023
26. The Brexit vote and inflation – updated evidence, cepr.org, 2 Mar 2020
27. ONS, Business investment (time series NPEL), ons.gov.uk, 22 Dec 2023
28. [De]Globalisation and inflation, p. 17, bankofengland.co.uk, BOE, 18 Sep 2017
29. GDP first quarterly estimate, 15 Feb 2024; GDP quarterly national accounts, UK: Oct to Dec 2023, 28 Mar 2024
30. Survey of Adult Skills, p. 272, comparison of 55–64 and 16–24 year-olds, oecd-ilibrary.org, 8 Oct 2013

Chapter 2: Brexit blues: how to devalue a country

1. The UK's border with the EU, UK in a Changing Europe, ukandeu.ac.uk, 30 Jan 2024
2. HM Treasury analysis: the immediate economic impact of leaving the EU, assets.publishing.service.gov.uk, 23 May 2016
3. EU referendum: Osborne warns of Brexit budget cuts, bbc. co.uk, 15 Jun 2023
4. Sunak, Rishi on Twitter, 3 Apr 2023
5. Speech by Nigel Lawson, ukandeu.ac.uk, 12 Jan 2016
6. The EU-South Korea Free Trade Agreement and Its Implications for the United States, everycrsreport.com, 1 Dec 2011
7. The UK's new Trade Agreements: Curb your Enthusiasm, blogs.sussex.ac.uk, 8 Nov 2021
8. What has happened to UK-Japan trade one year after signing the CEPA FTA?, blogs.sussex.ac.uk, 8 Aug 2022
9. The NFU has responded to the UK and Australia trade deal, nfuonline.com, 17 Dec 2021
10. Australia and New Zealand Trade Deals, hansard.parliament. uk, 14 Nov 2022
11. Impact assessment of the FTA between the UK and Australia: executive summary, gov.uk, 10 May 2022

12. EU Exit Analysis, January 2018, Cross Whitehall Briefing, p. 14, committees.parliament.uk
13. Prime Minister's statement on EU negotiations: 24 December 2020, gov.uk; What does it mean for UK automotive? David Bailey, Centre for Brexit studies, 28 Dec 2020
14. CPTPP: impact assessment, para 2.1, gov.uk, 17 Jul 2023
15. The UK's approach to trade negotiations with the US, pp. 32, 57, gov.uk, 2 Mar 2020
16. EU trade policy, www.consilium.europa.eu, 11 Jan 2024
17. CE Marking, gov.uk, 1 Aug 2023; UK government climbs down on post-Brexit product mark, ft.com, 2 Aug 2023
18. Middle Temple's Treasurer's Lecture: The State We're In, johnmajorarchive.org.uk, 9 Nov 2020
19. The Retained EU Law (Revocation and Reform) Bill 2022, www.gov.uk, 22 Sep 2022
20. UK plan to scrap all EU laws suffers new setback, ft.com, 8 Nov 2022
21. Schedule of retained EU law, gov.uk, 15 May 2023; Why the watered-down EU law bill remains mired in controversy, ft.com, 19 May 2023; 'No longer relevant to the UK': list of 600 EU laws to be scrapped is published, theguardian.com, 15 May 2023
22. HM Treasury analysis, pp. 59, 63, April 2016
23. The economic consequences of Brexit, OECD April 2016, p 7, oecd.org, 2016
24. VAT rules and rates, europa.eu
25. Developments in the outlook for household living standards, March 2022, Chart F, obr.uk
26. https://ukandeu.ac.uk/2016-a-review/
27. Johnson sees no deal as better than surrender, thetimes.co.uk, 4 Sep 2020
28. Breaking international law is no way to protect peace in Northern Ireland, instituteforgovernment.org.uk, 11 Sep 2020; Brexit: UK and EU reach deal on Northern Ireland border checks, bbc.co.uk, 8 Dec 2020
29. GDP – International Comparisons: Key Economic Indicators, commonslibrary.parliament.uk, Economic indicators, 15 Feb 2024

30. OECD, Global revenue statistics database, oecd.org, accessed 1 Mar 2024

31. HM Treasury analysis: the long-term economic impact of EU membership and the alternatives, p. 9 for role of EU in reducing barriers to trade; pp. 87–93 for alternatives to EU membership; p. 138 for estimated impact, assets.publishing. service.gov.uk, 18 Apr 2016

32. Boris Johnson: UK will 'prosper mightily' even without a Brexit deal, www.politico.eu, 4 Sep 2020; Why a 'Canada Minus' deal still matters, Citigroup, 24 Dec 2020

33. Brexit analysis, obr.uk

34. UK trade in the wake of Brexit, p. 2, cep.lse.ac.uk, Apr 2022

35. Sources for box: New customs rules for trade with the EU, commonslibrary.parliament.uk, 7 Sep 2023; Cabinet Office, The Border with the European Union, p. 22, assets.publishing.service. gov.uk, Jun 2022; Brexit trade deal not delivering, pp. 19–20, britishchambers.org.uk, 21 Dec 2022; Brexit at three: fresh trade challenges growing, pp 30–32, britishchambers.org.uk, 19 Dec 2023; Letter: Brexit trade performance and why models matter, ft.com, 24 Jan 2024; and reply: Few Brexit crumbs of comfort for this cake lover, ft.com, 26 Jan 2024

36. EFO – March 2024, pp. 38–41, obr.uk, 6 Mar 2024; EFO – March 2022, pp. 62–4, obr.uk, 23 Mar 2022

37. CBI member survey reveals huge support for remaining in EU, theguardian.com, 14 Mar 2016; Boris Johnson challenged over Brexit business 'expletive', bbc.co.uk, 26 Jun 2018

38. What would 'trading on WTO terms' mean?, p. 5, ukandeu.ac.uk, Dec 2018

39. Letter to *Sunday Times*, alistairlexden.org.uk, 21 Dec 2020

40. PM speech in Greenwich, gov.uk, 3 Feb 2020

Chapter 3: Debt Wish

1. Fiscal risks and sustainability report, pp. 15–17, 100–101; and presentation by Richard Hughes, obr.uk, 13 Jul 2023

2. Peterson, Peter, *Gray Dawn*, pp. 70–72, Random House/Times Books, 1999

3. Review of the impartiality of BBC coverage of taxation, public spending, government borrowing and debt, pp. 4, 13–14, bbc.co.uk, Nov 2022

4. Public sector balance sheet tables, Appendix N, Table 4, ons.gov.uk, 21 Mar 2024

5. Autumn budget and spending review, 2021, pp. 149–154, gov.uk, 27 Oct 2021

6. OECD, Economic Outlook, Statistical Annex 114, Nov 2023

7. 300 years of UK public finance data, obr.uk, 20 July 2023

8. Forecasting the balance sheet: public sector net worth, pp. 16–21, obr.uk, Oct 2021

9. Kindleberger, Charles, *A Financial History of Western Europe*, p. 165, George Allen & Unwin, 1984

10. Debt Management Report 2022–23, pp. 17–19, assets. publishing.service.gov.uk, Mar 2022

11. Buiter et al., 'Excessive deficits': sense and nonsense in the Treaty of Maastricht, CEPR discussion paper 750, cepr.org, Dec 1992

12. High loan to income mortgages: if the cap fits . . . , fca.org.uk, 17 Feb 2020

13. Public sector finances databank, Table 2, obr.uk, Mar 2024; HMT Public Expenditure Statistical Analyses (PESA), Table 5.2, gov.uk, 19 Jul 2023

14. Repayment of £2.6 billion historical debt to be completed, gov.uk, 27 Mar 2015

15. Fiscal risks and sustainability, pp. 103–104, obr.uk, 13 Jul 2023

16. Labour unveils £8bn plan for green investments with private sector, ft.com, 25 Sep 2022; Labour cuts £28bn green investment pledge by half, theguardian.com, 8 Feb 2024; Keir Starmer and Rachel Reeves, Circumstances have changed, theguardian.com, 8 Feb 2024

17. London's new lord mayor calls for UK wealth fund to back fast-growing businesses, ft.com, 11 Nov 2022

18. Revenue from North Sea oil and gas as a share of GDP over time, ifs.org.uk, 9 Jun 2021

19. The Government Pension Fund Global: About the fund and its market value, nbim.no

20. Heseltine: Thatcher blew UK's North Sea windfall, heraldscotland.com, 11 Oct 2018

21. Accounting devices and fiscal illusions, imf.org, 28 Mar 2012

22. PFI and PF2 report, pp. 17, 23–25, nao.org.uk, 18 Jan 2018

23. If the ONS judged that insufficient risk had been transferred to the public sector, PFI projects could add to debt and borrowing, but these were the exceptions. In March 2010, £5 billion out of a total £40 billion of PFI contracts was recognized in the headline figure for debt. See: Private finance initiative: Seventeenth Report of Session 2010–12, pp. 11–12, publications.parliament.uk, 19 Aug 2011

24. Budget 2018: Philip Hammond's speech, gov.uk, 29 Oct 2018

25. Student loans and fiscal illusions, especially pp. 10–12, 15–17, obr.uk, Jul 2018

26. Public sector finances September 2019, section 10, ons.gov.uk

27. Fitch Ratings dataset, fitchratings.com, Dec 2023

28. Debt Management Report 2022–23, op. cit., p. 20

29. Lawson, Nigel, *The View from No. 11*, pp. 114–118, Bantam Press, 1992

30. Fiscal Risks Report, pp. 12, 56, 251–259, 278–279, assets. publishing.service.gov.uk, Jul 2017

31. Asset purchase facility quarterly report – 2021 Q4, bankofengland.co.uk, 4 Jan 2022

32. The direct fiscal consequences of unconventional monetary policies, obr.co.uk, 13 Mar 2019

33. EFO, March 2024, p. 120, obr.co.uk, 6 Mar 2024

34. Spring Budget 2024: initial IFS response, ifs.org.uk, 6 Mar 2024; This will be the biggest tax-raising parliament on record, ifs.org.uk, 29 Sep 2023

35. OBR, July 2023, Fiscal risks and sustainability report, op. cit., pp. 109–111

36. 'A fine balance' speech by Mark Carney, bankofengland.co.uk, 20 Jun 2017

37. Moody's lifts UK's outlook to 'stable' on restoration of policy

predictability, reuters.com, 20 Oct 2023; Fitch affirms United Kingdom at 'AA-'; outlook negative, fitchratings.com, 2 Jun 2023

38. Fiscal rules in the UK since 1997, instituteforgovernment.org. uk, 16 Mar 2022
39. Fiscal sustainability report, Chart 2.4, p. 31, obr.uk, 14 Jul 2020
40. Public finances data bank, obr.uk, March 2024
41. EFO – March 2024, p. 135, op. cit.; EFO – November 2023, p. 137, obr.uk, 22 Nov 2023
42. Solidarity and wealth tax, p. 3, europarl.europa.eu, Apr 2022
43. Commons Library, Tax statistics, p. 6, commonslibrary. parliament.uk, 28 Mar 2024
44. Spring Budget speech, gov.uk, 6 Mar 2024

Chapter 4: The City: blessing or curse?

1. Co-operation in production, p. 14, jbs.cam.ac.uk, Sep 2016
2. Soaring City bonuses 'hit £8.8bn', news.bbc.co.uk, 30 Oct 2006
3. Mervyn King, publications.parliament.uk, HC524-II, 2008, p. 3
4. Royal Bank of Scotland Group PLC – Annual General Meeting/General Meeting, investors.natwestgroup.com, 3 Apr 2009
5. Chairman Howard Davies looks back at the financial crisis, natwestgroup.com, 12 Sep 2018
6. Public sector net debt (including public sector banks), ons.gov.uk, Mar 2024
7. Bank rescues of 2007–09: outcomes and cost, commonslibrary. parliament.uk, 8 Oct 2018
8. Adair Turner, How to tame global finance, prospectmagazine. co.uk, 27 Aug 2009
9. FCA hit by rising vacancies and falling morale, ft.com, 22 Aug 2022; Annual report and accounts 2022–23, p. 81, FCA, 19 Jul 2023
10. Augar, Philip, pp. 317–326, *The Bank that Lived a Little*,

Penguin Books, 2019; Treasury Select Committee, Fixing
LIBOR, Volume II, pp. 60-61, 18 Aug 2012

11. Capital City, economist.com, 19 Oct 2006
12. New economy, new finance, new Bank, bankofengland.co.uk,
     21 Jun 2018
13. Amsterdam ousts London as Europe's top trading hub, ft.com,
     10 Feb 2021; Amsterdam retains share-trading supremacy over
     London a year after Brexit, reuters.com, 6 Jan 2022
14. Resilience in the City of London: the fate of UK financial
     services after Brexit, Table 1, tandfonline.com, 30 Oct 2021
15. EY Financial Services Brexit Tracker: Movement within UK
     financial services sector stabilises five years on from Article 50
     trigger, ey.com, 29 Mar 2022
16. Has the City of London benefitted from Brexit?, p. 3,
     grahambishop.com, 4 Jul 2023
17. European Commission implementing decision, eur-lex.europa.
     eu, 8 Feb 2022; France backs UK as banking mecca, denying
     Germany win in Brexit surprise, politico.eu, 21 Feb 2024
18. Listening up to level up, fca.org.uk, 20 May 2022
19. Threat to UK financial services watchdogs off the table,
     theguardian.com, 23 Nov 2022
20. 8 December 2021, Work of the Financial Conduct Authority –
     Oral evidence, committees.parliament.uk, 8 Dec 2021
21. UK Listings Review, pp. 28-31, Mar 2021
22. Other sources for box:
     SPACs were all the rage. Now, not so much, nytimes.com, 2 Jun
     2022; Where next for UK market structure, fca.org.uk, 3 Mar
     2022; Are UK SPACS starting to unwind?, Shearman & Sterling,
     27 Apr 2023
23. Government sets out plan to make UK a global cryptoasset
     technology hub, gov.uk, 4 Apr 2022; Keynote Speech by John
     Glen, Economic Secretary to the Treasury, at the Innovate
     Finance Global Summit, gov.uk, 4 Apr 2022
24. Crypto assets are helping illegal activity, BoE's Bailey says,
     reuters.com, 8 Nov 2021
25. The risks of token regulation, fca.org.uk, 6 Sep 2021

26. 'He knew it was wrong': Sam Bankman-Fried sentenced to
    25 years in prison over FTX fraud, theguardian.com,
    28 Mar 2024; Sam Bankman-Fried found guilty of defrauding
    FTX customers out of billions, theguardian.com, 3 Nov 2023
27. Stop blaming everything on pension funds, schroders.com,
    28 Mar 2023
28. Legal & General chief executive Nigel Wilson to retire, ft.com,
    30 Jan 2023
29. Lloyds Banking Group moves into the private rental sector
    with launch of Citra Living, lloydsbankinggroup.com,
    7 Jul 2021
30. Dismantle 'ring-fencing' rules to safeguard competitiveness, say
    Britain's banks, reuters.com, 1 Oct 2021
31. UK's 15 biggest mortgage lenders hit by price war, ft.com,
    12 Aug 2019
32. Bank of England deputy governor Sam Woods: 'I will defend
    ringfencing of banks to my last drop', telegraph.co.uk,
    12 Jan 2020
33. Aligning the ring-fencing and resolution regimes: Call for Evi-
    dence, gov.uk, 2 Mar 2023
34. Brexit: the European Investment Bank, chapter 2, publications.
    parliament.uk, 31 Jan 2019; Brexit Britain will miss cheap EU
    funds for infrastructure, ft.com, 11 Aug 2016
35. UK infrastructure bank framework document, paras 6.4 and
    6.5, ukib.org.uk
36. Fundamental Spreads – speech by Sam Woods,
    bankofengland.co.uk, 20 Feb 2023
37. Revolut valued at $33bn to become UK's biggest-ever private
    tech group, ft.com, 15 Jul 2021
38. UK payment markets summary 2023, UK Finance, Sep 2023
39. Regulatory sandbox, fca.org.uk, 27 Mar 2022
40. Revolut investor cuts book value by 40%, ft.com, 15 Jun 2023

Chapter 5: Whatever happened to 'Made in Britain'?

1. Manufacturing: statistics and policy, researchbriefings.files. parliament.uk, 10 Jan 2020
2. UK trade, 1948–2019: statistics, researchbriefings.files. parliament.uk, 10 Dec 2020
3. World Bank, manufacturing value added (current US$), 2022, data.worldbank.org
4. UK manufacturing: the facts, 2023, makeuk.org, 13 Sep 2023
5. Wiener, Martin J., *English Culture and the Decline of the Industrial Spirit* 1850–1980, CUP, 1981
6. Empty shelves, economist.com
7. Work, Production and Capitalism since 1970, davidedgerton. org, 24 Jan 2022
8. Unctad, World Investment Report, 2023, Annex Table 2, p. 200, unctad.org
9. Bank of England, 2017, op. cit., Haldane, Productivity puzzles, p. 14
10. Update, excel table, oecd.org, Jan 2024
11. Trade and investment core statistics book, gov.uk, 20 Mar 2024
12. UK attractiveness survey, figure 50, assets.ey.com, Jun 2023
13. Harrington Review of Foreign Direct Investment, pp. 26–29, 48 for later reference to policy instability, assets.publishing. service.gov.uk, Nov 2023
14. A Mini part's incredible journey shows how Brexit will hit the UK car industry, theguardian.com, 3 Mar 2017
15. Trade in value-added: UK, oecd.org, February 2022
16. Industrial strategy: building a Britain fit for the future, p. 194, gov.uk, 27 Nov 2017; Build back better: our plan for growth, p. 54, gov.uk, 3 Mar 2021
17. GSK announces new global headquarters in central London, gsk.com, 12 Dec 2022; R&D locations, gsk.com
18. The Cambridge entrepreneur ecosystem: a recipe for success, jbs.cam.ac.uk, 19 Dec 2019; arm.com/company
19. The university spinout report 2021: which UK universities top

the rankings for turning innovation into commercial success?, sourceadvisors.co.uk, 16 Sep 2021

20. Chancellor Jeremy Hunt's speech at Bloomberg, gov.uk, 27 Jan 2023

21. The impact of Airbus on the UK economy, oxfordeconomics. com, 29 Mar 2022

22. IFS, Green Budget, 2018, chapter 7, ifs.org.uk

23. Defence expenditures of Nato countries (2014–2023), nato.int, 7 Jul 2023

24. UK motorsport industry in pole position for F1's 70th anniversary, gov.uk, 12 Aug 2020

25. Bank of England, 2017, Productivity puzzles, op. cit., p. 13

26. Industrial Strategy, gov.uk, op. cit., p. 172

27. Unlocking UK productivity: Internationalisation and innovation in SMEs, pp. 18–24, goldmansachs.com, 16 Nov 2015

28. Education at a glance 2020, Table A.1.1, p. 50: EU-23 average, oecd.ilibrary.org

29. What is holding back UK productivity? Lessons from decades of measurement, niesr.ac.uk, 9 Nov 2018

30. Bossonomics, cep.lse.ac.uk, Autumn 2009

31. Narrowing the productivity gap, blogs.deloitte.co.uk, 22 May 2023

32. Financing growth in innovative firms: Consultation, pp. 9–14, assets.publishing.service.gov.uk, Aug 2017

33. Britain is a great place to start a company, but a bad one to scale it up, economist.com, 21 Jun 2022

34. From trailblazer to basket case – how it all went wrong for Marconi, *Guardian*, 5 Sep 2001

35. Thames Water crisis could hit UK investment, ministers warn, ft.com, 2 Jul 2023

36. England's water groups slashed investment in sewage network in recent years, ft.com, 22 Dec 2021

37. Wind generated a record amount of electricity in 2022, bbc.co.uk/news, 6 Jan 2023

38. Hinkley Point nuclear agreement reached, bbc.co.uk/news, 21 Oct 2015

39. The energy supplier market, pp. 7-8, nao.org.uk, 22 Jun 2022;

Investigation into Bulb Energy, 29 Mar 2023

40. Industrial Strategy: Cable outlines vision for future of British industry, gov.uk, 11 Sep 2012

41. Sajid Javid heralds Thatcherite approach to business policy, ft.com, 16 Sep 2015

42. Industrial Strategy, especially pp. 4–20, 29, 67–69, 79–81, 94–103, 165, 192–202, gov.uk, 27 Nov 2017

43. New Industrial Strategy Council meets as membership announced, gov.uk, 1 Nov 2018

44. Kwarteng scraps Industrial Strategy Council and hints at BEIS rebrand, civilserviceworld.com, 5 Mar 2021

45. Build back better: our plan for growth, gov.uk, 3 Mar 2021

46. Haldane, Manufacturing puzzles, op. cit., pp. 18–20

47. Business groups back new IPPR blueprint to end flip-flopping and to get serious about green industrial growth, ippr.org, 17 Nov 2023

48. Jeremy Hunt's speech at Bloomberg, 27 January 2023, HMT, op. cit.

49. Jeremy Hunt's growth plan mixes welcome realism with speculative cakeism, instituteforgovernment.org.uk, 1 Feb 2023

50. The crucial thing missing from the vaunted UK business investment bonanza, ft.com, 22 Nov 2023

51. UK government pays £500mn in subsidies for Tata battery plant, ft.com, 19 Jul 2023. With link to article by Kemi Badenoch

52. Nissan to lead £2bn electric car investment in Sunderland plant, ft.com, 24 Nov 2023

53. Lawson, Nigel, op. cit., pp. 354–5.

54. The global industrial arms race is just what we need, ft.com, 26 Jun 2023

Chapter 6: Battle hymn to public services

1. Peter Brookes cartoon, 'Bright Future', *The Times*, 2 Sep 2023

2. Consultant-led Referral to Treatment Waiting Times Data 2023–24, england.nhs.uk

3. DWP benefits statistics: August 2023, gov.uk, 15 Aug 2023. Note: the benefit statistics exclude Northern Ireland; the rise in the school-leaving age is in England, as is the childcare package

4. Public services productivity progress report: February 2024, ons.gov.uk, 20 Feb 2024

5. OBR: Government spending plans beyond 2025 'worse than fiction', civilserviceworld.com, 24 Jan 2024

6. Public sector employment, UK: December 2023, ons.gov.uk, 12 Mar 2024; Is pay higher in the public or private sector?, ons.gov.uk, 16 Nov 2017

7. Public service productivity, UK: 1997 to 2022, ons.gov.uk, 17 Nov 2023

8. HMP Wandsworth: Prison told to make changes after alleged escape, BBC News, 8 Jan 2024

9. Unsafe and inhumane conditions at HMP Wandsworth, imb. org.uk, 11 Oct 2023

10. UK prison population statistics, p.15; p. 28 for comparison with other European countries; p. 27 for cost per prisoner, commonslibrary.parliament.uk, 8 Sep 2023

11. Germany refuses to extradite man to UK over concerns about British jail conditions, theguardian.com, 5 Sep 2023

12. Proven reoffending statistics: October to December 2021, gov.uk, 26 Oct 2023

13. The long-term sustainability of the NHS and adult social care, pp. 52–5, publications.parliament.uk, 5 Apr 2017

14. Performance Tracker: Spring 2017, instituteforgovernment.org. uk, 25 Feb 2017

15. Performance Tracker: 2023, pp. 5–18; p. 75 for later comment on inexperienced staff in NHS hospitals, instituteforgovernment.org.uk, 30 Oct 2023

16. PIRLS 2021: England rises up rankings, and 8 more findings, schoolsweek.co.uk, 16 May 2023

17. England among highest performing western countries in education, gov.uk, 5 Dec 2023

18. PISA 2022: Rise in maths, but warning over inflated results, schoolsweek.co.uk, 5 Dec 2023

19. Ruth Perry: Prevention of future deaths report, judiciary.uk, 19 Dec 2023

20. Education commission, thetimes.co.uk, 15 Jun 2022

21. Britain's education system is 'failing on every measure' – with 'shocking' regional disparities uncovered, news.sky.com, 15 Jun 2022

22. Educating for the modern world, CBI/Pearson Education and Skills annual report, November 2018, p. 23, cbi.org.uk

23. 'Maths to 18' in England, researchbriefings.files.parliament.uk, 27 Nov 2023

24. Sources for following section include: IfG/CIPFA 2023 performance tracker, op. cit., pp. 11, 46–47, 51–55, 59–64, 88–89; NHS England statistics A&E attendances; Access to GP appointments and services, nuffieldtrust.org.uk, 14 Dec 2023; Stressed and overworked, health.org.uk, Mar 2023; NHS hospital bed numbers: past, present and future, kingsfund.org, 5 Nov 2021

25. Health at a glance 2023, pp. 68–69; 78–79 for infant mortality, oecd.org, 7 Nov 2023

26. Final Ockenden Report, p. xi, ockendenmaternityreview.org.uk, 30 Mar 2022

27. Public satisfaction with the NHS and social care in 2022 and 2023: results from the British Social Attitudes survey (covering England, Wales and Scotland), kingsfund.org.uk, 29 Mar 2023 and 27 Mar 2024

28. After the gold rush, economist.com, 10 Dec 2009

29. Public investment is too low and too volatile thanks to Treasury 'fiscal fine tuning', resolutionfoundation.org, 30 Mar 2023

30. The NHS estate continues to deteriorate, kingsfund.org.uk, 14 Dec 2023

31. NHS capital investment cuts leave England's hospitals crumbling, ft.com, 17 Aug 2023; New Hospital Programme, Oral evidence, committees.parliament.uk, 7 Sep 2023

32. Excel: Why using Microsoft's tool caused Covid-19 results to be lost, BBC News, 5 Oct 2020

33. Test-and-trace reporting error triggers health department probe, ft.com, 5 Oct 2020

34. Impact of the 2015 Spending Review on health and social care, p. 4, nuffieldtrust.org.uk, Jan 2017

35. Just half of secondary teacher recruitment target met, schoolsweek.co.uk, 7 Dec 2023

36. GreenBudget, pp. 194–197, ifs.org.sites, Oct 2022

37. Le Grand, Julian, *Motivation, Agency and Public Policy: Of Knights & Knaves, Pawns & Queens*, Oxford University Press, 2003

38. More doctors and nurses alone will not heal the NHS, ft.com, 7 Jul 2023

39. Improving schools' performance: Are multi-academy trusts the answer?, lordslibrary.parliament.uk, 23 Sep 2023

40. The 'redisorganisation' of the NHS, bmj.com, 1 Dec 2001

41. The health and care act: six key questions, kingsfund.org.uk, 16 May 2022

42. The future of public health – speech by Matt Hancock, gov.uk, 18 Aug 2020; Jeremy Farrar on Twitter, twitter.com, 19 Aug 2020

43. 'The world's biggest quango': the first five years of NHS England, p. 26, assets.kingsfund.org.uk

44. PM speech on the NHS: 18 June 2018, gov.uk

45. How does UK health spending compare across Europe over the past decade?, health.org.uk, 16 Nov 2022

46. What does the government spend money on?, ifs.org.uk, 1 Dec 2023

47. US general warns British Army no longer top-level fighting force, defence sources reveal, news.sky.com, 30 Jan 2023

48. The Royal Navy's surface fleet, researchbriefings.files.parliament.uk, 15 Dec 2022

49. Defence funding boost 'extends British influence', says PM, bbc.co.uk/news, 19 Nov 2020

50. God save the British military, wsj.com, 19 Dec 2023

51. Battling for survival, thetimes.co.uk, 22 Jan 2024

52. Letter to thetimes.co.uk, Curing NHS ills, 16 Nov 2023

Chapter 7: Is more immigration the answer?

1. Reddaway, W.B., *The Economics of a Declining Population*, p. 15, George Allen & Unwin, 1939
2. International migration: A recent history, ons.gov.uk, 15 Jan 2015
3. The impact of EU enlargement on migration flows (2003), p. 58, ucl.ac.uk
4. Second thoughts, economist.com, 24 Aug 2006
5. Migration Advisory Committee (MAC), EEA migration in the UK: final report, p. 73, assets.publishing.service.gov.uk, Sep 2018
6. The changing picture of long-term international migration, England and Wales: Census 2021, ons.gov.uk, 27 Jan 2023
7. MAC, Sep 2018, op. cit, pp. 2–3
8. Replacement migration: Is it a solution to declining and ageing populations? pp. 68–9, un.org, 21 Mar 2000
9. MAC, Sep 2018, op. cit., pp. 29–33
10. MAC, Sep 2018, op. cit., pp. 68–70
11. The economic impact of immigration, pp. 5–6, 25–26, publications.parliament.uk, 1 Apr 2008
12. Migrants set up one in seven UK companies, study reveals, ft.com, 4 Mar 2014
13. Foreign-born founders behind 39% of the UK's fastest-growing companies, forbes.com, 22 Aug 2023
14. Judy asks: Is Brexit bad for Europe?, carnegieeurope.eu, 11 April 2019
15. Home Secretary announces new UK points-based immigration system, gov.uk, 19 Feb 2020
16. The UK's 2021 points-based immigration system, p. 5, migrationobservatory.ox.ac.uk, 17 May 2021
17. Small boat crossings to UK fell by a third in 2023, ft.com, 1 Jan 2024
18. Long-term international migration: year ending June 2023, ons.gov.uk, 23 Nov 2023. For this and following figures
19. Sources for box from ons.gov.uk:

23 Nov 2023, Understanding international migration statistics; Methods to produce provisional long-term international migration estimates; Estimating UK international migration: 2012 to 2121; 28 Feb 2023, Reconciliation of mid-year population estimates with Census 2021: England and Wales; Apr 2014, Quality of long-term international migration estimates from 2001 to 2011

20. Legal migration, hansard.parliament.uk, 4 Dec 2023; Net migration measures: further detail, gov.uk, 21 Dec 2023

21. Statement of changes to the Immigration Rules: HC 1019, gov.uk, 24 Jan 2022. Explanatory memorandum

22. Visa journeys and student outcomes, ons.gov.uk, 29 Nov 2021

23. London Assembly (Mayor's Question Time), meetings.london.gov.uk, 23 Oct 2013; Boris Johnson: The only way to take back control of immigration is to Vote Leave on 23 June, voteleavetakecontrol.org, 26 May 2016

24. Seldon, Anthony with Newell, Raymond, *May at Ten*, pp. 13, 17–18, Biteback Publishing, 2019

25. Legal migration statement: estimated immigration impacts (accessible), gov.uk, 21 Dec 2023

26. Shortage occupation list, Richmond Chambers, 27 Dec 2023

27. Home Office, Statement of changes in immigration rules, (HC 1019), Explanatory memorandum, p. 2, gov.uk, 24 Jan 2022

28. Home Office, Statement of changes in immigration rules, (HC 813), Explanatory memorandum, pp. 22–25, gov.uk, 22 Oct 2020

29. MAC, A points-based system and salary thresholds for immigration, pp. 8, 148, 267, assets.publishing.service.gov.uk, Jan 2020

30. How Asian doctors saved the NHS, news.bbc.co.uk, 26 Nov 2003

31. NHS Long term workforce plan, p. 13, 30 Jun 2023

32. Who cares?, resolutionfoundation.org, Jan 2023

33. Alan Manning: 'Achieving growth by just having more people is not what we should aim for', ft.com, 8 Mar 2023

34. National population projections: 2021-based interim, ons.gov.uk, 30 Jan 2024

35. Migrant workers and skills shortages, pp. 26–29, cipd.org, May 2023
36. International students boost UK economy by £41.9 billion, hepi.ac.uk, 16 May 2023
37. The changing picture of long-term international migration, England and Wales: Census 2021, op. cit., Figure 2
38. Reducing Net Migration Factsheet – February 2024, homeofficemedia.blog.gov.uk, 1 Feb 2024
39. Long-term international migration, op. cit. sections 5 and 6, ons.gov.uk, 23 Nov 2023
40. Population estimates for England and Wales: mid 2022, ons.gov.uk, 23 Nov 2023
41. Why are the latest net migration figures not a reliable guide to future trends?, migrationobservatory.ox.ac.uk, 14 Dec 2023
42. Who are 'economically inactive' people, and could they join the work force?, fullfact.org, 20 Feb 2020
43. Fiscal risks and sustainability report, p. 25, obr.uk, Jul 2023
44. Annual figures for unemployment and inactivity based on reweighted LFS data, ons.gov.uk, 13 Feb 2024; EFO, pp. 41–42, obr.uk, Mar 2024
45. Rising ill-health and economic inactivity because of long-term sickness, UK: 2019 to 2023, ons.gov.uk, 26 Jul 2023
46. Comparisons of all-cause mortality between European countries and regions, op. cit., from start of 2020 to week 26 in 2022
47. Fiscal risks and sustainability, September 2023, op. cit., p. 7, obr.uk
48. obr.uk, op. cit., pp. 45–47
49. Employment support launched for over a million people, gov.uk, 16 Nov 2023
50. Workplace health: long-term sickness absence and incapacity to work, nice.org.uk, Mar 2009
51. Immigration policy won't cure Britain's labour market ills, ft.com, 26 Oct 2022
52. Covid-19 vaccine: First person receives Pfizer jab in UK, bbc.co.uk/news, 8 Dec 2020

53. German researchers advance coronavirus vaccine, dw.com, 9 Nov 2020
54. Rishi Sunak's parents, politics.co.uk
55. Prime Minister's keynote speech at the Global Investment Summit: 27 November 2023, gov.uk

Chapter 8: Levelling up – or down?

1. PM statement in Downing Street: 13 December 2019, gov.uk, 13 Dec 2019
2. Regional gross value added (balanced) by industry, updated from 19 December 2019, Table 1c, ons.gov.uk, 23 Apr 2023
3. London's population over time (1931–2035), trustforlondon.org.uk
4. Big cities drive half of global economic growth, ft.com, 8 Dec 2022
5. Estimates of the population for the UK, England, Wales, Scotland, and Northern Ireland, Spreadsheet 6, ons.gov.uk, 26 Mar 2024
6. The Great British Brain Drain: Where graduates move and why, centreforcities.org, Nov 2016
7. Plan for Growth, p. 72, gov.uk, Mar 2021
8. Regional labour productivity, UK: 2021, ons.gov.uk, 20 Jun 2023
9. *Closing the Watford Gap*, Channel 4 Television, 28 Feb 1993
10. How big are regional economic inequalities in the UK?, commonslibrary.parliament.uk, 10 Mar 2020; Poverty in the UK: Statistics, researchbriefings.files.parliament.uk, 8 Apr 2024
11. UK regional productivity differences: an evidence review, industrialstrategycouncil.org, pp. 9–12, 23–26, 4 Feb 2020
12. Left behind: can anyone save the towns the UK economy forgot?, ft.com, 16 Nov 2017
13. Regional and subregional productivity comparisons, UK and selected EU countries, ons.gov.uk, 26 Apr 2018
14. Enhancing productivity in UK core cities, oecd.org, 2020

15. Why big cities are crucial to 'levelling up', centreforcities.org, Feb 2020

16. Tackling the UK's regional inequality, p. 8, hks.harvard.edu, Mar 2023

17. Unequal Italy, pp. 2–7, library.fes.de, 12 Jul 2021

18. What levelling up policies will drive economic change?: The need for a long-term focus on skills and cities, pp. 15–17, instituteforgovernment.org.uk, 15 Jul 2022

19. What does it take to 'level up' places?, pp. 36–45, industrialstrategycouncil.org, 26 Jan 2021

20. The Eddington transport study: The case for action, pp. 22, 32, 48–9, news.bbc.co.uk, Dec 2006

21. Oakervee Review of HS2, p. 60, gov.uk, 11 Feb 2020; HS2 Cost and Risk Model Report: A report to Government by HS2 Ltd, p. 14, assets.publishing.service.gov.uk, Mar 2012

22. PM: 'In a hole the size of HS2, only thing to do is keep digging', news.sky.com, 31 Jan 2020

23. PM statement on transport infrastructure: 11 February 2020, gov.uk

24. HS2 rail leg to Leeds scrapped, Grant Shapps confirms, theguardian.com, 18 Nov 2021

25. HS2 and Euston: Tenth Report of Session 2023–24, HS2 and Euston, p. 5, committees.parliament.uk, 7 Feb 2024,

26. Industrial Strategy, 2017, gov.uk, op. cit., pp. 140–141

27. Rishi Sunak on twitter.com, 4 Oct 2023

28. IPPR North: Broken transport promises come as new evidence shows widening transport spending gap, ippr.org, 18 Nov 2021

29. Gear shift: International lessons for increasing public transport ridership in UK cities, centreforcities.org, Nov 2023

30. Rail needs assessment for the Midlands and the North, pp. 5, 55–56, Annex B, nic.org.uk, 15 Dec 2020

31. Wouldn't TransPennine Express passengers rather have a reliable rail service than 'random acts of kindness'?, independent.co.uk, 24 Oct 2023

32. The Transpennine route upgrade programme, pp. 4–7, nao.org.uk, 20 July 2022

33. Chancellor: 'We need a Northern powerhouse', gov.uk, 23 Jun 2014

34. Spatial disparities across labour markets, pp. 6-7, ifs.org.uk, 2 Feb 2022

35. The determinants of migration flows in England, pp. 50–51, 58, geog.leeds.ac.uk, July 1998

36. University spinout report 2021, op. cit.

37. The results are in: Mayor Steve Rotheram hails success of Eurovision as report reveals £54m economic boost to city region, liverpoolcityregion-ca.gov.uk, 26 Oct 2023

38. Higher education student numbers, pp. 4, 25, researchbriefings.files.parliament.uk, 2 Jan 2024

39. Motorsport Valley: How the Midlands Become the Epicentre of Formula 1 Manufacturing, businessinthemidlands.co.uk, 22 Sep 2021

40. Interview with Michael Heseltine, www.channel4.com/news, 20 May 2020

41. Birmingham City Council effectively files for bankruptcy, itv.com, 5 Sep 2023

42. The life and legacy of Joseph Chamberlain, birmingham.ac.uk

43. OECD Fiscal Decentralisation Database, Table 1, oecd.org

44. Everything you need to know about metro mayors, centreforcities.org, 29 Feb 2024

45. Government unveils levelling up plan that will transform UK, pp. viii–xxvii, 1–5, gov.uk, 2 February 2022

46. Will the levelling up missions help reduce regional inequality?, instituteforgovernment.org.uk, 30 Mar 2022

47. What levelling up policies will drive economic change?, 15 Jul 2022, op. cit., website summary and pp. 4–7, 25–26, 30

48. Boris sends the House of Lords up north, thetimes.co.uk, 19 Jan 2020

49. Structural change and future prospects, bonn.de

Chapter 9: Boosters and gloomsters: could Britain bounce back?

1. Prime Minister's keynote speech at the Global Investment Summit: 27 November 2023, gov.uk
2. Keir Starmer's speech at Labour Conference, labour.org.uk, 10 Oct 2023
3. Nobel prizes and laureates, nobelprize.org, accessed 12 January 2024; Nobel prizes by country 2024, worldpopulationreview.com
4. International comparison of the UK research base, 2022, assets.publishing.service.gov.uk, May 2022
5. The Times Higher Education World University Rankings 2024, timeshighereducation.com, 27 Sep 2023
6. Plan to forge a better Britain through science and technology unveiled, gov.uk, 6 Mar 2023
7. S&T – Is the UK a world leader in science?, jameswphillips. substack.com, 10 Mar 2023
8. UK joins Horizon Europe under a new bespoke deal, gov.uk, 7 Sep 2023
9. Horizon Europe: how the UK's delay in rejoining EU funding scheme is damaging scientific research, theconversation.com, 21 Jul 2023
10. Why basic science matters for economic growth, imf.org, 6 Oct 2021
11. MHRA, Archive, updated 22 November 2023, Information for UK recipients on Covid-19 Vaccine AstraZeneca (Regulation 174)
12. WineGB Industry Report 2022-23, winegb.co.uk
13. UK Viticulture report, rural.struttandparker.com, 28 Jun 2023
14. English wines win record number of awards in global tasting competition, theguardian.com, 22 Sep 2020
15. Industrial Strategy, gov.uk, 2017, op. cit., pp. 61–67; Plan for Growth, gov.uk, 2021, op. cit., p. 53
16. ONS releases on R&D, 29 September 2022 and 22 November 2022

17. Research and development expenditure (% of GDP), data.worldbank.org, 27 Nov 2023, accessed 12 January 2024

18. Global innovation index, wipo.int, 2023

19. World trade in services, Eurostat figures, July 2023, for shares in 2012 and 2019; Unctad, December 2023, for 2022

20. Richard Baldwin et al., Deconstructing deglobalisation: The future of trade is in intermediate services, Asian Economic Policy Review, 10 October 2023

21. Global Trade Outlook, pp. 19, 21, wto.org, 5 Apr 2023

22. Brexit, four years on: answers to two trade paradoxes, cer.eu, 25 Jan 2024

23. Who does the UK trade with?, ons.gov.uk, 3 Jan 2018

24. Industrial analyses, table 2.2, professional and support services, ons.gov.uk, 2023; The rich world's Bangalore, economist.com, 11 Nov 2004

25. Industrial Strategy: government and industry in partnership, pp. 5–7, 35–36, assets.publishing.service.gov.uk, July 2013

26. Universities UK response to official figures on education export revenue, universitiesuk.ac.uk, 21 Mar 2024; tuition fees, table 6, hesa.ac.uk

27. Creative industries need another Great British Rebrand, ft.com, 5 Jan 2024

28. Future funding for UK universities under examination, universitiesuk.ac.uk, 2 Nov 2023

29. Lord Patten's letter of retirement to the Vice-Chancellor, Professor Irene Tracey, ox.ac.uk, 6 Feb 2024, the letter is dated 26 Jan 2024

30. Efforts to reduce universities' dependence on China stalling, report says, kcl.ac.uk, 13 Sep 2023

31. Budget 2016: George Osborne's speech, gov.uk, 16 Mar 2016

32. Tory leadership race: what are candidates' promises on tax?, theguardian.com, 10 Jun 2019

33. OBR, EFO, Mar 2020, p. 95; Nov 2023, pp. 95–101

34. Build back better: our plan for growth, pp. 44–45, gov.uk, 3 Mar 2021; OECD, Education at a glance 2020, Table A1.1. educational attainment of 25–64-year-olds, oecd-ilibrary.org;

OECD, 2020, Raising the basic skills of workers in England, pp. 14–16, oecd.org, 18 Dec 2020

35. PM's skills speech: 29 Sep 2020, gov.uk
36. Annual report on education spending in England: 2023, pp. 69–70, ifs.org.uk, 11 Dec 2023
37. All change: Why Britain is so prone to policy reinvention, and what can be done about it, pp. 5–9, instituteforgovernment. org.uk, 14 Mar 2017
38. Over 1.1 million homes with planning permission waiting to be built – new LGA analysis, local.gov.uk, 8 May 2021
39. House building UK: permanent dwellings started and completed by country, Table 3b, ons.gov.uk, 30 Jan 2024
40. Britain's failure to build is throttling its economy, economist.com, 1 Sep 2022
41. Housebuilding market study, Main report, Figure 4.1, p. 57; Summary, p. 6, gov.uk, 26 Feb 2024
42. Delivering net zero, climate resilience and growth, p. 10, nic.org.uk, 2023
43. State of the profession 2023, pp. 5, 31, rtpi.org.uk, Nov 2023
44. Revealed: capacity and churn issues facing planning teams, lgcplus.com, 16 May 2023
45. Big projects struggle to get off ground amid budget blowouts and setbacks, ft.com, 27 Jan 2024
46. Generative AI set to affect 300mn jobs across major economies, ft.com, 27 Mar 2023
47. Ending Stagnation, p. 93, economy2030.resolutionfoundation. org, Dec 2023
48. Labour's share – speech by Andy Haldane, pp. 12–13, 33, Bank of England, bankofengland.co.uk, Nov 2015
49. The risk of automation for jobs in OECD countries, esp. pp. 4, 8, 14, 33, oecd-ilibrary.org, May 2016
50. Machine learning in UK financial services, especially chart 12, bankofengland.co.uk, 11 Oct 2022
51. The AI revolution's first year: has anything changed?, ft.com, 29 Dec 2023

52. Times Health Commission, a 10-point plan for health, thetimes.co.uk, 5 Feb 2024
53. The dismantled National Programme for IT in the NHS, publications.parliament.uk, 18 Sep 2013
54. Coronavirus test, track and trace plan launched on Isle of Wight, gov.uk, 4 May 2020
55. Post-pandemic economic growth: Industrial policy in the UK, p. 10, committees.parliament.uk, 28 Jun 2021

Chapter 10: A ten-point plan to save the economy

1. Ten years of automatic enrolment in workplace pensions, DWP, 26 Oct 2022
2. Spring Budget 2024, p. 68, gov.uk, 6 Mar 2024
3. Releasing resources to the front line, webarchive. nationalarchives.gov.uk, Jul 2004
4. HMT, Spending Review, July 2000, Public service agreements, 2001–04, p. 35
5. Starmer says 'vast majority' of Labour members back his plans for government, labourlist.org, 23 Feb 2023
6. Government counts mailouts to hit 100,000 testing target, hsj.co.uk, 1 May 2020; NHS Providers, The NHS needs an updated testing strategy, nhsproviders.org, 30 Apr 2020
7. The new hospital programme, p. 7, publications.parliament.uk, 17 Nov 2023
8. Mirrlees review, Tax by design, Ch. 20, ifs.org.uk, 13 Sep 2011
9. Kay, John, *Obliquity*, Ch. 3, Profile Books, 2010
10. Records created or inherited by the Department of Trade and Industry, The National Archives, reference NK; Rishi Sunak breaks up UK business department to refocus on energy and science, ft.com, 7 Feb 2023
11. Rishi Sunak's reshuffle – February 2023, instituteforgovernment.org.uk, 7 Feb 2023
12. FCA, Discussion paper on a duty of care, July 2018, p. 11 and Annex 2, p. 37; Feedback statement, April 2019, p. 18;

December 2021, A new consumer duty, pp. 77, 90, 92
Commons Library, 7 May 2021, Financial Services Act 2021,
pp. 8, 68

13. Can Keir Starmer plant the seeds of growth?,
    prospectmagazine.co.uk, 1 Nov 2023
14. UK's industrial policy: learning from the past?, p. 25,
    productivity.ac.uk, Oct 2021
15. White heat redux, economist.com, 14 Jan 2010
16. Written evidence submitted by British Business Bank,
    committees.parliament.uk/writtenevidence, Sep 2023
17. The health of nations: the contribution of improved health to
    living standards (2002, originally published November 1999),
    elischolar.library.yale.edu
18. Trends in life expectancy in the EU and other OECD
    countries: Why are improvements slowing? p. 20, oecd-ilibrary.
    org, 28 Feb 2019
19. Health survey for England 2018: Overweight and obesity in
    adults and children, files.digital.nhs.uk, 3 Dec 2019
20. Smoking age should rise from 18, by one year every year –
    Rishi Sunak, bbc.co.uk/news, 4 Oct 2023
21. George Osborne, March 2016, Budget speech, gov.uk, 16 Mar
    2016; Sugar tax, instituteforgovernment.org.uk, 14 Nov 2022
22. New obesity strategy unveiled, gov.uk, 27 July 2020; Tackling
    obesity, p. 23, instituteforgovernment.org.uk, 5 Apr 2023
23. What has happened to college teacher pay in England?, ifs.org.
    uk, Mar 2023
24. No train, no gain, edsk.org, Nov 2022
25. *The Knowledge: 2020 Vision*, bbc.co.uk, transmitted 2 Jul 1995
26. International profiles of health care systems, pp. 83–92,
    commonwealthfund.org, Dec 2020
27. The Dutch health care system, english.zorginstituutnederland.
    nl; Health systems in transition, Netherlands review 2016,
    pp. xx–xxi, 23–25, 66–76, iris.who.int
28. Mirror, mirror 2021: Reflecting poorly, commonwealthfund.
    org, 4 Aug 2021. This ranked the Netherlands second overall
    among eleven high-income countries and fourth in health care

outcomes; the UK was ranked fourth overall and ninth for outcomes.

29. Lawson, Nigel, op. cit., p. 613

30. The NHS in crisis: evaluating the radical alternatives, kingsfund.org.uk, 31 Jul 2023

31. Le Grand, Julian, op. cit., pp. 161–162

32. NHS finances can be fixed by breaking with Treasury orthodoxy, ft.com, 9 Feb 2018

33. Health and social care levy, commonslibrary.parliament.uk, 22 Nov 2022

34. Gordon's way, economist.com, 1 Dec 2005; Blair, Tony, *A Journey*, pp. 584-589, 608-609, Hutchinson, 2010

35. Pimlott, Ben, *Harold Wilson*, pp. 277–281, 360–364, 474–482, Harper Collins, 1992

36. Treasury 'orthodoxy': What is it? And is it a problem for government?, especially pp. 4–5, instituteforgovernment.org.uk, 19 Jan 2024

37. Power with purpose, instituteforgovernment.org.uk, 10 Mar 2024

38. Here's how to stimulate UK growth: give away power, ft.com, 12 Jan 2024

39. Dani Rodrik: doing industrial policy right, ft.com, 9 Feb 2024

40. A central role for local government? The example of late Victorian Britain, historyandpolicy.org, 2 May 2002

41. Modernisation, managerialism and the culture wars: reshaping the local welfare state in England (2004), p. 3, oro.open.ac.uk

42. Mortality in England and Wales: Average life span, 2010, ons.gov.uk, 17 Dec 2012

43. Local government funding in England, instituteforgovernment.org.uk, updated July 2023

44. Why hasn't UK regional policy worked?, pp. 3–5, 10, 51–52, hks.harvard.edu, Oct 2023

45. AEB devolution: 2022 to 2023, gov.uk, 13 Sep 2023

46. Labour wants to make Brexit work better. What does the EU think?, economist.com, 1 Feb 2024

47. Labour's European conundrum, cer.eu, 10 Dec 2023

48. UK halts trade negotiations with Canada over hormones in beef ban, bbc.co.uk, 26 Jan 2024

49. Northern Ireland Protocol: UK Legal Obligations, hansard.parliament.uk, 8 Sep 2020

50. Northern Ireland protocol bill passes Commons vote, theguardian.com, 27 Jun 2022; Windsor Framework unveiled to fix problems of the Northern Ireland Protocol, gov.uk, 27 Feb 2023

51. Double majority fact sheet, aec.gov.au

52. Referendums and the constitution, p. 57, consoc.org.uk, 2017

53. Cameron, David, *For the Record*, pp. 625–6, William Collins, 2019

54. Opinion: grassroots members should not choose party leaders, ucl.ac.uk, 7 Feb 2020

55. William Hague, Tory members must not pick next leader, thetimes.co.uk, 1 Nov 2022

Acknowledgements

They say it takes a village to raise a child, and much the same applies to this book. First and foremost, I want to thank publisher and editor Sameer Rahim, who came up with the overall design and title, transforming my mundane proposal and first draft into something altogether better and livelier. Thanks, too, to everyone else at Little, Brown, who have contributed to this project, including copy editor Jon Appleton, publicist Katya Ellis, and especially Frances Rooney, who calmly guided *Tanked* through various tough deadlines to the finished product.

Commissioned in 2023, this has in many ways been a book long in the making and inspired by some exceptional editors. While my main beat at *The Economist* during the 2000s was covering the British economy and public finances, I was also encouraged by Britain editors Emma Duncan and Merril Stevenson to write about the public services, especially the NHS. During that time, I also wrote international surveys of pensions and health-care funding, overseen by the sadly deceased Barbara Beck. More recently, I have worked closely with Tom Clark and Alex Dean of *Prospect*, Ouida Taaffe of *Financial World*, and Arlene Getz while she was commentary editor at Reuters. My thanks to them for setting me challenging assignments on a range of issues, including many of those covered in this book.

Throughout, I have been able to draw upon research by super-clever people at the Institute for Fiscal Studies, Institute for Government, Resolution Foundation, and UK in a Changing Europe. Invidious though it is to pick out individuals working at these think-tanks, I would like to acknowledge the help I have long received from Carl Emmerson and Ben Zaranko of the IFS; Gemma Tetlow of the IfG; and Jill Rutter of UK in a Changing Europe. I would also like to thank three other experts who read parts of the book and commented on it. Any errors are my responsibility alone.

None of this would have been possible without my wife and family, who have supported me so much throughout this project.

Index